FROM RAILS TO TRAILS
THE MAKING OF AMERICA'S ACTIVE TRANSPORTATION NETWORK

PETER HARNIK

University of Nebraska Press
LINCOLN

Library of Congress Cataloging-in-Publication Data
Names: Harnik, Peter, author.
Title: From rails to trails: the making of America's active
transportation network / Peter Harnik.
Description: Lincoln: University of Nebraska Press, 2021. | Includes
bibliographical references and index.
Identifiers: LCCN 2020034266
ISBN 9781496222060 (paperback)
ISBN 9781496226532 (epub)
ISBN 9781496226549 (mobi)
ISBN 9781496226556 (pdf)
Subjects: LCSH: Rail-trails—United States—History. | Rails-to-Trails
Conservancy—History. | Bicycle trails—United States—History. |
Railroads—Abandonment—United States—History. | Railroads—
Right of way—Multiple use—United States.
Classification: LCC GV191.4 .H37 2021 | DDC 796.60973—dc23
LC record available at https://lccn.loc.gov/2020034266

Set in Scala OT by Laura Buis.

A simple idea
Pathways of peace and beauty
Rail-trails forever

—LISA HEIN

CONTENTS

ILLUSTRATIONS

Figures

Maps

Following page 84

Illustrations

TABLES

ACKNOWLEDGMENTS

WRITING THE FIRST-EVER HISTORY OF A MOVEMENT IS A DAUNT-ing enterprise. As I got started my feelings on the matter fluctuated widely: Was the topic too insignificant to be worth chronicling? Why had no one tried it before? Or was the task too difficult to undertake? Had many others perhaps tried and given up in defeat? Was I ahead of the curve—or behind it? As I did my research I alternated between elation over the freedom I had in charting uncharted waters and the frustration that no one else had taken the plunge ahead of me.

Fortunately, as with everything else in my life, I leaned on and learned from a wonderful circle of friends, collaborators, former colleagues, and new acquaintances to unearth the stories and elucidate the analysis of this fascinating young movement. Naturally I take full responsibility for all errors of fact, judgment, and omission, but if it hadn't been for the encouragement, information, enthusiasm, and support of these folks, this book would have foundered and sunk. They include:

Mark Ackelson, Sallie Adams, Anthony Allison, Shirley and Butch Anson, Keith Argow, Stan Bales, Henri Bartholomot, Annemarie Bauer, Karl Beard, George Bellovics, Ralph Benson, Kathy Blaha, Kay Blankenship, Mark Borleske, Rick Boucher, Roland Bowers, Linda McKenna Boxx, Mark Boyle, Becky Bremser, David Brickley, Jonathan Broder, Chris Brown, Kitty Cole Brown, Ken Bryan, Emory Bundy, Tim Burke, Champe Burnley, George Burrier, Brian Burwell, David Burwell, Sarah Campbell, Paul Ceruzzi, Ray Chambers, Doug Cheever, Jeff Ciabotti, Karin Cicelski, David Clanton, Andy Clarke, Buzz Constable, Derrick Crandall, John Crompton, Mark Cross, Dan Cunning, Paul Cunningham, Jeff Davis, Sharon Davis, Craig Della Penna, Jim Denny, Matt Dickey, Bill Dickinson, John DiMura, David Dionne, Jim Donovan, Tom Downs, Ed Dressler, Paul Dyer, Tom Eksten, Steve Elkinton, Bruce Epperson, Craig Evans, Matt Fisher, Chuck Flink, Marianne Fowler, Joan Frey, Patti Friday, Karen Gantz, Ben Gessel, Michael Gessel, Parris Glendening, David R. Goode, Kingdon Gould Jr., David Greenwood, Eli Griffen, Dorian Grilley, Gerald Grinstein, Dana Gumb, Jr., Margaret Guroff, Bill Hall, Bob Hansen, Jan Hartke, Duncan Hay, Lisa Hein, Ben Helphand, Rita Hennessey, Bob Herbst, Hal Hiemstra, Axie Hindman, Darwin Hindman, John Horsley, Brandi Horton, Oliver Houck, David Ingemie, Gabrielle Ivanier, Gerry Johnson, Roy Jones, Bob Karotko, Linda Keenan, David Kelly, Richard Kendall, Roy Kienitz, Evelyn Kitay, Randy Kline, Carl Knoch, Ron Kucera, Paul Labovitz, Joe LaCroix, Pete Lagerwey, Ray LaHood, Jean Lauver, Larry Leach, Josh Lehman, Judy Lemons, John Leshy, Greg Lindsey, Amanda Livingston, Gwen Loose, Dave Mankamyer, Greg Maxted, Cate Mayfield, Ed McBrayer, Alan McClennen, Paul McCray, Lee McElvain, Connie McGuire, Kevin Menke, Ed Merlis, Bill Metzger, Gabriel Meyer, John Milliken, Kevin Mills, David Moore, Maryanne Moore, Hugh Morris, Tom Murphy, Yvonne Mwangi, Andy Neault, Doug Nelson, Charles Newman, Ed Norton, Karen Nozik, Caroline O'Boyle, Richard Orsi, Gus Ose, Kelly Pack, Bill Palmer, Pat Parenteau, Hank Parke, Bob Patten, Louis Pear, Robert Peck, Clay Peters, Dave Peterson, Tom Petri, Don Phillips, Cleve Pinnix, Paul Pritchard, John Rathbone, Peter Raynor, Tom Ridge, Barbara Robinson, Ellis Robinson, Jarrod Roll, Andy Sansom, John Sayler, Frederick Schaedtler, Fred Schaeffer, Bill Sepe, Tom Sexton, Rick Sharp, Jamie Simone, Ron Steffey, Roger Storm, Ben Sullivan, Robert Taft, Bob Thomas, Steve Thompson, Tommy Thompson, Glenn Tiedt, Wes Uhlman, Ivan Vamos, Fred Wagner, Dave Watts, John Wengert, Carol Werner, Fred Wert, David Wiggins, Mac Wilkerson, Bill Wilkinson, Frank Wilner, Steve Winslow, Sandy Wood, Robert Yates, Lori Yeich, Ron Yesney, and Lori Zoller.

I want to particularly thank Keith Laughlin and Ryan Chao, along with the entire staff of the Rails-to-Trails Conservancy, for their unstinting support and for opening up the organization's files and databases to me. I also want to give my deepest thanks to my geo-

Acknowledgments

graphic advisor Derek Strout; my railroad advisors Dan Cupper, Charlie Marshall, and Mark Reutter; my legal advisors Matt Cohen, Andrea Ferster, Charles Montange, Simon Eristoff, and Danaya Wright; my editorial advisors Jim Conroy, Diane MacEachern, Jan Schaeffer, Charles Bookman, Debby Baldwin, and Ted Mastroianni; my University of Nebraska Press team of Rob Taylor, Ann Baker, Elizabeth Zaleski, Tish Fobben, and Debbie Anderson; and very special thanks to my most creative and indefatigable research assistant Tim Balton. Lastly, as always, I salute the love and forbearance provided me during this lengthy labor by my wonderful wife, Carol Ames Parker.

INTRODUCTION

THERE WAS A TIME IN NEW YORK CITY, BACK IN THE 1890s, when bicycling was a glamorous sport of rich daredevils—physically superior men and socially courageous women—but by the time I was growing up there, in the 1950s and '60s, cycling had deteriorated into a low-status fringe activity. While biking in parks and on beachfronts was great fun for children and a source of nostalgic pride for parents standing by with Band-Aids and "it's all better" hugs, cycling on roads with cars was too frightening for most people. And in the 1960s, there was no such thing as a road without cars.

Since I was a teen and thought myself immortal, I was never overly fearful of competing with cars. Also the average speed of traffic in Manhattan was about 8 miles an hour, and that didn't seem too terrifying. My mother was pretty relaxed about letting me do what I wanted, which included biking to my high school from West 78th Street. I grew up with a European heritage that rather honored cycling, and as a teen I was the proud recipient of my Austrian uncle's old three-speed, which he had somehow taken along when he escaped Hitler. Fortunately I never had a bad run-in with a car, so my various close calls never rose to the level of visceral, cold-sweat-at-night fear. Despite all this, and even though cycling itself was an unmitigated joy, I didn't find riding in the streets of New York to be all that much fun.

For one thing, the buses. Riding behind them was a smelly and often hot torture, not to mention a frustrating seesaw of starts and stops, passing and being passed. And then, the taxis, which would precipitously pull in and out with no warning. Red lights were of course an annoyance, made worse by the almost inevitable honk the moment the signal turned green. Plus, from a social perspective, it was frustrating that cyclists couldn't ride side by side. On the other hand, if you could get up at sunrise on a summer weekend and outflank most of the cars, it felt like a miracle. There was even the opportunity to talk about fantasies like, "Wouldn't it be cool if there were full-time streets without cars?"

Then, one Sunday in 1966, the miracle happened. New York City mayor John Lindsay closed to cars the main loop road in Central Park. It was just one day, an experiment, but it was a revelation.

Even with cars, Central Park was a wonderland for millions of city dwellers. But very few New Yorkers had any memory of what that 843-acre mecca was like before it had become an auto speedway. Actually, asking a New Yorker to notice the cars in Central Park was like asking a fish to notice water. The cars were as much a Central Park fixture as the trees, meadows, lakes, horse buggies, and surrounding apartment towers. Timed signals kept the one-way park loop flowing so that the bursts of traffic came in reliable waves, a few minutes of roaring swoosh followed by a few seconds of silence. The park also had pedestrian trails so, naturally, we children on bikes used them, but they were curvy, steep, uneven, root-bound, crowded with walkers and baby carriages, and periodically interrupted by steps. There were cinder-covered horse trails in the park, but our one-speed kids' bikes and three-speed English racers weren't designed to make it through the ruts and soft sand. All in all, the winding pathways of Central Park weren't a great place to bring a bike if you were much over the age for training wheels.

That all changed with one mayoral signature.

Suddenly a thundering circular speedway—six miles long, three lanes wide, with a jostling throng of yellow cabs—became a promenade. The quiet was profound. Birdsong in the city—whoa! Who knew? Yes, there were noises—squealing children, barking dogs, transistor radios, shouting teens, the eerie continuous clicking of bicycle sprockets coasting down hills. But not the blanket dull roar of traffic punctuated by unmuffled outbursts from trucks and motorcycles. And, for cyclists, no fear of being sideswiped, forced into a guardrail, or flattened.

My initial enthusiasm grew through an unexpected delight: it turned out that the beneficiaries were far more than just cyclists. Eliminating cars unleashed an entire ecosystem of roadway users— walkers and runners and skaters and scooter riders and hula hoopers and pogo-stick bouncers and chalk-art drawers and musicians and dancers and drummers and painters. This was, after all, New York City, with every imaginable sport, activity, art form, and lifestyle. Although the wild menagerie put off the hard-core racing cyclists, some of whom openly longed for a return to the predictable flow of autos, most other people were fascinated by the unprecedented sights and sounds, and charmed by the fresh smell.

Mayor Lindsay's Central Park experiment set off firestorms of both rage and exultation. Motorists were shocked and opposed, both the professionals in taxis and the regular folks accustomed to a pleasure outing in their cars. But the even hotter emotion— jubilation—carried the day. It was just as Jane Jacobs in 1961 had pointed out in her book *Death and Life of Great American Cities*. After castigating the "erosion of cities by automobiles," she revealed that its good twin is the "attrition of automobiles by cities." She wrote, "Tactics are suitable which give room to other necessary and desired city uses that happen to be in competition with automobile traffic needs."

• • •

BY THE TIME I WAS ENSCONCED IN WASHINGTON DC IN THE 1970s, at a time when only a few hardy souls were pedaling at the edges of the city's broad avenues, the National Park Service had already used New York's example and taken the small step of closing one section of one road in 1,700-acre Rock Creek Park to cars. It wasn't much—one Sunday a month during the summer—but again it was a revelation. Suddenly the park's Beach Drive felt like a country road deep in West Virginia, minus the three-hour trek to get there.

As in New York, bicyclists had provided the initial agitation and the ongoing political muscle, but as soon as the barrier gates were closed, a much wider array of regular folks came out to enjoy the newfound space. Who were all these runners, walkers, stroller pushers, skaters, dog walkers, plein-air painters, and binocular-toting bird-watchers? Skateboards didn't exist yet, but eventually they would show up too. And where had they all come from? How did they get down to that hidden valley so far from transit and from most people's homes? This was a group of people attracted to something so special that they had made extraordinary efforts to get there without driving.

And yet . . .

Not all bicyclists enthused over special places for bikes. The bicycle organizations were surprisingly, almost mystifyingly, split on the issue. Within the groups, every time a proposal to support a mandated bike lane came up for a vote, a shockingly loud minority of voices called out against it.

At first, I didn't understand. The arguments were vitriolic, the combatants contemptuous of each other, the pat phrases repetitive. Once, at a pro–bike path speech I gave in California, I was publicly denounced by a committed cyclist in the audience as a "murderer." He claimed that more cyclists are wiped out on trails that intersect roads than on roadways themselves. His allies proclaimed that cyclists could never make political progress unless they marched arm in arm with the American Automobile Association. But then *they* were shouted down. The local politicians who convened the hearings were frustrated as well. At another tumultuous meeting an official called out, "Could you people please go back and figure out what it is you want from us?"

Gradually, painfully, I began to comprehend. Even though bike advocates all seemed to be marching together under a conceptual banner that cried, "Cyclists Demand a Better Deal," there was diametrical disagreement over what the deal was and what was being demanded.

On one side was the group I labeled "Macho Militants." Predominantly though not exclusively male, the Machos were well-educated white-collar professionals, they rode ten-speeds and tended to have quality equipment and good riding technique, and they had an unshakable conviction that bikes and cars were both roadway vehicles that must be treated as equals. The Macho Militant demanded automotive rights for cyclists and always rode in the middle of the lane. He was sometimes seen on a two-lane road chugging methodically up a hill, a line of cars crawling behind him. He signaled a right turn not by pointing in that direction but by crooking his left arm and raising it as we were taught in driver's ed. Although the Macho was impervious to car horns, air pollution, and loud motorcycles, his blood boiled at the driver who cut him off; his fantasy revenge was to wear steel-toed boots and kick in the taillight of the offending vehicle as it roared past. Yet all Machos owned cars. When they talked about "revolutions," they weren't preaching any kind of societal overthrow; they were referring only to their pedals.

In contrast were what I called the "New Age Activists," a more motley crew who tended to view cycling as much a social commentary as a means of transportation. Most would have identified themselves as environmentalists, appropriate technologists, and feminists (even the men). They tended to think of their bikes more as gentle, simple contraptions than as well-oiled machines. Their equipment was also motley, sometimes even ranging to hand-me-down one-speeds with frumpy accessories like baskets, mudguards, and kickstands. They weren't all flawless riders; more than a few would be seen standing by the curb waiting for a line of cars to pass before making a left-hand turn. What united New Agers was their hostility to cars. They tended to rant about bus fumes, truck noise, automobile velocities, and being surrounded by hot engines in August. Their vision included curb-separated bike lanes, 15-mile-per-hour speed limits, and car-free zones. When it came to fantasy retribution, the outraged New Ager would pour sugar into gas tanks. To her, debilitating an auto wouldn't seem all that heinous since she herself might not own one.

When Machos and New Agers chanted in unison, "Out of the gutter and into the streets!" the former meant *with* cars and the latter meant *instead* of them.

The bitterest debate erupted over bike lanes. Machos hated bike lanes. They saw them as roadway ghettos, a source of danger and confusion, a broken-glass-covered badge of second-class citizenship, and an insult to their riding ability. Where bike lanes did exist, Machos made a point of riding outside them, hoping to be ticketed so that they could take the case to court. Their favorite stories were of cyclists being injured due to bad roadway design or cowardly riding technique.

New Agers loved bike lanes. They dreamed of having them on every street, along with a special system of bicycle traffic signals. They dreamed that bike lanes would lure so many people out from behind the steering wheel that streets would gradually be given over to bikes and that someday it would be cars that got relegated to special lanes at the edge. They dreamed that all one-way streets would allow two-way travel for bikes. They dreamed of mid-block barriers that would detour autos but allow bikes to slip through. They dreamed of compact communities, easily reachable shops and offices, bike parking racks on every sidewalk, greenhouses, windmills, solar panels, and an entirely new world order.

The Machos' guru was a man named John Forester, the engineer from Palo Alto who had yelled "murderer" at me. Forester was a onetime president of the League of American Wheelmen, and his book, *Effective Cycling*, was his followers' bible. The New Agers leaned for inspiration more toward Barry Commoner, author of *The Closing Circle*; E. F. Schumacher, author of *Small Is Beautiful*; and for political coalition-building, Saul Alinsky, author of *Rules for Radicals*. Because the Macho Militants were the "old guard" of bicycling and because they had been involved in organizations for years, they tended to be in positions of power and leadership. In fact they also inhabited many of bicycling's bureaucratic and engineering positions in city, state, and federal governments. The New Age Activists, younger and more recently converted to cycling, had less historical knowledge and data, but they demanded attention by claiming to speak for the millions of potential cyclists who would emerge as soon as they were protected from cars.

Once, in a fit of exasperation after a lengthy argument with one of the ultra-knowledgeable Macho Militants who sat with me on the board of the Washington Area Bicyclist Association, I, who had pitched my tent in the New Age camp, said, "Look, let's peel this debate back all the way to the very basics and see where our positions begin to diverge." He was willing.

"Okay, beginning at the very beginning, we both love bicycling, right?"

"Yes."

"And we both agree that we would like to see more people cycling, right?"

"No."

Well, that was a surprise. And a revelation. He was a militant, but he wasn't out to change the world. He wanted to ride his bike in peace, endangered neither by arrogant drivers nor by clueless pedalers. He had no problem with cars per se. In fact he felt car drivers could often be good companions: predictable and relatively consistent people who knew the rules of the road, unlike the untamable mixture found in car-free places: novice bikers and racers, children and seniors, stroller pushers and skaters, runners, family groups, walkers, tricyclists, and skateboarders who traveled at inconsistent speeds, stopped at will, changed direction randomly, talked heedlessly with each other, and never looked behind.

I, on the other hand, did actually want to change the world, at least a bit.

To me, it was difficult to be pro-bike without being anti-car, since cars seemed to be the implacable adversary that had us beat every which way we turned. At the time I didn't know what they were doing to the upper atmosphere and the climate, but I figured it must be bad. Even parked, a car was an adversary, gobbling up precious real estate and threatening cyclists with being "doored." Drivers sometimes came up behind and honked; other times they passed aggressively with only inches to spare; occasionally a passenger would make rude gestures or throw something. Even without that kind of malice, the spinning tires would frequently hurl little stones or, on dirt roads, fill the air with dust.

We needed leaders, or at least heroes. One of mine was a man named Bob Silverman, leader of an anarchical Montreal group called Le Monde à Bicyclette, the World on Bicycles. After the Parisian ecology group Les Amis de la Terre turned the French word for bike—*velo*—into the universal word "velorution," Silverman's group adopted it as their rallying cry, elevating the revolution against cars to an art form. "To be arrested in the cause of the bicycle is an honor," he would say, proudly exhibiting a warrant with his name on it. (He had actually turned himself in, hoping for a publicity trial, but the police waved him away, saying the judge hadn't signed the document. Silverman stage-whispered, "The judge knows how embarrassing it is for the authorities to put a bicyclist in jail.")[1]

In the late 1970s Le Monde à Bicyclette staged one catchy event after another, managing to keep issues of bicycling inequity on the front pages. One day members got up before dawn, purchased a full line of parking spaces by putting coins into every parking meter on a block, set out orange traffic cones, and created an instant downtown bike lane. To protest the impossibility of crossing the St. Lawrence River without a car, they first staged a "fly-in," attaching wings to their bikes, donning bird costumes, and frantically flapping their arms before the TV cameras. When that didn't work, they put their bikes into canoes, ending up miles downstream after struggling against the fierce current, again in front of cameras. Finally they dressed up as Moses and the Israelites, pedaled to the shoreline, and sought to part the waters. Solemnly, bilingually, they chanted the Seven Plagues of the Automobile:

> "L'automobile pollue!"
> "The automobile makes too much noise!"
> "L'autombile gaspille l'energie!"
> "The automobile monopolizes urban space!"
> "L'autombile dévore les resources naturelles!"
> "The automobile threatens a resource war!"
> "L'automobile vous laisse endetté!"

The other group that caught my fancy was Berkeley-based Urban Ecology, a similar collection of creative misfits pushing the envelope against auto domination. Led by West Coast visionary Richard Register, Urban Ecology originally made a name for itself by removing the seats, hood, and trunk cover of a 1968 Pontiac GTO, then filling it with soil and converting it into the Vegetable Car, a community garden.

It was, of course, a sensation. It was, of course, ticketed. But at 4,000 pounds (and motor-less), it was virtually immovable, forcing Berkeley's finest to tow it away. At the time I was first alerted to the story, in 1981, Urban Ecology was circulating a petition to have the Vegetable Car rescued and declared a portable historic monument.[2]

But Urban Ecology didn't just poke fun. The group was an early exponent of smart growth and compact development—the kind of community design that would obviate the need for a car and stimulate the growth of cycling. One elegant idea was the Slow Street, a road with a 12-mile-an-hour speed limit. In a rigorously gridded community like Berkeley, having an occasional Slow Street would be a minor inconvenience to drivers who could simply use the next street over. Bicyclists and skaters, meanwhile, could also go a block or two out of their way for a relaxed and pleasant roadway environment. It would almost be like a . . . trail system.

Sadly, neither Le Monde nor Urban Ecology made much headway beyond headlines. The ideas were there, but the political muscle wasn't. I, sitting stodgily in Washington DC and now part of a loose coalition of bicycling activists, may have been envious of the vision, the humor, and the pointed messages, but I recognized that our somewhat more plodding, by-the-book style—writing letters, turning people out to hearings, and holding the occasional rally—was having more on-the-ground success.

• • •

BACK TO ROCK CREEK PARK. WE SO LOVED THE CAR-FREE moments on Beach Drive that we kept pushing for more—more hours, more days, more miles, more events. And for a while we made progress. The road closure was expanded to every Sunday during the summer, then every weekend during the summer, then every weekend year-round, then every holiday year-round. There was some pushback from drivers, but the groundswell of support was overwhelming, and a remarkable Park Service superintendent named Jim Redmond was astute enough to recognize the alignment between his park mandate and the political benefit he gained from having so many happy and positive users. (Redmond also got some more mundane benefits, like less litter and reduced roadkill burdening his minimal budget.)

Then in 1983 we hit a wall.

The bicyclists' proposal that Beach Drive be permanently closed to cars ran into the fierce opposition of weekday auto commuters. Jim Redmond contracted liver cancer and was suddenly gone. His successors, unable to navigate the political tightrope, relegated the issue to a series of studies that dragged on fecklessly for decades. Two political lessons were revealed. First, that city people absolutely love car-free roadway surfaces and are willing to work hard to get them. Second, that car drivers really, really, *really* don't want to give up any roadway space. Even though bicycling was good for the environment, good for the city, good for personal health, quiet, fun, rewarding, inexpensive, a great social experience, a fine family outing, and an outstanding way to get to work, there was almost no place to do it. It was at the extreme bottom of the decision makers' lists. They were happy to provide a car-free venue for bicycling, but only if absolutely no one else had any use for the location for anything else, even for parking.

Yet, against all odds, there was a glimmer of hope. Very softly, almost subliminally, whispered messages occasionally drifted in from the Midwest, showing up in obscure columns in new age magazines or stories from friends of friends. Some town in Wisconsin or Illinois or Minnesota had taken over an abandoned railroad track and converted it into a trail. People were now biking and cross-country skiing on it. Or something like that. Well. That definitely sounded like a lark . . . in a very theoretical, far-away, and generally irrelevant way. Do they bike on the ties? Next to the tracks? *Do they balance on the rails?*

It seemed somewhat akin to fantasizing about surfing in Hawaii. It might be fun . . . if we ever get out to some obscure corner of the countryside in the upper Midwest and happen to have bikes with us. Or maybe we could rent a bike. (They rent bikes in the Midwest, right?) . . . Isn't it fun what people can do when they live so far from real-life places?—they can even dismantle old railroads. . . .

• • •

BY THE WAY, DID I MENTION THAT MY CHILDHOOD APARTment in New York City was on Riverside Drive? And that for my early years I walked, biked, sledded, played, fought, watched the boats go by, and daydreamed in Riverside Park? I also spied on trains.

New York's Riverside Park is, in a weird way, a rail-trail. Or, more accurately, a "rail-under-trail." For nearly a hundred years, beginning in 1846, a noisy, smoky, and intrusive railroad line snaked between Riverside Drive and the Hudson River. Then, in 1937, New York City parks commissioner and "power broker" Robert Moses undertook a $100-million park expansion program that included covering those New York Central tracks. By the time I was a first-grader, in the mid-1950s, the trains were so out of sight and out of mind that virtually no one knew about them anymore. Except me. I would be playing with my sand bucket, hear the far-off train horn and the deep underground rumble, jump up with a squeal, run over to the steel grating in the walkway, throw myself stomach-first onto it, cup my eyes with my hands, and watch the trains rumble past beneath me. I could only see the roofs and the glint of the couplers, but there was no missing the exciting squeaks, groans, wails, thumps, clicks, and goose-bump-generating shrieks of steel on steel. And the smells! What a nose-wrinkling mixture of dank stone and cement, diesel exhaust, rotting coal and wood, and God knows what else. My mother, embarrassed by my fixation, would come over to pry me away from the grate, but I would wiggle and resist.

"It's so dirty," she would say. "Trains!" I would say, transfixed.

I never put two and two together, at least not for more than fifty years. I loved bicycling in Riverside Park and I loved thinking about the trains that rumbled below. I never considered that trains had supplanted bicycles or that bikes might ever supplant trains. All I knew was that I loved them both.

FROM RAILS TO TRAILS

1

The Queen of Trails

SAY YOU CLIMB ONTO YOUR BICYCLE AT SIXTEENTH AND K Streets NW, three blocks from the White House, with the intention of pedaling westward. The first mile and a half is about as unpleasant as it gets: narrow lanes; dense, fast automobile traffic teeming with buses and trucks; a prohibition on sidewalk riding; five stop signs and twelve signalized intersections made treacherous by complex turns and turning regulations; and occasional sewer grates wide enough to snag a bike's tire and send its rider tumbling.

After that, bliss. For the next 328 miles, all the way to Pittsburgh, there is barely a stoplight or a motorized vehicle.

What's more, on that journey you'll be treated to more than a hundred bridges, including massive steel structures spanning major waterways, and you'll pass through dozens of overpasses and tunnels, three of which transect mountains so long and so pitch-dark in the center you'll need to bring a light. And almost never in the five- or six-day journey up and down river valleys and over the precipitous folds of the Allegheny Mountains will you be pedaling on a grade steeper than 2 percent.

You'll be on a rail-trail, the queen of all America's pathways.

Building a bicycle route of such extraordinarily high engineering quality from scratch today would cost around $4 billion—a political impossibility. Yet there it is. Half that route to Pittsburgh is an old canal towpath. The other half is a continuous series of abandoned railroad corridors. The components were graded and built more than a century ago by muscle and sweat. Today's trail was established on the bones of that old skeleton through persuasion and lobbying. It took twenty-six years and cost about $80 million. Like almost every rail-trail, this one—the Great Allegheny Passage—is a collaboration between nineteenth-century physical brawn and late twentieth-century political skills.

Some aspects of rail-trails are obvious and sensory: they are flat, or very nearly so, even to the point of being magical. If you're cycling on a trail and it's getting dark, and you're on the verge of being late enough to get a reprimand when you come home, but the rhythm of your legs and the cadence of your lungs are so perfect, and the glimpse of the view around the broad next bend is so enticing, and you haven't had to shift gears for what feels like forever or make more than the barest tweak to the angle of your handlebar, and the bridges fly over the passing streams with implacable authority, and you simply can't bring yourself to turn around or stop, then it's a rail-trail.

Rail-trails are subtle and thought provoking too. Do you notice that waterways are hugged tightly enough to provide the flattest possible profile and lowest possible construction costs, but not so close that rising stormwaters would have washed away the ballast, ties, and tracks? How about those overturned granite, cast steel, or concrete posts, inscribed with a *W* and lying forlornly in the underbrush? They were whistle posts, each one positioned hundreds of yards ahead of country road crossings, to remind a locomotive engineer to sound the whistle. I've seen dads on tandems instruct their children to go "Wooooooo-Woooooooo-Woo-Wooooooooo"— that's the proper rule book cadence—as they whiz past the posts.

The rail-trail is laid onto the detritus of a surpassed technology. Today's bicyclists, walkers, runners, skaters, skiers, equestrians, and even snowmobilers are merely Johnny-come-lately beneficiaries of a surface network created by radically different people for a totally different purpose. For a nineteenth-century Irish, Black, or Chinese railroad worker to look up from the bed of a rock-hewn tunnel or iron truss bridge and see a twenty-first-century Lycra-clad cyclist gliding silently by on a feather-light bicycle would have been as jolting then as it is, today, to read of scientists' claims that birds somehow evolved from dinosaurs.

Rail corridors, even the ones now forlornly rusting in bushes and below berms, originally provided the structural underpinning of the greatest industrial lattice created up to that time. And since they were built to carry some of the heaviest rolling loads ever devised, the roadbed engineering had to be astoundingly precise. In the 1850s, engines weighed 20 to 30 tons and pulled loads more than twice that size. By the 1890s there were tracks and ballast strong enough to support ten-wheel Consolidation-type locomotives weighing 100 tons pulling tenders that carried 8 tons of coal and 3,500 gallons of water, plus 4 million pounds of freight over the crest of the Rockies.

Getting heavy trains moving from a standstill was so difficult, and preventing downhill train runaways so critically important, that grades were constructed with tolerances in the fractions of inches. In Washington DC if you bicycle today on the Capital Crescent Trail—the old Baltimore & Ohio Georgetown Branch line—from Key Bridge the 2.2 miles to Fletcher's Boat House, it feels so flat that you would swear a drop of mercury would sit still on the pavement. Not so. At the start of the ride, the adjoining Chesapeake & Ohio Canal lies 24 feet above the old rail line; at Fletcher's the two transportation modes are directly side by side. Another half mile and the track flies over the canal on a bridge measuring at least three mules' shoulders above the towpath. That's a steady, unwavering uphill grade of 0.2 percent, one inch of height gain for every 41 feet traveled forward, perfectly measured, cut, dug, filled, and laid by laborers working with donkeys and using hand tools. Bicycling, the legs don't notice it. But rolling along, the curious mind might.

You say there's a canal at the top of that steep bank? I can't believe a waterway would be perched above us like that.

Then: *The brush is dense, but, you know, I think the embankment isn't as high as it was a few minutes ago.*

Then: *Is the hillside getting shorter? I think I just saw someone walking up there.*

Then: *Oh! Now her feet are at the level of my head. In fact, I think I can see the gravel of the towpath.*

Then: *Hey, I can see over the towpath to the water in the canal. What's going on?*

Then: *Now we're at the exact same level! How did that happen? The canal must be flowing downhill.*

No, canals don't flow downhill. Every pool of a canal is perfectly flat from one lock and spillway to the next. That's how canals work. And there is no lock between Georgetown and Fletcher's. It is the rail-trail that was imperceptibly climbing as we pushed our pedals.

The steepest incline ever constructed on a main-line railroad was the Saluda Grade outside Asheville, North Carolina. Abandoned now, it was a 4.2 percent incline, meaning just over 4 feet up for every 100 feet forward, or a climb of 222 vertical feet over the distance of one mile. Maybe one day it will become a trail. If so, you would definitely feel the grade in your legs, but it wouldn't be a killer. If someone constructs a trail and wants to comply with the Americans with Disabilities Act, the federal government's steepness limit is 5 percent. Capitol Hill in Washington DC is about 7 percent. Bunker Hill in Boston is about 14 percent. San Francisco's Filbert Street between Hyde and Leavenworth is 31.5 percent, and Pittsburgh's Canton Avenue, reputed to be the steepest street in the country, has a grade of 37 percent. The Manitou Incline in Colorado Springs has an *average* grade of 43 percent.

On my bike I couldn't ascend most of those grades, nor could the trains. For railroad companies, grades were a trade-off of construction expense versus operating cost: the more they spent leveling out their hills, the less they had to spend running their locomotives. Steep climbs needed more powerful engines that burned more coal, or the addition of helper engines—"pushers"—at the bottoms of long hills. Or companies could use a process called "doubling the hill"—splitting long freights into sections, pulling each one up the hill separately, and then reassembling the train on top (while also cautiously tightening all the brakes for the descent). Conversely, flattening the grade in mountainous regions necessitated extra miles of long, winding routes, such as the famous Horseshoe Curve near the crest of the Alleghenies in Pennsylvania, whose course was deliberately lengthened to keep the grade at 1.86 percent, about 93 feet per mile. When the federal government got into the conversation in the 1850s because of incessant railroad requests for financial support, it set the maximum allowable grade at 116 feet per mile, just under 2.2 percent.

So how exactly is the steepness of a grade controlled?

In extreme terrain the railroads used bridges and tunnels. Over gently rolling hills they got by with fills and cuts, something that most trail users don't even notice. I've had friends say to me, "Isn't it amazing how the railroads were able to find such flat places to lay down their tracks?" Good eyes, wrong conclusion. The railroads grappled with the terrain and mastered it.

What really drove it home for me, the first time, was a bicycle outing on the Torrey Brown Trail heading north out of Baltimore. Riding toward the Pennsylvania state line, my wife and I were spinning through forestland and fields up a slight incline, a slope so gradual it was barely noticeable. To my right, through the trees, I heard the roar of a car engine in low gear. I noticed, to my surprise, that the country road paralleling us wasn't really parallel at all. We were gently rolling along while the nearby drivers had to negotiate steep rises and sharp drops—uphills that would have been quite unpleasant on a bike, followed by downhills that could have required some tight braking. *Hey!* I thought. *The state of Maryland has provided a higher-quality route for bikers than they give to cars!*

Well, it wasn't the state of Maryland. It was the Baltimore & Susquehanna Railroad (the B&S), chartered in 1828, that began the hefty engineering needed to traverse the rolling countryside. Then, when the B&S went under and was supplanted by the Northern Central Railway, the route was completed up to York, Pennsylvania (and eventually through connections via steeper mountains all the way to Lake Ontario). It was the engineering of the Northern Central that made this first a great train route (used by Abraham Lincoln in 1863 on his way to speak in Gettysburg) and then a great trail. Maryland is a fine state, but there is no way that its department of transportation would spend countless millions blasting and filling for a pitch-perfect cycling, walking, and skiing route along the Gunpowder River. If Maryland *did* decide to build a new bike path (as it has in several parks around the state), it would budget perhaps a few hundred thousand dollars and begin by looking for a nice passageway winding through the trees. It would then cut away the undergrowth and lay a roller-coaster ribbon of asphalt directly on the irregular contours of the ground. At the crossing of major roads, the state would look for a stream, curve the trail

Table 1. Genealogies of selected rail-trails

Cannon Valley Trail (1986) Minnesota	Farmington River Trail (1996) Connecticut	Trolley Trail (2012) Portland, Oregon	West Ashley Greenway (1993) Charleston, South Carolina
Minnesota Central RR (1857)	Connecticut Western RR (1868)	East Side Railway (1891)	Charleston & Savannah RR (1854)
Wisconsin, Minnesota & Pacific RR (1883)	Hartford & Connecticut Western RR (1881)	Portland City & Oregon RR (1900)	Savannah & Charleston RR (1867)
Chicago Great Western RR (1920)	Central New England & Western RR (1883)	Portland Railway Light & Power (1906)	Charleston & Savannah Railway (1880)
Chicago & North Western RR (1968)	New York, New Haven & Hartford RR (1927)	Portland Electric Power (1924)	Savannah, Florida & Western RR (1901)
	Penn Central RR (1968)	Portland Traction Company (1946)	Atlantic Coast Line (1902)
	Conrail (1976)	Union Pacific/ Southern Pacific (1962)	Seaboard Coast Line (1967)
	Guilford Rail (1980s)		CSX (1980)

Source: Tim Balton, 2019

down to it, and skim the shoreline by squeezing under the inevitable tightly fitting auto bridge. It would then erect signs saying, "Low Bridge—Watch Your Head," "Beware of High Water," and "Slow—Dangerous Corner."

There is no authentic rail-trail in the nation that has a sign about low bridges, high water, or sharp corners. If the old train was able to fit, you can fit. If the train could handle the curve, you can too. Superior engineering—the cuts, fills, bridges, tunnels, and sumptuously soft arcs—took care of those issues and many others as well.

Every rail-trail in the country has a genealogy akin to the one that preceded the Torrey Brown.

Almost as soon as they were developed, trains became the fastest vehicles known to humanity. Even in 1830, when the tiny Tom Thumb steam engine was challenged to a race by a horse and stagecoach, the little engine leaped into the lead, losing only when it malfunctioned and ground to a halt. (For the stagecoach company, it was a pyrrhic victory; horses were soon left in the soot, and what remains today is the quaint measurement scale of engine strength: horsepower.) In fact, by the end of the century train velocities were almost beyond comprehension. In 1893, near Batavia, New York, a New York Central & Hudson River steam locomotive, No. 999, reached 112.5 miles per hour. (Happily, that engine is preserved in the Chicago Museum of Science and Industry, although most of its brethren have been scrapped.) To safely handle the force of that speed, track curvature had to be as smooth and gentle as a baby's bottom. Even the grade and radius standards of today's interstate highways are lax in comparison. Putting fast trains on the bed of twisting Interstate 68 through Cumberland, Maryland, or on serpentine Interstate 40 on either side of Asheville, North Carolina, would result in a pile of busted pistons, decapitated smokestacks, and mangled steam cylinders.

When the topography became severe—Berkshire Mountains severe, Appalachians and Rockies severe—railroad companies had to unleash the ingenuity of their best engineers and the brawn of their best laborers to dig tunnels and erect trestles. The first great excavation began in 1850 with the Crozet Tunnel in Virginia, which was soon followed in Massachusetts when the nearly five-mile-long Hoosac Tunnel was laboriously blasted through the Berkshires to connect New England with points west. That mammoth effort, which took twenty years and killed nearly two hundred workers, resulted in the then-longest tunnel in the western hemisphere. It also set the stage for even longer tunnels in the Rocky Mountains. Although the Hoosac still serves trains of the Pan Am Southern Railroad, many other tunnels sit silent now, welcoming only cyclists and walkers, from West Virginia and Pennsylvania to California and Washington State. (The Crozet Tunnel, replaced and abandoned in 1944, was finally reopened as a trail in 2020.)

For many trail users, a primeval, pitch-black tunnel, with maybe a pinhole of light beckoning from deep in the distance, represents the memorable thrill from a day's outing. But it is a massive trestle or bridge that usually wakes up the naïve or oblivious cyclist to the fact that she isn't on a run-of-the-mill bike path.

"Wow! The government built this half-mile-long columnar rock-and-steel structure across the Ohio River for us two-wheelers?"

Well, no. And it wasn't the government, either. Opened in 1895 and featuring the longest truss spans ever built to that time, the Big Four Bridge from Louisville, Kentucky, to Jeffersonville, Indiana, was designed by William Burr for the Cleveland, Cincinnati, Chicago & St. Louis Railway (the "Big Four"). We are the lucky beneficiaries. Other unforgettable railroad bridges now servicing bikes and pedestrians include the mile-long Walkway Over the Hudson at Poughkeepsie, New York; the Stone Arch Bridge in Minneapolis; and the Western Maryland Railway's mammoth Salisbury Viaduct across the floodplain of the Casselman River in Pennsylvania. If the railroads hadn't built these, no one would have.

It's not just engineering that makes rail-trails so special. It's also the locations of the very routes themselves. Trains, after all, were built for economic motives. To serve shippers and travelers most tracks had to run from city to city, connecting towns in between. So rail-trails today regularly intersect towns, and when they do they go to where the action is. Of course the rail depot isn't always the most scenic, parklike prospect—it is frequently accompanied by a lumberyard, warehouses, or similar industrial relics—but it's often one of the most interesting. Ideally the trail is adjoined by an old railroad station, several preserved historic buildings, a few non-chain restaurants or other shops, maybe even a little museum. The location can make for a very nice resting point for an ice-cream break, a meal, or even a bed-and-breakfast for the night. Also, even though the trail may traverse the center of a town, it very likely avoids the majority of grade crossings through the use of overpasses, underpasses, berms, and the plain old pattern of urban design. (Railroad companies were as anxious to avoid troublesome intersections back then as cyclists are today.) Then, just past the other side of town, the route might shoot back into deep woods or across open farm fields, or perhaps alongside a lovely rivulet for the next five or six bucolic miles.

Of course not every inch of rail-trail is beautiful. Some places clearly demonstrate their other-side-of-the-tracks visage, with tumbledown houses, bleak stretches of chain-link fence, and long stretches

The Queen of Trails

of asphalt. After all, railroad corridors were industrial lifelines serving every manner of commerce that built up and maintained our nation. Railroad companies didn't control what sprouted, flourished, or decayed beyond their right-of-way property lines, nor did they employ landscape architects to beautify their facilities, except around some stations. Nevertheless, taken together, these trails are about as real as America gets, and even the grittiest ones—as we shall see—exhibit a remarkable capacity for recovering their natural beauty over time.

But what is the story here? If rail corridors were so important, why have so many of them been abandoned? And of those abandoned, why have some been turned into parklike trails? To understand, we must trace the full arc of this unique technology and the social, environmental, economic, and political impact the rail companies had on life in the United States in the two centuries following 1830—how the land was acquired, how the routes were laid out, and why many of the corridors didn't survive.

2

Why Were There So Many Rail Corridors?

YOU CAN'T HAVE A RAIL-TRAIL IF YOU DON'T HAVE AN OLD railroad line. There will never be a rail-trail in Central Park. Or down the side of the Grand Canyon. Or from the Hollywood sign over to Malibu. In none of those places did a railroader ever engineer a corridor that would later serve as the base for a trail.

But there aren't many places that didn't have a railroad. Yosemite? Yes, it had one. Yellowstone? Yes, several. New York to Chicago? Definitely; in fact there were seven different routes. The Okefenokee Swamp? Naturally. Up and over the Rocky Mountains? Affirmative, in at least five separate places.

Railroads were developed to get natural resources from the mine, the forest, or the farm field to the processing plant, commercial market, or city. They were invented because laying stones to build a high-quality macadamized (Roman-type) road was almost impossibly expensive in wilderness America with its long distances and scarcity of available workers. Also, the great modern binder material asphalt wasn't known and wouldn't start to come into use until 1887 when the mother lode of natural asphalt, Pitch Lake on the Caribbean island of Trinidad, would be leased to an American to begin providing the new material for "blacktop" roads in the United States and Europe.

Even if an outstanding hard surface could have been constructed in the early nineteenth century, the road wouldn't have been able to compete with a railroad for the low-friction efficiency of iron-on-iron and its relative comfort compared to wooden wagon wheels on rutted dirt and stones. (Air-filled pneumatic tires weren't perfected until 1885.) Moreover, road-based wagons couldn't hold very much and in muddy conditions could turn over and spill an entire load, sometimes more than once in the course of a four- or five-mile trip to market.

The best transportation alternative was the river, on which barges could smoothly carry scores of travelers or many tons of freight. And where rivers were too fast, too rough, or too shallow, canals could be dug alongside with periodic lift locks to handle the grade change. Even though canals were extraordinarily challenging to design, excavate, shore up, and maintain, they could efficiently carry a prodigious amount of goods, making the investment worthwhile. Beginning in 1825, with the opening of the 357-mile Erie Canal on the lowland passage between Albany and Buffalo, New York, canal mania gripped the United States. Although the Erie Canal cost $7 million, took eight years to complete, and resulted in the deaths of perhaps a thousand of its primarily Irish laborers, it was instantly profitable to its investors and to the nation as a whole, it resulted in the rapid development of the trans-Appalachian northwest, and it launched New York City into undisputed national preeminence. Other states were forced to reckon with the immense power of trade, and it certainly appeared that the canal would be the next big thing.

Maryland broke ground on the Chesapeake & Ohio Canal, taking advantage of its geographic position far to the west of New York and thus closer to Ohio, which at that time was the frontier. Pennsylvania began a complex and ambitious rail-and-canal project, "Main Line of Public Works," between Philadelphia and Pittsburgh. Richmond, Virginia, tried a canal along the James River. The fever also spilled into the West—Ohio, Indiana, and beyond.

But canals suffered from drawbacks that made them only marginally more useful than roads. They froze in winter. They were susceptible to droughts and especially to floods. They leaked and needed constant attention. The slow-moving water became putrid. And every eastern state except New York had the impediment of the Appalachian Mountains. The frenzy instigated by the Erie Canal was short-lived. Instead of being a technological salvation, the canal turned out to be a stepping-stone for inventors working on solid ground. Those men were experimenting with the laying of iron rails.

Compared to roads, rails were almost magical. A single horse or mule could pull much heavier loads using wood or metal wheels on a metal rail, and teams of animals could pull multi-carriage trains. On the other hand, there were numerous technical challenges in keeping the tracks straight and even, anchoring them to the ground, keeping them from breaking or wearing out, keeping carriages balanced on the iron bands, and agreeing on a uniform width, not to mention the logistics of handling two-way traffic. The earliest animal-drawn railroads were limited to pulling rock from quarries over to boats on waterways. (One mining company in the eastern Pennsylvania mountains was particularly ingenious, using mules to drag empty railcars up the incline. Workers then loaded the train with coal and rolled it down to the canal below—with the mules hurtling along in special open cars of their own.)

Then the steam-powered locomotive entered the scene. It had gone through a twenty-year gestation period of technical experimentation and growing industrial competence in England, and it made its first tentative appearance in the New World in 1829. The timing was propitious, particularly for the merchants of Baltimore, Philadelphia, and Boston who were panicked about losing their western trade competition to New York. Suddenly there was a technology that could really conquer distance, mountains, valleys, and weather. It wasn't the canal that was going to be the next big thing; it was the railroad.

And it became really big. From today's vantage point, where trains seem to be in the background or even, in some places, virtually underground, it is hard to comprehend the power and centrality of the railroad industry in the nineteenth century. In no particular order of importance, railroads literally opened the country to settlement and transported the majority of immigrants; they consumed the largest share of all foreign investment in the U.S. financial markets; they essentially created the cities of Chicago, Indianapolis, Omaha, St. Paul, Fort Worth, Atlanta, and hundreds of smaller places; they consumed 75 percent of the nation's steel production as well as vast quantities of coal and wood; they provided the crucial logistical difference between the armies of the North and the South in the Civil War; they forced the creation of uniform time zones and redefined the public's sense of time; they served as the backbone of the post office; they revolutionized Americans' diets

Why Were There So Many Rail Corridors?

with fresh produce and meat; they created the first streetcar suburbs; they created millions of jobs but also resulted in tens of thousands of accidental deaths; they destroyed untold numbers of local
economies and forced hundreds of towns into "ghosthood"; they
helped decimate the cultures of scores of Native American tribes;
they revolutionized the relationship between government and private corporations; and they precipitated several of the worst financial panics and depressions the nation had seen up to that time.

Although many Americans today have never set foot aboard
a train, and many others condescendingly view them as unreli-
able relics run by unsmiling crews, railroads from about 1890 to
1930 were at the pinnacle of American culture, setting standards
for speed, frequency, geographic coverage, luxury, capacity, efficiency, and panache. On November 21, 1914, the New York, New
Haven & Hartford Railroad, using sixty-five trains over a four-hour
period, transported 33,468 passengers to the Harvard–Yale foot-
ball game in the brand-new Yale Bowl. Three years earlier, the Milwaukee Road had unveiled the seventy-two-hour Chicago–Seattle
Olympian whose observation cars contained a ladies' tearoom, a
men's smoking room, a library, and a buffet, and also offered bar-
ber and bath services. Within a couple years further amenities
included a telephone for use in terminals, tailor service, and special "Olympian-grams" containing news and stock market reports.
Electric lighting was standard and all cars were vacuum cleaned
daily en route, according to Jim Scribbins in his book *Milwaukee
Road Remembered*. Some trains had pianos, and at least one Pull-
man Palace Car had an organ for Sunday church services. In 1934
the stainless-steel Burlington *Zephyr*, a three-car train so light that
its manufacturer devised the publicity gimmick of pulling it with
a ten-man tug-of-war team, made the 1,015-mile trip from Denver
to Chicago in thirteen hours and five minutes at an *average* speed
of 78 miles per hour. In 1894 St. Louis opened Union Station as
the largest station in the world, with forty-two track gates serving
eighteen different railroad companies. However, even at the height
of railroading, Americans indulged their pent-up frustrations and
their funny bones by coming up with humorous renderings of the
local trains they both loved and vilified. Converting the Minneap-

Table 2. Selected railroad nicknames

Railroad	Nickname
Maryland & Pennsylvania	"Ma & Pa"
New York, Ontario & Western	"Old & Weary"
Chicago Great Western	"The Great Weedy"
Nevada, California & Oregon	"Narrow, Crooked & Ornery"
Midland & Great Northern	"Muddle & Get Nowhere"
Hannibal & St. Joe	"Horrible & Slow Jolting"
Atchison, Topeka & Santa Fe	"All Tramps Sent Free"
Lake Erie & Western	"Leave Early & Walk"
Missouri & North Arkansas	"May Not Arrive"
Toronto, Hamilton & Buffalo	"To Hell & Back"

olis & St. Louis Railroad into the "Misery and Still Limping" was emblematic of the hundreds of affectionate zingers used to chastise the nation's most dominating industry.

Of course, the railroad wasn't just for passengers. In 1888 mail trains employed more than five thousand clerks who gathered, sorted, and distributed 6.5 billion pieces of mail over 126,000 miles of railway, often using iron posts to grab and toss mail sacks from trains moving as fast as 70 miles an hour. The mail cars also had slots where people could deposit letters while the train was stopped in the station. Among the most important trains in the 1920s were the special silk trains, which transported live Chinese silkworms in their cocoons from the port at Tacoma, Washington, to eastern markets. One Milwaukee Road silk train, with fifteen heated cars and traveling faster than a passenger train, was valued for insurance purposes at $4.8 million. If the worms either died or ate through their cocoons before the train reached the East, the shipment was ruined.

• • •

THE FIRST RAILROAD CORRIDOR TO EXPERIMENTALLY HOST A steam locomotive ran west for six miles out of Charleston, South Carolina, in December 1830. (Its locomotive, named *The Best Friend of Charleston*, was also the first to explode a few months later when its fireman, annoyed by the noise of the escaping steam, sealed closed the safety valve.) The first railroad constructed for U.S. common carrier (scheduled) service was built in 1830. Initially using horse-drawn coaches, the route stretched 14 miles west from Baltimore to the town of Ellicott Mills, and it was named the Baltimore & Ohio; "Ohio" being the river, not the state. The Ohio River, for eager Baltimore merchants and traders, was the gold at the end of the rainbow. When the Baltimore & Ohio reached Ellicott City it was in fact still 216 miles shy of the Ohio, but the name said it all. Eventually the B&O did arrive at its namesake river, after twenty-two years of grading, building bridges, and laying track. Not much later it far surpassed that destination and reached all the way to Cincinnati, St. Louis, and Chicago.

Incredibly, that very first rail corridor, known as the Old Main Line, still exists. Even though the B&O corporate entity itself has by now been subsumed and obliterated, the Old Main Line continues to carry an average of six freights a day. Not every B&O corridor has been so lucky, but that's for later. We're still nearly a century ahead of any rail corridor abandonments.

From today's vantage point, there are only a few high-profile corridors that get the lion's share of books, attention, and public television shows—the transcontinental railroad, from Omaha, Nebraska, to Sacramento, California; the Northern Pacific, from Minneapolis to Seattle; and the Atchison, Topeka & Santa Fe over Raton Pass at the southern end of the Rockies. But from the perspective of rail-trails, it was the workaday lines that are of greatest interest. *Why were so many of them built?*

The railroad system didn't have a master plan, certainly nothing decreed by the federal government, a state, or any other overarching entity. U.S. railroading from the very beginning until at least the 1890s was the ultimate expression of free-form capitalist entrepreneurship. Every town, farm field, mine, and forest was a potential source of profit, and entrepreneurs rushed to meet the opportunities. Moreover, every town father knew it, and businessmen and officials were equally eager to embrace the railroaders, lest their hamlet be bypassed and relegated to economic purgatory. As Richard Stone and Michael Landry have written, "While obtain-

Table 3. Rail network density by state at time of maximum build-out, 1916

Rank by density	State	Rail miles	State area (sq. mi.)	Line miles per 100 sq. mi.
1	New Jersey	2,338	7,417	31.5
2	Massachusetts	2,133	7,840	27.2
3	Pennsylvania	11,635	44,817	26.0
4	Illinois	12,742	55,584	22.9
5	Ohio	9,121	40,948	22.3
6	Indiana	7,475	35,867	20.8
7	Connecticut	1,000	4,845	20.6
8	Rhode Island	203	1,045	19.4
9	New York	8,493	47,214	18.0
10	Iowa	9,946	55,869	17.8
11	Delaware	335	1,954	17.1
12	West Virginia	3,974	24,078	16.5
13	Michigan	8,876	56,804	15.6
14	Maryland	1,428	9,774	14.6
15	Wisconsin	7,694	54,310	14.2
16	New Hampshire	1,252	8,968	14.0
17	Georgia	7,482	57,906	12.9
18	Louisiana	5,603	43,562	12.9
19	South Carolina	3,724	30,110	12.4
20	Virginia	4,799	39,594	12.1
21	Missouri	8,270	68,886	12.0
22	Vermont	1,073	9,250	11.6
23	Minnesota	9,153	79,610	11.5
24	Kansas	9,345	81,815	11.4
25	North Carolina	5,537	48,711	11.4
26	Alabama	5,495	50,744	10.8
27	Arkansas	5,294	52,068	10.2
28	Tennessee	4,091	41,217	9.9
29	Florida	5,280	53,927	9.8
30	Kentucky	3,836	39,728	9.7
31	Mississippi	4,439	46,907	9.5
32	Oklahoma	6,454	68,667	9.4
33	Washington	5,698	66,544	8.6

Why Were There So Many Rail Corridors?

34	Nebraska	6,169	76,872	8.0
35	North Dakota	5,275	68,976	7.6
36	Maine	2,263	30,862	7.3
37	Texas	15,867	261,797	6.1
38	South Dakota	4,279	75,885	5.6
39	Colorado	5,702	103,718	5.5
40	California	8,441	155,959	5.4
41	Idaho	2,873	82,747	3.5
42	Montana	4,848	145,552	3.3
43	Oregon	3,067	95,997	3.2
44	Utah	2,137	82,144	2.6
45	New Mexico	3,040	121,356	2.5
46	Arizona	2,410	113,635	2.1
47	Nevada	2,318	109,826	2.1
48	Wyoming	1,906	97,100	2.0
	Total U.S.	254,813	2,959,006	8.6

Note: Alaska and Hawaii were not states in 1916.

ing a railroad did not ensure prosperity, not having one ensured extinction."[1]

The lure was so strong and the feasibility of laying down first-generation rudimentary track was, in most circumstances, so relatively easy that every impresario with a stake of initiating capital, an aspirational route name, and a golden tongue could get himself started. The New York, Chicago & St. Louis? *That sounds rich.* The Central New England & Western? *Looks like limitless profit.* The Cape Fear & Northern. The St. Louis & San Francisco. The Seattle & International. The Ultima Thule, Arkadelphia & Mississippi (which reached none of its named places, though it got close to Arkadelphia). As a supreme expression of self-aggrandizement, dozens of hopefuls added "and Pacific" to their names, no matter how small their chance of reaching the West Coast. They were all aiming over the horizon, and there were hundreds of them.

It may have taken all of human history to bring forth the railroad, but once the pieces finally came together the development curve skyrocketed. From 23 miles in 1830, the network grew to 2,818 miles in 1840 and 9,021 in 1850. That's an annual growth rate of about 20 percent, resulting from a perfect storm of need, greed, and cash. The needy were western farmers and lumbermen with lots of land but almost no local market for what they could produce. The greedy were eastern merchants and shippers who coveted the western trade. And the cash was largely from England—English industrialists who had become ultra-wealthy from the booming cotton business and were looking for an investment outlet. Thus, an extended railroad fever took hold from 1830 until 1890, interrupted only by periodic panics and depressions. And in this environment, companies with the best endpoints, the loudest promoters, and the best-connected political lobbyists (and bribe distributors) fared the best.

Since it had early been established that it would be too unwieldy to allow multiple companies to use the same track—unlike the efficient sharing of today's highways—each new venture had to blaze its own route. Tracks had to be laid by individual companies, and shippers had to put their goods into the cars of individual railroads. Later, elaborate systems of buying and selling trackage rights were devised, and also of sharing and leasing interchangeable freight cars. But in the early days of cutthroat competition between the likes of William Vanderbilt, Edgar Thomson, James J. Hill, Jay Gould, and Jim Fisk, railroads struck out on their own, the number of parallel, redundant tracks be damned. In 1851 there was a route from New York City to Albany. In 1852 a competitor track was opened, running closer to the Hudson River. In 1884 another competitor opened, on the other shore of the river. It was worse in the Midwest. By the mid-twentieth century Chicago was connected to Omaha by seven railroads and to Kansas City by seven more.

In addition, since farmers, miners, loggers, and others had limited ability to ship their wares to distant loading depots, railroads were forced to put down a lot of track. In the Midwest, the general rule was a railroad depot no more than one day's journey from every farm (by horse-drawn wagon, round-trip, over rudimentary roads). In other words, tracks could run in parallel bands as little as 10 or 15 miles apart. Crossing a large state with bands that close yields a lot

Why Were There So Many Rail Corridors?

Table 4. Railroad mileage by state at time of maximum build-out, 1916

Rank by mileage	State	Rail mileage
1	Texas	15,867
2	Illinois	12,742
3	Pennsylvania	11,635
4	Iowa	9,946
5	Kansas	9,345
6	Minnesota	9,153
7	Ohio	9,121
8	Michigan	8,876
9	New York	8,493
10	California	8,441
11	Missouri	8,270
12	Wisconsin	7,694
13	Georgia	7,482
14	Indiana	7,475
15	Oklahoma	6,454
16	Nebraska	6,169
17	Colorado	5,702
18	Washington	5,698
19	Louisiana	5,603
20	North Carolina	5,537
21	Alabama	5,495
22	Arkansas	5,294
23	Florida	5,280
24	North Dakota	5,275
25	Montana	4,848
26	Virginia	4,799
27	Mississippi	4,439
28	South Dakota	4,279
29	Tennessee	4,091
30	West Virginia	3,974
31	Kentucky	3,836
32	South Carolina	3,724
33	Oregon	3,067
34	New Mexico	3,040

35	Idaho	2,873
36	Arizona	2,410
37	New Jersey	2,338
38	Nevada	2,318
39	Maine	2,263
40	Utah	2,137
41	Massachusetts	2,133
42	Wyoming	1,906
43	Maryland	1,428
44	New Hampshire	1,252
45	Vermont	1,073
46	Connecticut	1,000
47	Delaware	335
48	Rhode Island	203
49	District of Columbia	37
	Total	254,850

Note: Alaska and Hawaii were not states in 1916.

of track—12,742 miles in Illinois; 9,946 miles in Iowa; 9,121 miles in Ohio. In a 120-mile-wide swath of western Kansas in 1889, there were seven rail lines. As long as all the economic relationships kept clicking, it worked. But as soon as anything changed—from economic recession to price war to better roads to new transportation technology—some of the corridors began to lose money.

But that was later. We are now still in the construction phase, and private money was only a part of the flood of investable dollars. Another huge chunk came from governments, which became entwined in the mania both through constituent lobbying (or bribery) and through the general enthusiasm of intercity and interstate competition. According to Richard Stone in his book *The Interstate Commerce Commission and the Railroad Industry,* "The willingness of both the national and state governments to subsidize the railroads through land grants, loans, mail contracts and stock subscriptions made railroad speculation very lucrative and attractive. In fact, it was more profitable to build railroads than to operate them. Railroad construction often outran the demand for rail services."[2]

Why Were There So Many Rail Corridors?

Government participation was at every level—local, county, state, and national. It had begun back in the canal era when the federal government dabbled in land donation to help with waterway construction. While the Panic of 1837 had brought sober realities to the fore and made legislators a bit more cautious about extravagant claims, the giveaways continued. The first state to offer free land for a railroad (a strip 60 feet wide plus its accompanying timber) was Florida in 1835. Thanks to public frenzy and intense political pressure, the practice mushroomed, coercing both supportive presidents, like Millard Fillmore, and staunch fiscal conservatives, like Franklin Pierce. In 1850 Congress made its first full-fledged railroad land grant—a gift, in addition to the corridor itself, of alternate adjoining mile-wide sections to enable railroads to sell land that would raise money for actual construction. Since the government kept the alternative sections, it, too, benefited from development and resulting land sales. This grant, pushed by Illinois senator Stephen Douglas, was for the then-unprecedented route of the combined Illinois Central Railroad and the Mobile & Ohio Railroad, more than a thousand miles along the Mississippi River. The federal grant totaled more than 2 million acres.[3] Then the floodgates opened. During the Fillmore administration it jumped to 8.2 million acres. Under Pierce it grew to 19.7 million. During the Civil War it ballooned to 34.5 million, and after the war it reached an almost inconceivable 130 million acres, larger than Ohio, Indiana, Illinois, and Iowa combined. Moreover, this was matched with about 50 million acres of state lands in Texas, Florida, Minnesota, Michigan, Maine, Arkansas, Iowa, Nebraska, and Kansas, in descending order.

In 1871 the mammoth giveaway finally came to an end. Westerners had strongly supported the program because it both provided cheap land and facilitated making the land usable, but they soured on it when they realized that many railroads were taking advantage of the nation's largess. Some companies had never built anything after receiving their land. Others had stopped selling their acreage and were stockpiling it for mineral exploitation. By the time of the last grant, to the Texas & Pacific Railroad, the political tide had reversed, with the public beginning to clamor for the forfeiture of unsold grants.

The deal that had made these land grants more palatable to the public, particularly to easterners, was an agreement by all recipient railroads that they would freely carry both U.S. mail and American military troops, a practice that continued until 1946. Ever since, there has been an arcane and fierce debate between pro- and anti-railroad economists as to which side outmaneuvered the other. Many rail-trail advocates tend instinctively to claim that the now-abandoned land should be donated because "the railroads stole it in the first place" (and those donations sometimes do occur). However, the legal truth about ownership is complicated, varying from place to place and year to year.

The end of federal land grants didn't put an end to corridor construction. Although the northeastern network had already been largely filled in, the rest of the country saw an immense mileage of tracks laid in the 1870s and '80s. (The all-time pinnacle was reached in 1887 with 13,000 new miles in that single 12-month period.) The Chicago, Burlington & Quincy Railroad reached Lincoln, Nebraska, in 1870, Denver in 1882, and St. Paul in 1886. The Louisville & Nashville Railroad connected Pensacola, Florida, with the Appalachicola River by 1882. The Louisville, New Orleans & Texas Railway linked Memphis with New Orleans in 1884. The Wabash Railway, building both east and west, stretched from Detroit to Omaha by 1884. The Chicago, Rock Island & Pacific reached Colorado Springs in 1889, two years after the storied Atchison, Topeka & Santa Fe Railway made it all the way to Los Angeles.

As soon as the crest of track mileage for steam locomotives was reached, a new type of railroad came on the scene. This was the *interurban*, and with it began the next flood of corridor construction. A new genre of motive power, it began as the simple trolley in the late 1880s, an electrified single car (named after the roof-top "troller" that pulled electric power down from overhead wires) that was invented by Frank Sprague, a former colleague of Thomas Edison. The trolley had made its national debut in the unlikely location of Richmond, Virginia, as a replacement for the tracked horsecar. (The need to find a mechanical substitute for the horse had become acute in 1872 when an equine disease killed and disabled thousands of steeds throughout the eastern United States;

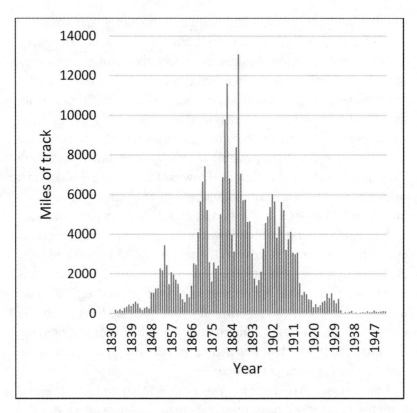

Fig. 1. Miles of track built per year. Data from National Bureau of Economic Research, http://www.nber.org/databases/macrohistory/contents/chapter02 .html, NBER indicator a02082a. Created by author.

many horsecar companies suspended business entirely, while others hired gangs of strong men to pull the vehicles by hand.) Sprague's invention, initially dismissed, became a sensation, and it was profitable too. Trolley companies became interwoven with electricity producers, which then added attractions like amusement parks, swimming pools, zoos, and concert venues to give residents even more reasons to use the rolling stock.

The slow, early trolleys ran on tracks laid within downtown streets. They became valuable cogs of a city's infrastructure, transporting passengers, mail, and coal; hauling garbage; and even serving as hearses. As the technology became more robust, the networks expanded into the countryside, using separate rights-of-way often laid out along the sides of roads. The 20- to 40-horsepower trolleys evolved into 50- to 160-horsepower vehicles that could go much faster and farther, even to distant towns—hence the name "interurban." Another Sprague invention, the multiple-unit control, allowed one engineer to operate two or more linked vehicles that could reach speeds of 60 or more miles an hour. With a headlight, a whistle, paid switchmen, and a set timetable, interurbans were effectively trains, except that since they ran on electricity and were smokeless and they connected with trolley lines, they were allowed to penetrate the centers of towns. The first interurban line, from St. Paul to Minneapolis, opened in 1891. By 1905 virtually every city and town had a network, and, at least in the Northeast and Midwest, nearly all the networks linked with one another. (By changing from one interurban to the next, an unhurried voyager could inexpensively travel from New York to Boston.) Interurbans scooped up much of the short-run passenger and light freight business from the steam railroads, and their business became quite prodigious: in 1914 the main terminal in Indianapolis had five hundred interurban departures and arrivals per day, carrying seven million passengers a year.

The railroads hated the interurbans, but they in fact benefited from their rise, since passenger and small-package service was not profitable. "Trolley mania" lasted until around 1920 and resulted in the construction of about 16,000 miles of free-standing track—that is, railway in its own corridor and not on city streets. The densest networks were in Ohio, Indiana, Illinois, Iowa, and southern Michigan, with other concentrations in the Northeast and on the West Coast. But the rise of automobiles, buses, and trucks led to the interurban's rather rapid demise. Later many of the tracks were obliterated when the adjacent roadways were widened—"rails-to-roads," not a political movement, just a reality. However, a few interurban corridors went into dormancy or were purchased by a local government and survived long enough to become rail-trails. Among the most famous former interurban routes are the Lafayette-Moraga Trail outside Oakland, California, the North Shore Bike Path outside Chicago, and the Baltimore & Annapolis Trail in Maryland.

Another source of rail-trail corridors was the narrow-gauge railroad. These were a variety of facilities built at several different

Why Were There So Many Rail Corridors?

less-than-standard track widths. Much has been written about the many-years-long process of settling on a single, standard 4-foot, 8½-inch track width (including the amazing story of the conversion of the entire Illinois Central main line from Cairo, Illinois, to New Orleans in a *single day* in 1881), but in steep terrain a narrower gauge was cheaper to build. Thus, narrow-gauge railroads were often used to transport logs off heavily timbered slopes, after which the temporary tracks were disassembled and reused. Some of these corridors were located on lands that later became national forests. The most primeval of them can be a bit hard to distinguish from today's traditional hiking trails, though the observant eye may spot the telltale berms, cuts, wide curves, and elevated stream crossings that make rail-trails special. Many can be found in New Hampshire, Pennsylvania, Michigan, and Colorado but also in other states with large tracts of logged national forestland.

In 1916, the year of the maximum extent of the U.S. railroad system, there were 254,037 miles of track—more than five times the size of today's interstate highway system. Many of those corridors were duplicative, particularly after competing railroads were merged or taken over. More than 137,000 miles of track are still operating, but that means that more than 115,000 miles, in thousands of different segments, have been abandoned all around the country. Many are lost forever, some have been saved as trails, some are in public ownership but rusting quietly in the bushes, and some are in an indeterminate limbo awaiting leadership from a local activist or state official. This network, along with any future abandonments from the currently active rail system, makes up the extent of the American rails-to-trails resource. How the trails were created—the political forces necessary to achieve success—is the story of this book.

3

Meanwhile, the Bicycle

WE NOW MUST DETOUR FROM HUNDREDS OF WHEELS TO TWO. From what was presumed to be the world's climax technology to what seems merely a simple elementary contraption: the bicycle.

At first blush, replacing a locomotive with a bike sounds like a joke. Upgrading a trail to a railroad, yes, that feels intuitive. However, the opposite? Going back *down* the technological ladder? But that's not what actually happened. It's not that the frail and wobbly bicycle muscled the robust railroad off its tracks. Rather, when the politics and economics of the railroad dinosaur were upended, it's the bicycling constituency that rushed in to snap up the key piece of infrastructure left behind. In ecological terms it's like an ancient redwood tree crashing to the ground and being replaced by a flimsy blueberry bush, the first pioneer plant to soak up the newly available sunlight.

Of all the instigators, the leading advocates for rail-trails were—and are—bicyclists. Even though bikers aren't as common as walkers or even runners, and they weren't the first group to discover abandoned railroad corridors, it is cyclists who most profoundly feel the need for safe, wide, gentle corridors away from car traffic. But the story of how they arrived at their zealotry is tortured and circuitous.

For starters the bicycle is both younger and more complex than most people realize. No, it was not originated by Leonardo da Vinci (that is a hoax from the 1970s). In fact it wasn't dreamed up at all, as Judith Crown and Glenn Coleman explain in their detailed study of the rise and fall of the Schwinn Bicycle Co. "The bicycle was developed, not invented," they report, its history "ruled by booms and busts, cutthroat competition and a near-Newtonian law of innovation that rewards the nimble and punishes the bland."[1]

The initial surprise is the chronology. Straddling a 28-pound bicycle at a railroad crossing on a country road, feeling the ground shudder under the lumbering weight of a gargantuan locomotive hauling a hundred cars and uncounted tons of coal, or standing by a fence and getting slapped by the wind shock from a 110-mile-an-hour Acela engine pulling six glistening coaches, it's rather hard to believe that the featherweight two-wheeler is the more recent invention. But as baseball manager Casey Stengel used to say, you can look it up. The steam-driven locomotive was developed in England in 1804. That was decades before the chain-driven bicycle finally emerged, also in England, in 1885. Yes, there had been bike precursors earlier in that century, including the pedal-less hobby horse and the one-speed high wheeler, but at the time the general population was first mastering the modern bicycle, locomotives weighing nearly 50 tons were already flying past at 70 miles an hour. Call it "bigger isn't always better," or "small is beautiful," but the bicycle is temporally younger—further along the evolutionary pathway—than the steam engine.

Youthfulness, of course, does not always supplant age, and it's not that bicycles have replaced trains or that trails have replaced all rails. Indeed U.S. railroading in the twenty-first century is a $70-billion-a-year industry, more than ten times larger than the U.S. bicycling business. The point is that the bicycle occupies a surprisingly recent position in planetary transportation development. And ever since it came on the scene, the world has tried to figure out how this newfangled technology fits in. From the traffic engineer's perspective, is it more like very fast walking—or very slow driving? Or something completely unique, with its own geometry and infrastructure? From the marketer's perspective, are its uses primarily purposeful—or recreational? ("Just for kids" is, finally, buried in the scrap heap of history.) From the consumer's perspective, is it primarily social, relaxing, and collaborative—or individualistic, intense, and competitive? To one line of thinking, the bicycle should be the building block for our entire short-distance transportation system, the link between walking and motor-based modes (not to mention the technology that stimulated the Good Roads movement at the turn of the twentieth century). To others, it is merely a toy to enjoy as time and money allow, something akin to the modern roller skate and skateboard. Throughout the decades of its history the bicycle has teetered between these characterizations as it followed a confounding rise-fall-rise-fall trajectory of sales and use. Understanding the technology's strengths and weaknesses is key to understanding why trails are so important to cyclists.

• • •

THE FIRST PRE-BICYCLE—SOMETHING WITH TWO PARALLEL wheels that was "sittable" and steerable—was invented in 1817 in Mannheim, in Baden (now Germany). The Germans called it the *Laufmaschine* (a running device); the French called it the Draisine, after its inventor, Baron Karl von Drais; and the English called it the dandy horse or hobby horse. It was one of those creations that seems to have been ready to emerge for years, but when it took shape it was more in the nature of a curiosity. There is a credible claim that its invention, in 1817, was directly due to the bitter cold of the year before—the famous "Year Without a Summer"—when a large number of horses froze to death or were eaten by starving peasants, leaving many citizens unable to get to market or otherwise travel.

Not that the invention was anything as dandy as a horse. The Draisine had no pedals, so to make it move one had to sit while running, a particularly discomforting form of locomotion. It was even worse going uphill. Rolling down, however, did provide an unparalleled thrill. It also provided the opportunity to gradually get the hang of balancing on two wheels—a counterintuitive maneuver that was truly something new under the sun.

Remember your first time on a bike? Probably not too clearly—you were most likely around six years old. Your mom probably didn't say, "Now, the trick to staying balanced is to make sure that your center of mass remains over the wheels." Your dad probably didn't elaborate with, "To successfully navigate a turn you must lean into it so that the frame can regain its position under your center of mass. This lean is induced by a method known as counter-steering and it happens dozens of times each minute, so subtly that you don't even notice it." And he certainly didn't say, "Actually, although the wheels provide a certain amount of gyroscopic force, scientists are still not 100 percent sure exactly how a bicycle stays up."[2]

Regardless of the physics and the thrill, the Draisine didn't catch on. In the United States it enjoyed a brief fad in New York in 1819, but that left no residue other than a law banning the contraption from sidewalks. It's not clear why developments on the bicycle front moved so slowly for so long. Some scholars blame railroading, with its excitement and potential profit, for sucking up nearly all the attention of inventors and investors in America and Britain. Others contend that the world simply had not yet developed sophisticated enough machine technology to create the necessary parts for a high-functioning bike. Nevertheless tinkerers kept working at it, and in 1855 the bicycle had its first revolutionary moment. A French carriage maker, Ernest Michaud, took the creative step of putting cranks on the front wheel. Good-bye Draisine, hello "velocipede," a concocted Latinization for "fast walking."

The velocipede was a marked improvement. However, don't confuse it with a bicycle of today. It was more comparable to the mechanism of a modern child's tricycle—one speed, no ability to coast, no brake. With a one-speed bike there are only two ways to go faster—by rotating your legs ever more feverishly or by increasing the diameter of the wheel. But as you enlarge the wheel you've got to raise the seat. Gradually the contraption will go from being slightly wobbly to ridiculously dangerous. And it was worse than that. Because the rider sat directly above the front wheel, any pothole or rock tended to throw him—and it was virtually always a *him*—forward, over the handlebar and onto his outstretched arms, bare face, and helmetless head.

At that point the ever-larger velocipede was given the more English appellation "high-wheeler" (and the humorous "penny-farthing," since it reminded Britons of the difference in size between their two common coins).[3] The high wheelers were made of wood, were heavy and undependable, and had no brakes. To stop, one backpedaled with a prayer. A few young daredevils became proficient riders and racers, and one, Pierre Lallement, emigrated in 1866 to America, where he started an intense but very brief high-

Fig. 2. The earliest two-wheeler, the "hobby horse," from 1817, could be powered only by walking or running, but balancing and speeding on the downhill was an intoxicating revelation. L. Brent Vaughan, *Hill's Practical Reference Library of General Knowledge* (New York: Dixon, Hanson & Company, 1906). Courtesy Florida Center for Instructional Technology, https://etc.usf.edu/clipart/.

wheeler craze in New York. That was boom-bust cycle number two, 1868–69. It lasted just long enough to frighten horses and pedestrians and to generate a spate of anti-bicycling ordinances in cities throughout the Northeast. (Actually, since bikes were banned from sidewalks, and since urban roadways were impassably clogged with horse manure and other obstructions, nearly all early cycling was done indoors, in rinks and gymnasiums.)

Despite its dangers and problems, the infant vehicle still had a certain cachet and allure among a small but influential group. In

Meanwhile, the Bicycle

Fig. 3. The addition of pedals in 1855 created the velocipede, but without gears, brakes, or air-filled tires this was still not a safe and comfortable bicycle. That would require another thirty-year wait. *Encyclopaedia Britannica*, 11th ed., vol. 7 (New York: Encyclopaedia Britannica Company, 1910). Courtesy Florida Center for Instructional Technology, https://etc.usf.edu/clipart/.

1876 five English penny-farthings were put on display at the great Centennial Exposition in Philadelphia (where, incidentally, also featured was Pennsylvania Railroad's locomotive *John Bull*; it was undoubtedly the first time a train and a bicycle—an iron horse and a pedal-driven hobby horse—were exhibited together under one roof). The number of fairgoers who were turned on by the exotic two-wheeler is unknown, but at least one of them, former Civil War soldier Albert A. Pope, who owned a factory in Hartford, Connecticut, was so impressed that he decided to convert his production from shoes and small mechanical parts to high-wheelers. Within two years he began producing the Columbia.

The timing was propitious. It was a small, fast-growing industry, and thanks to marketing genius and aggressive legal tactics, Albert Pope went on to dominate it for a quarter century. He became not only a manufacturing powerhouse and an accumulator of bicycle patents but also a political activist, stimulating the formation of local cycling clubs in Boston, Buffalo, New York, Providence, Hartford, and hundreds of other places. These clubs were made up of cyclists who, as Bruce Epperson writes in *Bicycles in American Highway Planning*, were overwhelmingly young, male, and affluent. "The *Columbia* in the late 1870s cost $90, which was nearly three months' wages of a skilled mechanic. Because of that, the members inhabited a particular niche," Epperson says. "Organized upon military lines, the early bicycle clubs offered their members a chance to escape their typically sedentary lives and participate in an activity that recalled the rigors and romance of the recent Civil War with only a hint of its lethal potential."[4] Soon after, high-wheel aficionados gathered in Newport, Rhode Island, and with the unwavering backing of Pope, formed the League of American Wheelmen (LAW), an organization that would ebb and flow in its leadership of cyclists for well over a century, even up to today.

The bicycle was a sensation, but still more to be gawked at than to be used. It was largely the machine of a fringe and somewhat antisocial portion of the population showing off, riding too fast, operating too dangerously in crowded conditions, frightening pedestrians and horses alike, and asserting rights to the public space that seemingly hadn't been earned. The rest of society stood by, watching warily and labeling the daredevils "scorchers."

Then suddenly, finally, inventiveness plus the capabilities of new machining equipment led to a cornucopia of breakthroughs and moved the bicycle into the mainstream. The freewheel was invented in 1869, tensioned wire spokes in 1870, rubber-covered pedals in 1871, rim brakes in 1876, the bike saddle in 1882, the chain in 1885. At last, in that same year—1885—in Coventry, England, two men, John Kemp Starley and William Sutton, combined all the previous decade's modular inventions into the great breakthrough, the "safety bicycle." Named *Rover*, it was an apparatus sporting two roughly 30-inch wheels, a chainring connected to pedals, a chain to the rear wheel, a seat just ahead of the rear wheel, a diamond-shaped frame, axles filled with ball bearings, and a steering column. Three years later Sutton and Starley doubled the pleasure by softening the standard iron and wood wheels with pneumatic tires invented in Ireland in 1888 by John Boyd Dunlop. At last there was a two-wheeled, human-powered transportation technology that was comfortable, made sense, and really worked. In no time it found its way across the Atlantic and started filling what revealed itself as a huge, pent-up demand in America for a "bicycle for the rest of us." Suddenly men who were older, more timid, or less physically fit could all partake of the bicycle's pleasures without risking their lives or their pride. More important, so could women.

The first safety bicycle arrived in the United States in 1887. By the next spring there was a lady's version with a skirt-friendly dropped frame. In 1890 the pneumatic tire crossed the Atlantic and within a few years became standard equipment. By the mid-1890s the average weight of a bicycle dropped from 50 pounds to 23, and speeds shot up so much that by 1894 the fastest cyclist, John Johnson, set a mile track record that was one-tenth of a second faster than the record for a horse. The creative floodgates opened further, inventions poured out, and bicycle sales skyrocketed. In 1895 three hundred American companies sold more than 200,000 bicycles; the number produced more than doubled the next year.[5] Concomitantly the League of American Wheelmen mushroomed in size, peaking in January 1898 with a stunning membership of 103,298.

Almost overnight bicycling became an intoxication and bicycles were everywhere. As documented in Margaret Guroff's great history, *The Mechanical Horse,* the safety bicycle changed America in numerous ways, from women's clothing to social mores, from patterns of consumption to dating rituals, from attitudes toward physical activity to new conceptions of distance. With the freedom and the quick reach it provided, first to wealthier people and soon after to most others, bicycling struck an American nerve like almost nothing before.

The bicycling boom also provided the impetus to pave America's roadways—the so-called Good Roads movement. Choking summer dust and up-to-the-axle springtime mud were bad enough for farm wagons, but for those balancing on two wheels the obstructions could be downright fatal. There was an outcry for smoother and better-laid roads, both in town and out in the country, with LAW making that platform one of the centerpieces of its advocacy.

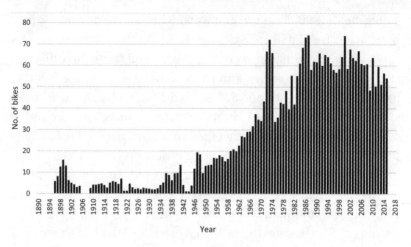

Fig. 4. Estimated number of bikes sold per 1,000 persons in the United States. Created by author.

Of course, it was easy for the city slickers to complain—it wasn't they who had to do the physical labor. Back before there were highway departments or even an expectation that the government had responsibility for roads, convention held that every farm family would donate a few summer days to local highway repair. Comparable to jury duty, it was about as much loved. Thus, being badgered by wealthier urban cyclists to fix the roads was not received kindly in the hinterland. Even though cyclists were creative advocates for good roads, pointing out the potential economic benefit of having travelers who would need food, accommodations, and other services out in the countryside, rural opposition uniformly crushed all early efforts to mandate taxpayer-funded paving.[6] It was one of many struggles between city folk and farmers, presaging some similar battles over rail-trails many decades later.

Then, against all expectation, the bicycle boom went bust. The excitement died off, bike sales declined, the market became glutted, sellers slashed prices, and manufacturers went under in droves. America moved on.

Why? Like so much else in the United States, uneasiness based on race and class was partly to blame. The first cyclists were wealthy young whites, but as bike prices dropped and as a used-bike market emerged, African Americans in the South and immigrants and

Meanwhile, the Bicycle

lower-wage laborers in the North and Midwest began buying bikes, undermining the social status of the original scorchers.[7] This was a period of virulent Jim Crow attitudes, and the League of American Wheelmen itself was riven by the passage of a motion from the Kentucky chapter to ban Black members—at which, the important New York and Massachusetts chapters immediately resigned. Founding club members began falling away, the industry's profitability started shrinking, and the entire business was undermined. Even Albert Pope himself, shocking his competitors, got out of production in 1905. (He got back in a few years later, however.)

Cyclists themselves were guilty of political fragmentation, failure to compromise, and inability to articulate their views to the general public. Bruce Epperson charts numerous tactical missteps within the nascent, divided bicycling community, culminating with this freighted quote from a former president of LAW in the late 1890s: "Some of the greatest political parties have made mistakes. It cannot be expected that an organization comprised chiefly of young men should be entirely free from error."[8] The truth of this observation has been evident within the cycling community for more than a century.

But while racism, classism, and ageism all played roles in bicycling's clumsy leap out of the starting gate, I have a more straightforward theory for the problem: for most people, bicycling proved simply too difficult. It didn't *seem* that hard, and at first the excitement eclipsed everything else. Cycling around town, up and down hills, and into the countryside was life-changing and certainly reason enough, for those who had some money, to splurge on such a major purchase. But keep in mind that the bikes of those days weren't equivalent to today's. Most had no gears, no brakes, and no freewheel. The only way to relieve your legs from constant cranking, even when you went downhill, was to lift your feet and let the pedals spin wildly. Plus the tires punctured easily and so did the inner tubes. The roads were bumpy, muddy, dusty, and rutted. The gearless bikes became hard to pedal the moment a grade was encountered—and roads back then, unlike the better-engineered railroad corridors, were steeply contoured. Without brakes, stopping required pedaling backward (like today's challenging "fixies"). There were no lightweight waterproof garments, and since umbrellas weren't feasible on a bike, rain was a significant setback. Without effective bike lights and almost no streetlights, the hours of darkness in autumn, winter, and spring became a major impediment. Over the seasons and years the day-to-day challenges gradually wore most people down. Taken together, bicycling in the 1890s was a wonderful pastime celebrated in text, song, and social mystique, but ultimately it was not quite worth the travails for many people.

There was another problem. Cyclists couldn't come to agreement on a vision of their place on the roadway. The strong ones adamantly wanted access to every inch of roadway, no matter how cluttered it was with crisscrossing wagons, trolleys, horsecars, carriages, pedestrians, and the occasional newfangled automobile. (Not to mention the fact that there were neither traffic signals nor such rules as driving on the right, passing on the left, or yielding before turning.) Weaker, more timid cyclists were gratified if they were offered specially demarcated bicycle paths, separated from all the other users; they even formed an advocacy organization called the Sidepath League. But when towns with bike paths began banning cycling on regular roadways, the bikers' mild disagreement erupted into a fierce philosophical divide. These were the early battles of a debilitating war that hamstrung the bicycle movement for three-quarters of a century and then, ironically, set the scene for the rails-to-trails movement.

The showdown first played out in Brooklyn, New York. Frederick Law Olmsted, the father of landscape architecture, after designing Prospect Park laid out 5.5-mile-long Ocean Parkway and in 1895 endowed it with the nation's first bike path. It was an immediate sensation that attracted thousands of pedalers from all over. To keep the entire parkway from becoming clogged, the park commission decreed that cyclists had to use the path. For the majority of pedalers this was no insult, as the bike path had a better surface than the carriageway. But a small, vocal group of firebrands was enraged over the restriction and staged voluble protests.

That political split, multiplied in numerous places around the country, was catastrophic to the League of American Wheelmen. By 1900 membership plummeted to 77,000, and by 1902 to an astonishing 8,700. Even worse, the group lost the mantle of the leadership of the Good Roads movement. What had once been a ral-

Meanwhile, the Bicycle

lying cry unifying all the various types of cyclists was lost in the din of partisan bickering, and representatives of the nascent automobile industry grabbed leadership of the potent street-improvement issue, eventually even leaving bicycle officials out of the Good Road coalition's leadership.

Succeeding generations of bicyclists would play out this enervating boom-and-bust pattern at least three more times in the twentieth century. First came a Hollywood-induced mini-boom of the 1930s (due to the enthusiasm of celebrity couple Joan Crawford and Douglas Fairbanks Jr.). By that time bike riding was easier and more pleasant, thanks to better tire, brake, and gear technology. But the advocates refused to unite around a sidepath policy, and by then the roads were already buzzing with far too many autos for the average cyclist to feel comfortable. Another bust. Then with World War II's gas and rubber rationing and the prohibition of automobile manufacture came the next bike boom, this one born of necessity and convenience. By that time prices had come way down and the bike was no longer a status symbol. Theoretically a concerted effort for sidepaths during this period of auto dearth could have been politically painless and potentially successful, but it was not to be. As soon as the war ended, not only were bicycles cast aside and record numbers of new automobiles purchased, but the nation then embarked on history's greatest highway-building program, resulting in 42,000 miles of interstates that explicitly banned bikes. Another bust, at least for the adult portion of the market. (The children's market, flourishing on new suburban sidewalks and cul-de-sacs, was what rescued the bike industry from complete annihilation.)

The third boom occurred in the late 1960s and early '70s. Thanks to a combination of technological upgrades (to so-called English racers), concern for clean air and healthier living, and (after the 1973 oil embargo) surging gasoline prices, bicycle sales reached all-time highs above twenty million per year. For pedaling aficionados like myself it really seemed that the millennium was arriving, except for one factor—there was still no place to comfortably ride. And by then traffic had become a truly serious impediment. Not only that, but the ultra-logical "vehicular cyclists"—the expert riders who fervently believed that bikes were to be treated as the equal of cars in every way—had by then taken firm control of all the cycling institutions, from the League of American Wheelmen to the bicycle offices in the city and state transportation departments. Naïve eco-boosters emotionally asking for a place away from autos were stunned to find themselves shouted down by fellow cyclists who said that the problem wasn't cars but rather ignorance. Bust number three, leading to millions more bikes collecting cobwebs in basements and garages.

During each boom, the intoxicating lure of bicycling's promise generated publicity, enthusiasm, and sales, and after each, the sobering reality of the physical and social challenges nipped the excitement in the bud. Bad roads, societal opprobrium, sartorial difficulties, inequities of class and race, rural-versus-urban mores, and then cars, cars, and more cars. It was a bit like repeatedly taking a candle outside into the wind, each time hoping the flame will finally maintain the perfection it demonstrates in still air. The indoor flame is the boom, the outdoor flame the bust.

Most people agree that silently pedaling down a gentle and smoothly paved incline on an optimally fitted bike in perfect weather, shirt flapping in the breeze and scenery flitting by at a delightfully eye-catching pace, is among life's pinnacle experiences. That's nirvana, the candle burning brightly. Then there are the other realities—the soaking rain, the numbing cold, the grinding hills or painfully bad road surface, the roasting sun, sticky humidity, relentless wind or impenetrable darkness. Worse than those, for most people, are the cars—cars that are so seductively comfortable and easy to use as a bike replacement, and, conversely, that are so fast, heavy, and obliviously driven—or worse—that they make cycling scary and unpleasant. That's the candle flame cringing in the wind.

By 1950 the nation was heading into the teeth of the automobile age. There was actually a fourth bike boom with the development of the macho, knobby-tired mountain bike in the 1980s, and there were years when bikes outsold cars, but the purposeful bicycle and the recreational bicycle—precision tools that needed a precision environment to enfold and nourish them—were already engulfed by auto traffic. The early advocates never learned how to unite and provide the milieu they needed. And they wouldn't get a second chance until abandoned railroad corridors started appearing, like a discarded miracle from heaven.

Meanwhile, the Bicycle

4

Dark Days and a Seismic Shift

"I want to go to Chicago in the worst way."

"You want to go to Chicago in the worst way?"

"Yes."

"Take the Erie!"

IT WASN'T SUPPOSED TO BE LIKE THAT CYNICAL JOKE. AS WORLD WAR II ended, the railroads were expected to flourish. Specifically for our purposes here, there was a brief, fleeting moment when U.S. transportation policy could have fused suburban bicycling and intercity railroading into a seamless, perfect fit. After all, the convenient, nimble, space-conserving bike is ideal for covering the "first mile" from home or the "last mile" to work, while the muscular, efficient high-speed train is perfect for moving multitudes the longer distance between. For decades consummating this theoretical union had been thwarted by impediments—company takeovers, uncyclable roads, railroad nationalization during World War I, economic collapses, and then during World War II a vastly overcrowded track network. Finally, after the war, it seemed that the rainbow of this marriage might be visible at the end of the highway.

But it was not to be. Despite the elegance of the bike-train-bike minuet, most Americans felt the whole rigamarole could be eliminated by the effortless, all-weather, one-step solution of buying an automobile. Which they did by the millions. Driving in the early years felt like a nearly free lunch; only in the 1960s would severe societal impacts begin showing up—clogged highways, smoggy air, road rage, the distortion of urban life as buildings were torn down for gargantuan parking lots and high-rise garages, and a massive collective expense. This was America's second Great Disruption (the first one, 100 years earlier, being due to the railroads). The automobile, combined with each state's highway program and every city's urban renewal scheme, was redesigning virtually every facet of our culture. And with almost no warning, both trains and bikes found themselves brusquely bulldozed aside.

Bikes, already on shaky ground, went first. They had taken a big hit in the early years of the twentieth century, and despite small waves of resurgence from technological improvements, health claims, or Hollywood glamour, the overall effect was like the occasional hopeful ripple in a rapidly receding tide. The Depression led a few people to pedal rather than drive, but of course those were people far down the social order who didn't set any trends. The economic earthquake of World War II democratized things a bit and led to a short bicycling rebirth when Detroit was ordered to make military tanks rather than autos and when gasoline and tires were severely rationed. In fact the bicycle proved itself to be an outstanding emergency vehicle in scores of applications, both on road and within sprawling production facilities. But it didn't last. Those soldiers embracing their girlfriends in Times Square on vj Day might well have been kissing their bikes good-bye. With the rise of auto traffic, on-street cycling came almost to an end, while off-street trails were essentially nonexistent. The adult bicyclist came close to obliteration.

For railroads the carnage was more surprising, more tortured, and profoundly ironic since the 1950s could have been the decade when the sector's many battered stars would finally align. Here was a business that had dominated the industrial, economic, and cultural life of the United States for nearly a century. It had carried settlers west. It had survived price wars as vicious as one in 1887 between the Southern Pacific Railroad and the Santa Fe Railway, where a ticket from Chicago to Los Angeles could be had for $1. It had transported millions of soldiers free of charge as repayment for lands given to railroads by the federal government. It had been nationalized during World War I and reprivatized immediately after. It had struggled through the Depression with catastrophic drop-offs in shipping, travel, and revenue, and then during World War II, turned around to transport unprecedented billions of tons of war materiel plus hundreds of millions of soldiers and civilians in outmoded equipment on tracks that had been under-maintained for years. Despite all the glories of song and film, railroading had suffered and barely survived a jujitsu assault.

Industry optimists predicted a postwar corporate resurrection that would be led by the diesel-electric locomotive, the powerful new technology that simplified railroad operations and greatly increased the ability to haul long trains and heavy loads. With diesels the requirement for coal-shoveling firemen or for helper engines at steep grades was cut, and there was no need at all to stop at water tanks for refilling. Enthusiastically the companies scrapped tens of thousands of hulking old steam engines, switched to diesel, and began pouring investment into all facets of their physical plants, including lightweight passenger trains, welded-rail tracks, and safer crossings.

The table was set, but the guests didn't show. Many of the invitees were waylaid by shiny new government-funded highways and airports. Shippers were increasingly choosing trucks, short-distance passengers were using cars, and long-distance travelers were rapidly shifting to airplanes (if they had money) or to intercity buses (if they didn't). The U.S. Post Office Department shocked the industry in 1967 by ending the fast railway post office cars that had financially propped up the long-distance passenger trains; mail thenceforth went by truck, airplane, or freight rail.

Historians have long debated the role of the federal government in the slow-motion disaster. Without doubt, massive federal subsidies for the competitive modes of highways, waterways, ports, and airports served as a weighty finger on the other side of the balance, proving nearly ruinous to the private rail enterprise. Moreover, a fairly consistent string of rulings by the Interstate Commerce Commission in favor of shippers and small towns forced the railroads to continue spending millions of dollars maintaining and operating unprofitable routes. On the other hand, the industry's long and often sordid history of rate manipulation, stock fraud, town and shipper intimidation, political machination, and other noxious tactics had left a residue of bitterness toward the business that may well have fostered enthusiasm for alternatives.

The deterioration in passenger service, both long distance and commuter, became obvious to the general public, and it played into the vicious cycle of auto buying, road building, more auto buying, and train decline. Interestingly that warning bell didn't overly alarm the rail companies (other than at New York's virtually passenger-only Long Island Rail Road). Insiders well knew that passenger service was a problematic, low-profit, and thankless subspecies of the business that was kept alive mostly through the mandates of regulators and politicians. The more people shifted to cars and buses, the railroads thought, the more they would be able to focus on their freight-hauling strengths and compete with trucks, boats, and cargo planes.

They were wrong. All the railroads struggled, and some didn't even come close to making it. The first company to abandon its entire system, in 1957, was the hapless 541-mile New York, Ontario & Western Railway. Next, three years later, was the Lehigh & New England, 177 miles. The dominoes were teetering.

Scrambling to avoid liquidation, most companies began to negotiate mergers. The combinations were very big news, and for a while they gave the impression that smaller regional carriers were becoming massive nationwide players. Between 1957 and 1968, for instance, the modest Chicago & North Western Railroad (C&NW), under the aggressive leadership of Ben Heineman, gobbled up both feeder lines and side-by-side competitors. Among these were the Chicago, St. Paul, Minneapolis & Omaha Railroad, the Litchfield & Madison Railroad, the Minneapolis & St. Louis Railroad, the Chicago Great Western Railroad, the Des Moines & Central Iowa Railroad, and the Fort Dodge, Des Moines & Southern Railroad. These were smaller systems, but Heineman came close to also acquiring the huge Chicago, Milwaukee, St. Paul & Pacific Railroad and the Chicago, Rock Island & Pacific Railroad. C&NW would have become a 30,000-mile behemoth, even though it was so financially fragile that it soon thereafter sold itself to its own workers and then was later taken over by the Union Pacific Railroad.

It also happened in the East. The Chesapeake & Ohio swallowed the Pere Marquette in 1947 and then fifteen years later did the inconceivable by absorbing the venerable Baltimore & Ohio, eventually even eliminating its famous Capitol dome logo. Changing its name to the Chessie System, the conglomerate next picked up the Western Maryland Railway in 1968 and the Seaboard Coast Line Railroad and Louisville & Nashville Railroad in 1980, whereupon its name changed once more, to the sterile and anonymous csx Corporation (C for Chessie, S for Seaboard, and—I'm guessing—X for some undefined ominous speculation of what the future might hold).

And in the West. In 1970 four of the great names in northwest railroading—Chicago, Burlington & Quincy Railroad, Great Northern Railway, Northern Pacific Railroad, and Spokane, Portland & Seattle Railroad—combined into the huge Burlington Northern system. (The other famous northwestern line, the Milwaukee Road, which was left out of the merger, went into bankruptcy seven years later and became the source of the single longest rail abandonment ever, from eastern Montana almost to the Pacific Ocean.)

The grandest and most catastrophic merger took place in 1967, following ten years of negotiation—the unification of archrivals Pennsylvania Railroad and New York Central (plus the frail, commuter-heavy New York, New Haven & Hartford) into the Penn Central. On paper it looked like the mightiest railroad of all time, representing well over a hundred years of unparalleled railroad leadership, but after only three years of failing to marry two clashing cultures and losing $1 million a day, it collapsed in the largest corporate bankruptcy to that point in American history.

The mergers were touted as cost-cutting victories and administrative streamlining breakthroughs, but they were actually corporate restructurings heavy with worker layoffs, union setbacks, and small-town debacles. It was the seismic, painful redesign of America's largest industry from a "serve everyone with everything they need over every distance" model to a limited framework that focused on the steady, long-distance movement of large-volume, lower-value commodities like coal, gravel, grain, oil, and lumber. Within the merged entities, schedules were reduced, maintenance slashed, speeds cut, services eliminated, and of course duplicative track scrutinized.

Famous passenger trains came to an end—the Milwaukee's *Olympian Hiawatha* between Chicago and Seattle in 1961; the New Haven's *Cape Codder* between New York and Hyannis in 1964; the

Lackawanna's *Phoebe Snow* through the cleaner-burning coal region between Hoboken, New Jersey, and Buffalo (with its advertising jingle, "My gown stays white / From morn till night / Upon the road of anthracite") in 1966; the New York Central's *Twentieth Century Limited* between New York and Chicago in 1967; and the gleaming, stainless-steel, three-railroad *California Zephyr* vista-dome streamliner between Chicago and Oakland, California, in 1970. It was the loss of the *Zephyr* that accelerated the formation of Amtrak, the federally sponsored skeletal national intercity rail passenger system. But while Amtrak saved some trains at its start-up on May 1, 1971, its creation came at the price of many dozens of others that were discontinued, taking with them famous names and long-standing traditions—Norfolk & Western's *Wabash Cannonball* from Detroit to St. Louis; the B&O's *National Limited* from St. Louis to Washington; and the Union Pacific's combined *City of Los Angeles/City of San Francisco/City of Denver/City of Portland.*

Then the freight routes themselves started to falter. The Erie-Lackawanna ended its route across lower New York State after damage from Hurricane Agnes in 1972. The Lehigh & Hudson stopped all service after a fire knocked out the Poughkeepsie Bridge in 1974. Snoqualmie Pass in Washington was closed in 1975, and the rest of the long Milwaukee Road corridor across Montana and the Rockies was lost in 1977. A few years later the Denver & Rio Grande Western shut down its route through the Royal Gorge and over Tennessee Pass in southern Colorado. Hardest hit were states in the Northeast, Upper Midwest, and Great Plains, but even economically growing states like Texas, Florida, Georgia, and Tennessee saw significant reductions in mileage.

The public cried out in anger and confusion. Commuters seethed at the decline in service. Shippers lamented lost markets. Old-timers reminisced about past glory days of dressing up for the ride to the big city. Historians recalled the excitement of the massive engines' smoke plumes and steam. Children mourned the death of the caboose. Environmental scientists deplored the loss of the nation's second most energy-efficient transportation technology (after the bicycle). Even hobos remembered their shared hard times hopping on freight-train boxcars they called "side-door Pullmans."

Table 5. Percent of corridor miles abandoned, 1916–2010

State	Mileage, 1916	Mileage, 2010	Percent abandoned
New Hampshire	1,252	426	66.0
Connecticut	1,000	364	63.6
Iowa	9,946	3,897	60.8
Maine	2,263	896	60.4
Michigan	8,876	3,634	59.1
New York	8,493	3,479	59.0
South Dakota	4,279	1,754	59.0
Massachusetts	2,133	896	58.0
New Jersey	2,338	983	58.0
Rhode Island	203	87	57.1
Pennsylvania	11,635	5,071	56.4
Wisconsin	7,694	3,387	56.0
Colorado	5,702	2,688	52.9
Missouri	8,270	4,019	51.4
Minnesota	9,153	4,521	50.6
Oklahoma	6,454	3,273	49.3
Louisiana	5,603	2,858	49.0
Nevada	2,318	1,192	48.6
Kansas	9,345	4,891	47.7
Nebraska	6,169	3,236	47.5
Arkansas	5,294	2,797	47.2
Maryland	1,428	755	47.1
Vermont	1,073	590	45.0
Florida	5,280	2,907	44.9
Illinois	12,742	7,028	44.8
Mississippi	4,439	2,454	44.7
West Virginia	3,974	2,228	43.9
Washington	5,698	3,215	43.6
Idaho	2,873	1,627	43.4
Indiana	7,475	4,273	42.8
Ohio	9,121	5,303	41.9
North Carolina	5,537	3,245	41.4
Alabama	5,495	3,254	40.8
New Mexico	3,040	1,835	39.6

Dark Days and a Seismic Shift

South Carolina	3,724	2,293	38.4
District of Columbia	37	23	37.8
Georgia	7,482	4,679	37.5
California	8,441	5,307	37.1
North Dakota	5,275	3,346	36.6
Utah	2,137	1,356	36.5
Tennessee	4,091	2,656	35.1
Texas	15,867	10,384	34.6
Montana	4,848	3,173	34.6
Kentucky	3,836	2,526	34.2
Virginia	4,799	3,214	33.0
Delaware	335	227	32.2
Arizona	2,410	1,683	30.2
Oregon	3,067	2,395	21.9
Wyoming	1,906	1,860	2.4
Alaska	n.a.	506	-
Hawaii	n.a.	0	-
	254,850	138,691	54.4

In reply, leaders of the new "disruption" industries—automobiles, trucks, buses, and airlines—along with millions of pragmatic and fatalistic Americans, countered with "you can't fight progress" and "don't be a romantic—what you hear is the marketplace speaking."

In truth it was a heavily manipulated marketplace, and this time it was the railroads that were outmaneuvered. That story is beyond the scope of this book, although it is noteworthy that the loud public outcry was over what happened to the *trains*, not to the *tracks*. Almost no one paid attention to the inventory of rusty, trash-filled corridors or noticed that they were the only resource that was growing. Abandonments like Tuscaloosa to Boyles Yard in Alabama, 60 miles. Oakland to Richmond in California, 9 miles. Lewes to Rehoboth in Delaware, 5 miles. Foley Junction to Live Oak in Florida, 40 miles. Albany to Cordele in Georgia, 33 miles. Storm Lake to Rembrandt in Iowa, 13 miles. Pekin to Morton in Illinois, 40 miles. Hundreds of long stretches and thousands of small ones—to mills and mines and warehouses and factories. To grain elevators and quarries. To small towns and backwater suburbs. To the weaker destinations in big cities. To defunct military bases and to unviable ports.

There was a massive economic tug-of-war under way over the future of railroading, and the reluctant arbiter was the federal Interstate Commerce Commission (ICC), the nation's very first federal regulatory agency. Created in 1887 following the longtime agitation of farmers and their allies, the ICC had a long and tortured history as the politico-legalistic middleman attempting to referee the competing forces of shippers, railroads, workers, passengers, towns, other transportation modes, and even the environment.[1] For the first years, the railroads used the courts and other mechanisms to hold off almost all attempted reform. Gradually, after the turn of the twentieth century, progressives with the help of President Theodore Roosevelt instituted rule changes and increasingly harsh regulation that began to have a taming impact. That worked—and perhaps too well. By the 1960s the tightening noose, combined with technological and economic changes in the society, caused the industry to begin strangling, and neither Congress nor the ICC could find a way to untie the Gordian knot.

The story of the ICC and the railroads is fascinating and convoluted, but only one key issue concerns us here: the abandonment of railroad corridors. And, since the economics of railroading were always shaky, abandonment was no minor matter. (Even at the high point of American railroading in 1916, one-seventh of all the trackage—37,000 miles—was being operated by companies that were at that moment in bankruptcy.) Railroads wanted to shed any branch line that wasn't bringing in revenue, while shippers and small towns wanted to save every track, even for intermittent use or just for possible reactivation. Generally speaking, in the first two decades of the twentieth century, the ICC followed the wishes of local politicians and made it almost impossible to abandon track. But with the rise of trucking and taxpayer-funded roads, the equation began to change. Shippers finally had other options, railroads started to suffer from competition, and over the years Congress passed new legislation making it ever easier to abandon a track— first in 1920, then in 1958, 1972, 1976, 1979, and 1980.

First to go were obscure tracks that had snaked into old resource-extractive hinterlands—played-out mines and cut-over forests. Following shortly thereafter were many of the interurbans—the lower-quality tracks, often built along the sides of roads, that had been economically weak from the start. Then the Depression hit and the pace of business failures shot up. By 1940 more than 23,000 miles of track had already been abandoned, generally short segments serving defunct industries and near-ghost towns. Following the transportation frenzy of World War II there was another bump in abandonments, and by 1963 it had climbed to more than 49,000 miles.

By the time we get to the end of this book, near the conclusion of the second decade of the twenty-first century, railroad abandonments will have reached to nearly the 120,000-mile mark, and fifteen states will have shed more than half their original mileage. But even in the late 1960s and early 1970s a few visionary conservationists, naturalists, outdoor enthusiasts, and park lovers were beginning to think about putting some of these unique linear strips to a second use.

5

Is This Idea for Real?

"WE ARE HUMAN BEINGS. WE ARE ABLE TO WALK UPRIGHT ON two feet. We need a footpath. Right now there is chance for Chicago and its suburbs to have a footpath, a long one."

So began a 1963 letter to the editor in the *Chicago Tribune*. Written by May Theilgaard Watts, a prominent naturalist at the Morton Arboretum who had been inspired by hiking in England, the letter painted a romantic picture of a trail that would feature wildflowers, fruit trees and tallgrass prairie plants, waterbirds wading through mud banks, benches provided by the garden club, students studying ecological procession, Boy Scouts walking to earn merit badges, and cyclists flying by safe from traffic. But it also ended on an ominous note: "That is all in the future, the possible future. Right now the right-of-way lies waiting, and many hands are itching for it. Many bulldozers are drooling."[1]

The route that Watts had in mind was the corridor of a once-dynamic interurban, the Chicago, Aurora & Elgin Railroad (CA&E), whose business petered out due to massive suburban highway construction, and which ceased service in 1959. (Passenger service had stopped two years earlier with CA&E infamously shutting down its commuter trains midday, stranding its final passengers downtown.) A group of visionaries sprang up, astutely decided to name the corridor the Illinois Prairie Path, organized an exploratory walk along the tracks, and began agitating for its acquisition. The Illinois Prairie Path wasn't the nation's first rail-trail—Pennsylvania's Stony Valley Trail dates back to 1949 and South Carolina's short Cathedral Aisle fragment goes back even further, to 1939—but no previous rail-trail proposal had been located within a densely populated area and had gotten any kind of public attention.

Of course trails themselves weren't new. Long before the iron horse, the nation was crisscrossed with Native American and early white settler walking paths. In New England in the 1800s a cadre of robust trampers built a network of beautiful and thoughtfully designed mountain meanders. Europe, naturally, had a lengthy history of walking routes that cosmopolitan American travelers like May Watts discovered in places such as England and Switzerland. Then, starting in 1921, a small group of visionaries began creating the Appalachian Trail, the unprecedented backcountry mountaintop route proposed by planner and conservationist Benton MacKaye.

The concept of the Appalachian Trail, stretching from Maine to Georgia, was truly mind-expanding. It wasn't a purposeful town-to-town route, and it wasn't merely an up-to-the-summit path for a great view. It was something that gave people permission to fantasize about walking long distances. Few would actually do a full through-hike, but even setting foot on a small, hour-long portion of the trail in western Massachusetts or far outside New York City or above Charlottesville, Virginia, opened up the illusion and maybe even the desire of going onward, by foot, forever.

The proposed Appalachian Trail was not a rail-trail—in fact, the AT is decidedly the antithesis of a rail-trail. Benton McKaye's concept traversed the high country, it was rugged, it was remote, it meandered, and it depended upon the goodwill and handshake agreements of a continuous string of landowners. Rail corridors, in contrast, wend their way through the valleys, are essentially flat and run from town to town, pass through the thick of commerce, and are locked into a very specific route by bands of steel. Still, both could grab their users' imaginations, stimulating them to wonder what's around every next bend and to also dream of life in the past.

The Illinois Prairie Path's gestation wasn't easy. Watts was an extraordinary motivator, and she quickly attracted a cadre of smart, enthusiastic, and hardworking volunteers, but they were political novices dealing with an unprecedented idea and a resource that crossed the boundaries of three counties and a multitude of towns. Fortunately, the big player, DuPage County, didn't need much persuading to purchase the corridor, although its quick action was not for a love of trails. It snapped up the line (for $400,000) under a hazier mercantile justification—perhaps automobile parking, or utility poles, or a water or sewer line. Assuring that the land was saved for the kind of nature park the conservationists had in mind would require years of grassroots fund-raising and political struggle.

Meanwhile, three years after Watts's original letter to the editor and 500 miles to the east, two outdoor lovers in Rochester, New York, Waldo Nielsen and Ralph Colt, became entranced by a slightly different fantasy. Inspired with former president John F. Kennedy's widely publicized interest in physical fitness, Nielsen and Colt resolved to hike 50 miles in a single day. But where could they do it? Uninterested in the idea of circling a static track, they also couldn't stomach the thought of trudging endlessly along the shoulders of roadways. New York had hundreds of miles of mountain hiking trails, but the men worried that that much exertion would turn a rigorous challenge into an impossibility. Suddenly, Nielsen later wrote, "it occurred to Ralph and myself that there are ideal trails for adventure of this sort. Long stretches of level and clear paths— abandoned railroad rights-of-way!"[2]

The men were not aware of what was happening in the Chicago suburbs, but they had heard of the 1957 abandonment of the old New York, Ontario & Western Railroad after its failure to compete with trucks, boats, and cargo planes. They decided to try to hike one of those old tracks, from Fulton, New York, to Oneida. The rails were gone but the intrepid explorers still had to tramp over fist-size ballast and rotting ties, and then were forced to ford cold, waist-high streams where trestles had been removed. They did it in just under twenty hours. (Had they been even more intrepid, they could have gone farther; the abandonment actually extended another 210 miles past the Catskill Mountain Jewish resorts all the way to the Hudson River.) Nielsen was hooked. "The path," he wrote, "leads through cuts and takes one along embankments or fill many feet above the surrounding terrain. One passes farms and villages, crosses creeks and roads, and walks through heavily wooded sections."[3]

A New York City boy who narrowly escaped death in World War II, Nielsen had become an engineer for Eastman Kodak in Rochester. He was curious and energetic, and he loved history as well as every kind of outdoor recreation. He resolved to compile a listing and make a map of all the abandoned railroads in New York State. His purpose was twofold—to show other explorers where the corridors were and to stimulate government planners to consider acquiring the routes for trails. His method for taking on the daunting task was rudimentary but effective. He got hold of every decade's Rand McNally railroad atlas and carefully compared them, book by book, as each iteration steadily showed fewer and fewer live tracks. After finishing New York State he realized it only made sense to do the same for the entire country. The result, published in 1974, was *Right-of-Way*, whose cover sported a picture of Nielsen stooping over to study a row of trackless, decaying railroad ties. The first edition contained a listing of 35,000 miles of abandoned corridor, each one coded by its general decade of abandonment.

Waldo Nielsen, unlike May Watts, wasn't a political organizer. He was a methodical collector of data. His book took no account of issues of ownership, trespassing, fences, mounds of trash, or any of the other mishaps that can befall a track the moment it stops being used. (In fact only many years later was a part of his fateful first hiking route developed into a formal trail, and even today its quality is rather low.) But Nielsen made a different kind of mark. His book alerted people—including some of the folks who later started the Rails-to-Trails Conservancy—to be on the lookout for abandoned rails and to explore walking on them.

Meanwhile, while Watts and Nielsen were inching forward as individual citizens in Illinois and New York, the state of Wisconsin used its sovereign power to swoop in and purchase the track that became the nation's seminal rail-trail.

Elroy, Wisconsin, a small town halfway between Chicago and Minneapolis, was once a significant railroad stop. It was the place for steam locomotives to refuel, to refill their water supply, and to turn around, and the Elroy Beanery was the place where everyone ate. After dieselization, with no more need for water and coal, the trains ceased stopping in Elroy, and the town lost much of its purpose. By 1964 the Chicago & North Western Railroad was ready to drop some tracks in the vicinity, including the scenic, rugged, and somewhat problematic old corridor between Elroy and Sparta, Wisconsin. That 32-mile stretch was so hilly that its 3 percent grades

Is This Idea for Real?

required the use of extra "helper" locomotives, and its construction back in 1873 had even required the blasting of three tunnels, one of them three-quarters of a mile long. Moreover, since tunnels during the frigid northland winter often suffer from freezing and cracking, the railroad had installed Brobdingnagian wooden doors on their portals that had to be manually opened and closed when a wintertime train approached.

While tunnels and challenging grades were tough on railroads, they added excitement for would-be hikers in the scenic backcountry of rural Wisconsin. One man who jumped on that idea was Alan Thompson, vice-chair of the Juneau County Board of Supervisors and father of future Wisconsin governor Tommy Thompson.

"Dad loved that old track," Tommy Thompson reminisced in a 2019 phone conversation. "It ran alongside our ranch. Calvin Coolidge came through on it, and so did Harry Truman. When Truman stopped in Elroy to give a five-minute speech, my father had me sitting on his shoulders, and the president waved at me. Later, Vice President Richard Nixon also came through and spoke from the back of a train. For him it was a little different. He'd hoisted a child up on the balcony when suddenly the train started moving. I'll never forget seeing that panicked father running down the track and a nervous Nixon handing the boy to him."

The Thompsons were deeply committed to Elroy. If they couldn't keep the trains running, they wanted to at least save the corridor for its tourism value, so they appealed to the state conservation commission to buy it. There wasn't much of a plan—maybe it could be used for hiking and camping, or possibly just for backcountry access by hunters. The Boy Scouts chimed in, enthusiastically estimating that as many as a thousand hikers a year might use it. Neighboring Monroe County, which contained most of the mileage as well as the larger town of Sparta, was also supportive. But, the younger Thompson said, "We beat 'em to the punch! That's why it's called Elroy-Sparta and not the other way around. Still, we were all in it together. A few farmers worried about fencing for their cows, so the state said it would cover half the cost. It happened so fast no one had much time to think about it. The rail bed was swampy and not good for farming. There wasn't much controversy."

On June 25, 1965, the Wisconsin Conservation Department voted to buy the 32-mile, 420-acre corridor from the Chicago & North Western Railroad. The price was $12,000—now referred to as the deal of the century. Two years after, with the ballast nicely covered by a compacted layer of limestone screenings, it opened to the public. At first, only hiking and horses were allowed, but it quickly became apparent that cycling would be the most logical and popular use—as long as riders remembered to bring lights and ponchos for the dark, drippy tunnels.

By 1968 there was a total of perhaps thirty rail-trails in the country. Other than the Illinois Prairie Path and the Elroy-Sparta Trail, the rest were mostly obscure, backcountry logging routes that had been absorbed into surrounding state parks or federal forests. Almost indistinguishable from the other hiking trails around them, they weren't thought of as special. Rail-trails were not yet a "thing"; the name itself wasn't coined until 1986.

Nevertheless the trails movement as a whole was moving up in importance. As detailed in Steve Elkinton's *A Grand Experiment*, a fine history of the National Trails System, the new stirring in the air had begun in the late 1950s and gathered momentum when Congress created the Outdoor Recreation Resources Review Commission (ORRRC). In 1962 the commission had published its influential report, *Outdoor Recreation for America*,[4] which became the blueprint for a raft of visionary, unprecedented laws over the next few years—the National Wilderness Act, the National Wild and Scenic Rivers Act, the Land and Water Conservation Fund, and the National Trails System Act. President Kennedy and his Interior Department secretary, Stewart Udall, quickly followed the report by creating the Bureau of Outdoor Recreation. A few years later President Lyndon Johnson, under the influence of his conservation-oriented wife, Lady Bird, released a "Special Message to Congress on Conservation and Restoration of Natural Beauty." A remarkable document, it described a rather thrilling vision of a cleaner, healthier, and more beautiful America, from its urban centers to its rural expanses. The section on trails was emblematic and even jumped ahead of most Americans' knowledge base. It said, in part:

Is This Idea for Real?

The forgotten outdoorsmen of today are those who like to walk, hike, ride horseback or bicycle. For them we must have trails as well as highways. Nor should motor vehicles be permitted to tyrannize the more leisurely human traffic. Old and young alike can participate. Our doctors recommend and encourage such activity for fitness and fun. I am requesting, therefore, that the Secretary of the Interior work with his colleagues in the federal government and with state and local leaders and recommend to me a cooperative program to encourage a national system of trails, building up the more than hundred thousand miles of trails in our National Forests and Parks. There are many new and exciting trail projects underway across the land. In Arizona, a county has arranged for miles of irrigation canal banks to be used by riders and hikers. In Illinois, an abandoned railroad right of way is being developed as a "Prairie Path." In New Mexico utility rights of way are used as public trails. As with so much of our quest for beauty and quality, each community has opportunities for action.[5]

This message led to the White House Conference on Conservation and Natural Beauty, which led to an Interior Department study and the publication of *Trails for America*,[6] which led to congressional hearings and, finally, in 1968 to the congressional passage of the National Trails System Act. Memorably, President Johnson signed the bill into law on the same day he also approved the National Wild and Scenic Rivers Act.

The law gave trail advocates their first sliver of a seat at the table. Suddenly—finally—trails had legitimacy from both the White House and Congress. However, the Trails Act was heavily skewed toward the Appalachian Trail and other long-distance, backcountry routes, and it didn't specifically do anything for rail-trails. In fact the hiking-oriented bill barely made reference to any kinds of facilities for bicycling.

There were many reasons that the rails-to-trails movement got off to a slow start in the 1960s. First, trails were the province of walkers and hikers, and most of those constituents were searching for solitude, beauty, and views, if not full-fledged mountain-scaling exertion. (At this time bicycling, as previously noted, was still largely the realm of children on sidewalks and cul-de-sacs.) For hikers, flat rail corridors seemed uninviting, if not downright repellent, with their town-to-town alignments and warehouses, their chain-link fences and barking dogs, and their random, low-status vegetation—especially when the rusting, littered tracks were still in place.

Second, it wasn't easy to build publicity around the concept since most of the early rail-trail examples were located deep in the backcountry. Elroy-Sparta, for example, is almost a three-hour drive from Minneapolis and even farther from Milwaukee and Chicago. And there seemed no reason for the railroads themselves to mention the idea of a rail-trail. In fact the railroads had spent decades warning people to keep off tracks and stay away from railroad property.

Third, the large wave of railroad abandonments hadn't yet hit. About 1,300 miles went defunct in 1969 and 1,700 miles in 1970, but those yearly numbers would double and triple over the next two decades. (As for the many miles of interurban lines that had been laid, most had been paved over and incorporated into adjacent roadways, so they weren't sitting there vacant and tickling the imagination of would-be explorers.)

Finally, many Americans were profoundly conflicted about the whole idea of rail abandonment. Yes, abandoning tracks seemed like an economic fact of life, and many people admitted that trains had become so bad that they themselves rarely used them, but a surprising number still had allegiance to the memories and allure of railroads. Even though a thirty-second elevator speech about rails-to-trails was compelling, the response as the elevator door opened was frequently, "It's a great idea, but I love trains!"

Committed train lovers, known as "railfans," didn't go quietly into the night. And, in truth, many trail advocates even rooted for them, holding off on any agitation for a recreation facility until every rail preservation avenue was thoroughly explored. Generally the flow of events followed a five-step hierarchy of denial and grieving:

1. Try to convince the railroad not to abandon.

2. Attempt to use the government to prohibit the railroad from abandoning.

3. Look for a short-line railroad to buy the line and operate it, on

Is This Idea for Real?

the theory that a nonunion entity might be able to eke out profits that the major carrier couldn't.

4. Seek donations locally to create a new nonprofit entity for a seasonal tourist-train operation, on the theory that volunteer energy might generate enough cash flow to at least pay taxes and insurance on the operation.

5. Reluctantly give up. If angry, walk away. If merely sad, join with trail advocates and serve as advisor on keeping the corridor as historically accurate, well documented, and well remembered as possible.

This flow of events played out in hundreds of communities. As a matter of fact, a surprising number of corridors were saved in step 3—there are today more than six hundred short-line railroads throughout the country—and a few were even rescued in step 4. According to the website american-rails.com, there are about 180 tourist train rides in the United States. When the Rails-to-Trails Conservancy came into existence, its standard explanatory line was always, "We are pro-railroad and do not advocate abandonment. We only want to save the corridor if it can't be used for trains anymore."

There actually was one other wild idea to save the tracks and still use them for trails, and that was to pedal right on the rails. This charming Disneyesque fantasy led to the invention of the railbike. Of course no mortal person can balance a bike on a track, and even if one converted the rubber tires to track-hugging metal flanges and then locked the handlebar, the contraption would immediately fall over, since cycling requires continuous microscopic adjustments of the front wheel to stay balanced. But a modified bike with a third flanged wheel on a diagonal arm to the other track—a tricycle, really—can do it. So can a full-fledged, four-wheel flanged vehicle with pedals. Of course it's heavier than a bike, but that's partly canceled out by the benefit of low-friction metal-on-metal travel. When William Gillum of Colorado Springs built a railbike, after seeing an English prospector pushing a wagon full of tools on some mountain tracks, *Popular Mechanics* picked it up, and Gillum received more than two thousand inquiries from around the world, including one from the design shop at General Motors. Another railbiker made such a splash when he was spotted in New Hampshire that the story was featured on page one of the *Wall Street Journal*. The king of railbiking appears to have been Richard Smart, a dentist in Coeur d'Alene, Idaho, who logged 25,000 miles on his contraption, built up a large library of written and electronic materials, filed a patent for a new design, and sold twenty-nine of his creations.

The railbike is a great thought bubble, and it could be a fine amusement park ride, but in the real world it has drawbacks. Most problematically, on single tracks railbikes can't pass each other, even those going in the same direction, which leads to "track rage" and radically reduces the number of people who can participate. Also, railroad companies hate the idea. It's not easy to know if a track is truly unused or not. It's also possible to start out on an abandoned segment and suddenly end up facing a train on a live track. Smart, the dentist, had to stop making his railcycles after receiving a string of aggressive letters from railroad lawyers.

At first, railfans staved off advocates of rail-trails, but the tide was running against full-fledged preservation of the tracks. For one thing, the rails and ties had considerable value as scrap, and the financially marginal railroad companies wanted to cash in where they could. For another, much more contentious issues of land-ownership rose to the fore.

• • •

A RAILROAD CORRIDOR MAY LOOK LIKE AN IMMUTABLE ICON for the ages, but from a legal standpoint it has been compared to a bundle of sticks lashed together with twine. The tracks are the twine; when they are taken away, the corridor is often revealed to be a hodgepodge of legal agreements usually dating back a century or more. Some of the parcels were originally purchased by the railroad, in which case it still owns them. Others were given or sold as easements by adjacent landowners with the understanding that the land would be returned if the trains stopped running. Other parcels were condemned—taken for a fee—by the railroad if a crucial landowner refused to negotiate, and condemnation rules varied by state and by year in the nineteenth century. And still other parcels were given by a multiplicity of governmental agencies under a variety of rules. Add to this the fact that most original railroad companies went bankrupt, were bought out, or were merged several times over the years, putting the deeds into ever dustier corners of old filing boxes. Finally, the very definition of "abandonment" is surprisingly murky, even today. Companies have considerable latitude in how they legally define a track's status, and there have been cases where a railroad (or an adjacent landowner) deems a line abandoned only to be told by a court that it's not. Taken together, those factors can quickly turn a rails-to-trails debate into a community's quagmire and a lawyer's paradise.

The folks in Elroy and Sparta were blissfully unaware of the potential land mines around them, or perhaps they were lucky that none of the track's neighbors thought litigiously. A similar swift early victory was scored in neighboring Minnesota as soon as the commissioner of the Minnesota Department of Natural Resources, Robert Herbst, got involved. When Herbst learned in 1970 that the Chicago Great Western Railroad planned to abandon a 12-mile track from Rochester through farmland and villages to the town of Pine Island, his ears pricked up. "I knew about that track from my wife," Herbst reminisced almost fifty years later. "It ran right past her daddy's farm, and she told me that railroad was the way she walked to school every day."

Herbst, a classic Minnesota activist, had already created the state's new programs for wild and scenic rivers and for trails. He resolved to purchase the track. "It would be a present for her and for the whole state," he said. As in Elroy the railroad was amenable, and the corridor became the Douglas State Trail, the state's first rail-trail. Today as one of twenty-one Minnesota state rail-trails, it gets more than 100,000 users a year, not only locals but also recovering patients at Rochester's world-famous Mayo Clinic and their visiting family members seeking a break in the outdoors.

But not all trail creation efforts went so smoothly. In Iowa the early win–loss record was abysmal. Today it is a standout state with nearly eighty rail-trails totaling more than eight hundred miles, but as recently as 1984 Iowa had only one, with every other attempt foiled. Usually it was a farmer who wanted the land; other times it was a town that clamored for parking, a highway department that desired a wider road, or a community that was simply nervous about outsiders wandering behind their homes.

Iowa, like all the Midwest, was crisscrossed by so-called granger roads, railroads that had laid thousands of miles of relatively proximate tracks to haul out farmers' grain at harvesttime. Financially, the overextended granger roads were vulnerable, and when the economics started unwinding, companies like the Chicago Great Western (CGW)—"The Corn Belt Route"—felt the pain first. Even before the CGW went bankrupt and was taken over by the Chicago & North Western (C&NW) in 1968, it had already abandoned 118 miles of track in Minnesota and Iowa. But after the merger the company's routes were so redundant that the abandonments took off—479 miles in 1969, 364 miles in 1970, 471 in 1971, and on and on through the 1980s. By 1985 Chicago & North Western had abandoned 6,647 miles of track. Not all its routes were lost—there are today a slew of short-line railroads with some C&NW in their genealogy—but many became fodder for rails-to-trails proposals.

Geography is destiny, and topography played a role in the nature and intensity of the struggles. In hilly and mountainous places like Pennsylvania, West Virginia, and Idaho, railroads were run through stream valleys, thereby making the strips less desirable to adjacent landowners and more valuable to state conservation agencies. In flatter areas like Iowa, Kansas, Illinois, Oklahoma, and Texas, railroads ran across the countryside straight and even. Some of the affected farmers wanted to eliminate an annoying diagonal line through their property to simplify planting and harvesting; others wanted to rid themselves of the burden of maintaining a fence. And not a few harbored generations of resentment against the railroad that had originally taken their great-grandfather's land. (In one old joke a farmer comes home to find his barn burned down, his house carried off by a tornado, and his wife run off with the hired hand. He goes out to the tracks across his field, raises his fist and bellows, "That goddamned railroad!")

Whatever the reasons for the inability to save many corridors, two factors were paramount: trail advocates were still too few and far between, and most of them were not aware of what was about to happen with their local track. With no early-warning system,

Is This Idea for Real?

those who cared were caught off guard, and between the lack of notice, the intransigence of the railroads, and the opposition of the adjacent landowners, most trail efforts were over before they had even begun.

But as the calendar rolled into the activist 1970s, changes were coming.

6

Congress Steps In

THE CONVERSION OF ABANDONED RAIL LINES TO TRAILS WASN'T a Great Society–type program that came out of a mandate from Washington DC. It was an up-from-the-grassroots movement that bubbled out of modest places like Sparta, Wisconsin; Maywood, Illinois; and Rochester, Minnesota. It soon spread, as we will shortly see, to other modest places like Columbia, Missouri; Falls Church, Virginia; and Center Point, Iowa. Nevertheless, in rather short order, the rise of some thorny political and legal issues—not to mention exciting opportunities—elevated the issue to the U.S. Congress and the federal bureaucracy.

The first federal agency pulled into the fray was the harried Interstate Commerce Commission. The ICC had been dealing with abandonments for decades, but that had previously only been in the context of a binary conflict between railroads and shippers. The concept of a third interest group—post-abandonment corridor savers—was a new curveball that the commission was less than excited to take a swing at. For one thing, the ICC had long been lobbied by railroads to speed up its decision making on abandonments (ICC resolutions had averaged 420 days each), and the agency had recently complied. Suddenly there was pressure from local communities and citizen organizations to slow the process *down* to give them *more* time to try to rescue a line for a trail.

The other agency that pricked up its ears to the faint sound of rail-trails coming was the U.S. Department of the Interior, specifically its small and obscure Bureau of Outdoor Recreation. This bureau had been created in 1962 by Interior Secretary Stewart Udall to fill the space between the highly preservation-oriented National Park Service and the sports-and-crafts bent of local park departments.

With a motivated and entrepreneurial staff, the bureau had developed a culture of activism, doing outreach into low-income communities that were often political tinderboxes due in part to a lack of outdoor places to exercise. Rail-trails, which were national in scope but not "natural" enough to pass muster with the National Park Service, were a perfect fit for the Bureau of Outdoor Recreation, and in 1971 it published a visionary booklet called "Establishing Trails on Rights-of-Way." After explaining the benefits and giving some history, the booklet exhorted activism. It even gave the specific locations of hundreds of railroad corridors that had been abandoned between 1960 and 1970.

Meanwhile on Capitol Hill two unrelated tides were rising. One was aiming to solve the railroads' economic problems, while the other sought to meet the public's demand for more trails. If ever they fused, they would make waves. Ironically, when the union finally did happen, a new railroad law yielded a surprise trail program, and an innovative trail act broke new ground in railroad practice.

First up was the railroad bill.

By the time the Penn Central went bankrupt in 1970, the tightly regulated U.S. railroad industry was so deeply mired in crisis that Congress needed eleven years and five laws to devise a way out. Of many sticky questions, one was whether railroads would be allowed to abandon money-losing routes and, if so, how. In 1975 when a Senate subcommittee held fifteen days of hearings on the topic, virtually everyone who testified held one of two opposing concerns—keeping the lines open for the benefit of shippers and communities or sloughing off uneconomical routes for the benefit of railroads and their stockholders. But one committee staff member, Tom Allison, had something else on his mind.

Allison was a young lawyer, newly in from Seattle. He was a strong runner ("he would cut back to quarter-speed so that I could keep up with him," recalled one of his colleagues), he loved trains ("actually, he loved everything that went fast," his first wife later reminisced), and he was a clever tactician ("I have yet to find anyone who had his overarching understanding of the role of railroads," reminisced another committee colleague, "and he was driven by notions of the good things that government can do."). During his law school years at the University of Washington, Allison had closely followed a local controversy over the 1971 abandonment of a train track through the university's grounds. The fledgling effort to save it as the Burke-Gilman running and biking trail may have had particular resonance for him since he had suffered leg damage in a bicycle accident while in school.

When Allison passed the Washington State bar, he had the honor of being sworn in by the Supreme Court's pro-conservation justice, William O. Douglas; he then landed a clerkship with Senator Warren Magnuson (D-WA), chairman of the Senate Commerce Committee. In DC, in his free time, Allison ran on the Chesapeake & Ohio (C&O) Canal towpath, which had been saved and recently turned into a national park partly through the help of Justice Douglas. While running, Allison undoubtedly spotted the adjacent, little-used Georgetown Branch rail line, and he was probably also aware of efforts in nearby Virginia to create a trail out of the abandoned Washington & Old Dominion (W&OD) Railroad. He started wondering if he could use politics to combine his instincts for saving railroads with his interest in nature conservation. Fortunately at work he had recently been promoted to counsel for the Transportation Committee.

What Allison had in mind was preserving rail corridors after abandonment. He may or may not have known of the legal complexities involved, but under Senator Magnuson's co-sponsorship, the measure he drafted was introduced as the Conversion of Abandoned Rights-of-Way Act. Specifically, the bill called for identifying tracks without rail service (or where it would likely soon terminate) that were potentially suitable for biking or walking. It authorized $25 million for the Departments of Transportation and Interior to provide technical and financial assistance for the conversions. The concept was approved, and the small measure was folded into the much larger Railroad Revitalization and Regulatory Reform bill (known as the 4R Act).

Over in the House of Representatives, similar legislation was passed two weeks later. It included a provision to set up a smaller, $5-million rails-to-trails program within the Transportation Department. (Tellingly, at that time, the Department of Transportation didn't support the rails-to-trails provision, stating "While relatively small, these [rails-to-trails] authorizations cannot be justified in the context of the pressing need for financial assistance for other railroad programs." But the demurral was ignored.) Since the House and Senate bills were not identical, a conference committee was set up to iron out the differences and bring the two bills into alignment. The committee went with the more generous Senate rails-to-trails funding.

Before the final votes could take place, however, the Gerald Ford administration announced that the spending level was too high and threatened a veto. In response, the conferees returned for intensive negotiations, one consequence being a reduction of the trails portion to $20 million. But still it survived, and on February 5, 1976, President Ford signed the Railroad Revitalization and Regulatory Reform Act. Thanks to Tom Allison, the United States finally had a tiny national rails-to-trails program.

In reflecting on Allison's work, his colleague Sallie Adams said, "Tom was able to keep the micro, the macro and the public interest all in alignment." He had done that with this program—a small strategy that, if it could prove itself, held the seeds for something very big.

Sadly while Tom Allison had a very successful legal career—Congress, the U.S. Department of Transportation, and a long run in private practice in Seattle—his seminal, behind-the-scenes role in the rails-to-trails movement was not known during his lifetime. He died in 2012 before his achievement was recognized.

• • •

MEANWHILE AN EVEN MORE REMARKABLE STORY WAS STARTing to play out in the other chamber of the Capitol, on the trail side of the coin.

Pathways, as we have seen, had never had much resonance in Congress. Yes, there had been the 1968 National Trails System Act, but in comparison to canals, railroads, and roadways, trails had seemed laughably unqualified for funding. To the limited extent they ever got support, it was at the state or local level, and usually through private donations or volunteer labor.

Even the 1968 law, created with so much anticipation, disappointed its backers. Eight years after its passage, so little had occurred on the ground that frustrated conservationists prevailed upon Congressman Roy Taylor (D-NC) to schedule an oversight hearing. The hearing revealed that, in a typical Washington scenario, money had been authorized by Congress but then hadn't been obligated by the Nixon and Ford administrations. It was like being told to go shopping but given an empty wallet.

"In his gentlemanly way, Taylor pinned their asses to the wall," recalled Cleve Pinnix, the committee staffer who set up the hearing. He was describing the predicament of the bureaucrats who came up to testify. The record clearly showed that significant trail money was badly needed. The elderly Taylor retired soon thereafter, but his place was taken by a remarkable congressional bulldog named Phil Burton (D-CA).

Parks were not Burton's top passion. A labor lawyer, he was primarily interested in justice for the poor and downtrodden, but he did think of parks as refuges for the less fortunate, and as a San Franciscan he also had a particular interest in preserving the redwoods and in saving the green spaces around the Golden Gate. Burton wasn't an outdoorsman and didn't know much about parks ("the only time you'll find me in the woods," he said, "is if I have to walk in 50 feet to go to the toilet"), but he was a master deal maker and he was unstoppable. As described by former interior assistant secretary Bob Herbst, "Burton always had 50 bills in his right back pocket and 20 political IOUs in his left back pocket." Herbst recalled a phone call at midnight where Burton said, "I'm drunk, Bob, but hear me out. The longer I talk the more sense this will make."

Burton had Pinnix do much of the policy work while he did the political horse trading. The first outcome of the collaboration was the breathtakingly large National Parks and Recreation Act. (Memorably, when the $1.4-billion bill cleared a committee hurdle in only five minutes, a conservative congressman said, "Notice how quiet we are. We all got something in there.")[1] Passed in 1978, it still stands as the largest park bill ever voted out by Congress.

The following year Burton picked up where he had left off. Since seven trail bills had failed to make it into the previous bill, the con-

Congress Steps In

gressman and Pinnix pulled those concepts together as the nucleus of new legislation to amend the National Trails System Act. The bill mostly focused on the nitty-gritty needs of particular trails, but one section was different. It was lofty and nonspecific: "The Secretary of Transportation, in administering the Federal Aid Program, together with Chairman of the Interstate Commerce Commission and the Secretary of the Interior, in administering the Railroad Revitalization and Regulatory Reform Act of 1976, shall encourage State and local agencies and private interests to establish such trails using the provisions of such programs."

The bill passed the House on September 22. The vague "such trails" clause was hardly a centerpiece of the legislation; in the introductory comments, it was referred to only as one of "numerous technical and clarifying amendments." During the House floor debate it wasn't mentioned at all. The Senate also passed it. But time ran out before the two bills could be conformed, and the measure died with the end of the session.

Looking ahead to the next Congress, Burton planned to immediately reintroduce the amendments, but then came the political earthquake of the 1980 election. Not only was President Jimmy Carter defeated by Ronald Reagan, but the Democrats also lost their majority in the Senate as well as seats in the House. Because of the precarious new politics, Burton asked his staff and allies to take the bill around to all the remaining senators and to key members of the bureaucracy to make sure that no one had any problems with it. One of the young allies who literally walked the bill around the halls of the Interior Department was Craig Evans, the newly hired director of the American Hiking Society. Normally, Evans recalled, when he spent time at the sprawling Interior Department, it was at the National Park Service, but this time Burton specifically told him to go to a different corridor and show the bill to a young lawyer named Pete Raynor.

Raynor, from Long Island, New York, had graduated in 1969 from Cornell Law School and had been hired by a large New York law firm. But he soon decided that he wanted to work for the public good, settled for a lower salary, and landed a job in the solicitor's office at the U.S. Department of the Interior. There Raynor cut his environmental teeth on a lawsuit over the newly established Redwoods National Park. Through that work he connected with Congressman Burton.

"Burton was a brilliant, omnivorous, larger-than-life character with a steel trap mind," Raynor related. "Anything he read, he never forgot. If you wrote him a memo, he could recall what it said better than you could. He remembered the exact wording of early bill drafts that had long been discarded. Plus, he was aggressive and fearless. He rose late, rarely got to the committee room before 4 p.m. and then worked past midnight. I would go over there in the evening and we'd kick around ideas for hours. I was mesmerized."

Raynor, like Tom Allison, was a runner on the C&O Canal, which headed in the direction of his home in suburban Maryland. He soon noticed the lightly used Georgetown Branch railroad track that paralleled the towpath before curving off into the woods. "I thought, wouldn't it be cool if instead of having my wife drive to pick me up from the Canal, I could run on the tracks, which would take me almost right home." But, as a lawyer, he also realized that if the railroad ever stopped running, the easements underlying the track would likely disappear and the corridor would be broken up into individual parcels and lost.

One of Raynor's friends and mentors at the National Park Service was Chuck Rinaldi, the man in charge of land acquisition for the Appalachian Trail. At the time, the AT was painfully discontinuous, with many on-road sections substituting for proper natural routes. Rinaldi was a skillful negotiator and land purchaser. Spending time with him taught Raynor about the many legal problems that faced anyone trying to maintain a continuous route.

When Craig Evans carried Burton's draft bill over to Raynor's office and Raynor saw the sentence about railroad corridors, he knew immediately that it was not specific enough to make a difference in a legal dispute. Going to one of his superiors, he suggested the idea of something stronger. "How about a 'bank' for railroad corridors?" he hypothesized. "If they were in a bank, they wouldn't be officially abandoned but could be saved for the future." This was pushing an envelope that didn't even exist. This was railbanking.

The response he received was enigmatic. "Whatever your idea is on this, I don't want to know about it." To Raynor, that was a go-ahead to try it on Burton's people.

Pinnix liked the concept, as did his Republican staff counter-part, Clay Peters. To the theoretical worry that the railroad industry might have a problem with railbanking, the staffers recalled one of Burton's frequent responses: "I only deal with people at the table." The railroads weren't at this particular table (and not even aware of it). In any case, Raynor, whose old New York law firm had rep-resented the Pennsylvania Railroad, felt he was attuned to the rail industry's thinking about this issue.

"The railroads' main fear was liability," he said. "They didn't really care about a bank for the future. They just didn't want any-one using their tracks, getting hurt and then suing. As long as we could protect them from liability, they didn't worry all that much about the old corridors."

Raynor loves what he calls "simple little laws." When he sat down at his typewriter that day, the language that he banged out—only two sentences—were designed to do just that. To the bland origi-nal, which he left alone, he added some muscle: "*Such interim use shall not be treated . . . as an abandonment of the use of such rights-of-way for railroad purposes.* If a State, political subdivision, or quali-fied private organization is prepared to assume full responsibility for management of such rights-of-way . . . *the Commission shall impose . . . interim use . . . and shall not permit abandonment or dis-continuance . . . disruptive of such use*" (emphasis added).[2]

In the bill's accompanying report, Pinnix added a bit of explana-tion to the legalese: "The purpose of this section is to encourage the development of additional metropolitan area trails. . . . Interim use . . . should not necessarily constitute an abandonment . . . for railroad purposes."

This new language was added at the beginning of 1981; the bill came out of committee later that year and finally came before the full House of Representatives on May 11, 1982, with Burton as floor manager. He had worked his usual deal-maker magic, and the floor debate was a lovefest, with members of all political stripes show-ing support. It passed, 389–6.

In the Senate, three months later, the Public Lands Subcommittee held its own hearing on the Trails Act Amendment. Testifying were a cross-section of federal agencies and private hiking groups, and everyone strongly endorsed the bill, but again the railbanking provision received virtually no attention. The only person who flagged its importance—the only one who even mentioned the word "railroad"—was Jeanette Fitzwilliams of the Virginia Trails Council. A month later, the Interior Department's official response devoted only one pallid sentence to the topic: "While we strongly support the objectives of this provision, we defer to the views of the other agencies involved as to its enactment."

The measure was reported out of the Senate committee, but it again succumbed to the calendar. Failing to come up for a full vote in time, it expired with the 97th Congress. The legislation had to start over for a third time.

Finally, the next year the trail gods smiled. On January 27, 1983, the bill, unchanged, was introduced by Senators Jim McClure (R-ID) and Malcolm Wallop (R-WY). It passed the Senate by voice vote on February 3, passed the House in identical form, also by voice vote on March 15, and was signed by President Ronald Reagan as the National Trails System Act Amendments on March 28, 1983.

Two weeks later, on April 10, Phillip Burton died of an aneurysm.

7

It's Perfect! Who Could Be Against It?

ON OCTOBER 11, 1977, THE GOVERNMENT ANNOUNCED IT HAD $5 million in demonstration grants to divide among communities interested in creating a trail out of an abandoned railroad line.

This was the outcome of the rails-to-trails concept that Tom Allison had enshrined in the 4R Act the year before. Though greatly diminished, it had survived to become the frail foundation of a future edifice. Allison had envisioned that the program would be run by the Department of Transportation, but DOT, disinterested, had turned it over to the Department of the Interior. Similarly unenthusiastic, the Interior top brass passed it down to their less-than-renowned Bureau of Outdoor Recreation (BOR). Then, only weeks later, BOR was abolished and reorganized into something new called the Heritage Conservation and Recreation Service (HCRS).

It was an unpromising beginning. No one knew how much interest the grant program would unleash. Unlike most environmental issues, like air and water pollution, converting rails to trails wasn't a fix for an obvious health problem; it was more in the nature of a great opportunity growing from an old economic misfortune. Meanwhile the HCRS staffers, acutely aware of their own tenuous position within the Interior Department, needed some quick successes and positive newspaper headlines. They wanted projects that were virtually shovel-ready. The agency also wanted geographic diversity so that it could court as many Congress members as possible. Plus, HCRS was able to offer the public only a short two and a half months to find out about the announcement and make an application.

But the enthusiasm was instantly apparent: an astounding 135 requests poured in from around the country, collectively asking for

$70 million. Of course, many were akin to a wish and a prayer, and HCRS had to cull out numerous proposals, some from places where tracks had not yet even been abandoned. By mid-1978, nine winners were chosen—one each in California, Maryland, Missouri, New Jersey, New York, Ohio, Pennsylvania, Virginia, and Washington.

The program was born exuberantly, but it didn't save the star-crossed HCRS; the agency's demise occurred before any of the nine trails actually came on line. Following the election of Ronald Reagan (who had famously signaled his stance on the environment with, "You've seen one redwood, you've seen them all"), the service was dismembered and its bones were sent to a corner of the National Park Service, never to be re-funded. Recalling that moment of transfer, the Park Service's coordinator of national trails, Bob Karotko, said, "We knew nothing about rails-to-trails, and our higher-ups couldn't have cared less."

But, as in a Greek legend, the severed head sprouted, and all nine projects grew into successful trails. Several, in fact, can lay claim to outsized roles in the genealogy of the rails-to-trails movement. The Washington & Old Dominion Railroad Regional Park (W&OD Trail), in the Virginia suburbs of the nation's capital, became particularly influential; its fortuitous location introduced many government staffers and even some members of Congress themselves to the concept of running or biking on a rail-trail. (Years later, after the Rails-to-Trails Conservancy came into being and began sending advocates to Capitol Hill, many an aide's blank stare became a big smile with, "Ohhh! You mean like the W&OD?") North of San Francisco, in a relentlessly hilly region that previously provided the populace only a high-speed highway link, the Mill Valley–Sausalito Path utilized the area's small remaining amount of non-flooded flatland to demonstrate a solution for cyclists, walkers, tourists, and even schoolchildren. In the college town of Columbia, Missouri, the city's small but courageous park and recreation department created the Show-Me State's first rail-trail and then used that short-distance success to leverage interest and funding for the 200-mile-long Katy Trail. Outside Albany, New York, the Mohawk-Hudson Bikeway, pieced together from the old Crescent Branch of the New York Central Railroad and the defunct Schenectady &

It's Perfect! Who Could Be Against It?

Troy interurban, served as a linchpin of what gradually grew into a 360-mile behemoth rail-and-canal trail linking the state's capital to Buffalo. And outside Cincinnati, the state of Ohio conceptualized a 46-mile rail-trail alongside the pristine Little Miami River—a trail that has led to the creation of an entire cross-state Ohio River to Lake Erie pathway from Cincinnati to Cleveland.

Rarely—perhaps never—has a small, almost still-birthed federal program had such an outsized and lasting impact.[1]

But this was not a languid roll down the rails. Each of the nine projects faced daunting, near-mortal challenges, and on average each required an eight-year slog before ribbon-cutting. The struggles were a harbinger, but then so were the victories. They were proof that creating this kind of pathway was authentically difficult but also that the value of the final product was worth it. For rail-trails, the phrase "No pain, no gain" wasn't a platitude. It was a reminder that these were real conflicts, unlike many other efforts involving bicycles or pedestrians (such as the mere erection of green "Bike Route" or yellow "Thickly Settled" signs with a hope for the best). Creating a rail-trail could be a true community-changing and even a life-changing phenomenon. Significantly, for many who took the challenge on, politics was a kind of contest they had never engaged in before.

Emblematic of these twisting, turning journeys was the creation of Maryland's Torrey Brown Trail out of the old Northern Central Railroad.

The Northern Central can trace its lineage to 1828, virtually the beginning of U.S. railroading. After numerous technological and political struggles, reorganizations, and name changes, the tracks from Baltimore were allowed into Pennsylvania, reaching Harrisburg in 1851. (The delay was due to powerful Philadelphia merchants who saw no reason that the frontier trade should be siphoned off to a rival port in another state.) The route enjoyed a distinguished freight and passenger career, but by the 1960s it had deteriorated into a barely profitable segment of the Penn Central Railroad. After severe damage in 1972 from Hurricane Agnes, it was taken out of service.

When Penn Central applied for the line's abandonment, Baltimore County executive Ted Venetoulis leaped at the chance to acquire it.

He envisioned not only a trail through the bucolic Maryland countryside but also a possible route for a fiber-optic cable. The Maryland Department of Natural Resources (DNR) similarly liked the idea and agreed to acquire the line if the county would then lease it back. The Interior Department liked it too and awarded Maryland $400,000 for acquisition. "The competition was very stiff," said Mac Wilkerson, regional DNR administrator. "We got the money because our application stressed that it was a partnership between the county and the state."

But theory clashed with reality: the trail corridor itself was repugnant. Without corporate oversight and maintenance, it had become a dumping ground for trash and a haven for dirt-bike riders. The neighbors hated it, and virtually every local politician came out against public acquisition. When Venetoulis ran for governor in 1978 (and lost), his successor as county executive immediately repudiated the trail. Fortunately it was too late. The state had already purchased the land.

"One of the heroes in this battle was Governor William Donald Schaeffer," said Wilkerson. "He told us to just take the heat from the neighbors and wait. We had very poor title on the land, basically just a public use condition, but we proceeded as if we owned it. We identified over 200 adjacent property owners, getting land donations wherever we could. If they pushed back on us, we made them prove their legal interest. If someone had a legitimate claim, we would buy them out."

Wilkerson and his boss, Secretary of Natural Resources Torrey Brown, were deeply committed to the trail, but the legalities and the glacial pace caused the National Park Service (NPS), successor to HCRS, to worry that it would never happen. To avoid losing the grant, Wilkerson cannily arranged a financial swap—Maryland would use state money for the cost of the acquisition if NPS would hold its funds for development, whenever that would actually occur in the future.

NPS agreed, but then things went from bad to worse. Baltimore County backed out entirely, leaving the land in the state's hands. DNR Secretary Brown, in an attempt to placate the opposition, appointed a citizens advisory committee made up of adjacent land-

　　It's Perfect! Who Could Be Against It?

owners. "Unfortunately," Wilkerson recalled, "75 percent of them were against the trail. Every meeting devolved into a bitter debate. Fortunately the corridor ran through an existing state park, so we incorporated the project into that and gave it an administrative home." With support from runners, cyclists, and equestrians, the tide very gradually began to turn. "We started by cleaning up. Opponents had been saying, 'If it's this bad now, just think how bad it will be as a trail.' We showed them it was the opposite—we took out 600 tons of trash. *600 tons!* And we began restoring an old trail station as a visitor center. As the uproar settled down a bit, we used the Park Service money to develop the first 7.5 miles in 1984."

It had survived by a hair. A state agency with an unusually strong backbone, combined with citizen advocates who were just vocal enough, then combined with a management structure and plan that could push back against naysayers, carried the day. This structure—citizen advocacy plus government ownership plus a plan of action—later became the organizing model promoted by the Rails-to-Trails Conservancy. Not every campaign succeeded, but the battle for the Torrey Brown Trail set the pattern. Today it serves 550,000 users a year and is considered the queen of Maryland rail-trails—so influential in the state that it helped lead to the formation of the Maryland Greenways Commission and a slew of next-generation trails.

The original concept was to pave the Torrey Brown Trail with a hard surface, but Baltimore County is historically horse country, and equestrians were opposed to asphalt. The compromise was a locally quarried stone dust known as Crusher Run 8, which proved to be an ideal surface. With an "environmental" look, and cool under the summer sun, it's soft enough for comfort (and the whoosh of tires on gravel eliminates the startle of pedestrians), yet it's fine-grained and hard enough to support thin-tired bicycles at a reasonable and pleasant speed. The 20-mile trail was so successful that it stimulated neighboring York County, Pennsylvania, to pick up the same route on its side of the border and continue it another 20 miles, even though there was still some train service up there. (That solution—constructing a pathway alongside an active track—is known as "rails-*with*-trails" and will be discussed later in this book.)

None of the other trails had the exact same set of pitfalls, but each faced a serious struggle. The Marin County, California, effort got bogged down in endless negotiation with the Northwestern Pacific Railroad. The Columbia, Missouri, trail had to be shortened because of opposition from landowners at the far rural end of the corridor. (It was later completed.) The w&od campaign in Virginia struggled against a recalcitrant electric utility company that had pounced in to buy the land from the defunct railroad. (They are now a partner.) The New York project suffered because a sponsoring town had difficulty matching the federal grant. The trail in Washington was seriously damaged when a salvage company mistakenly removed a huge trestle over a deep river gorge. (That's still a problem today.)

For proposals that hadn't received a federal grant, the going was even tougher. Every effort before 1980 in Alabama, Arkansas, Delaware, Florida, Kansas, Missouri, Nebraska, and seventeen other states was blocked by lack of knowledge, lack of resources, public apathy, railroad resistance, neighbor opposition, or all of the above. About half the states were able to limp through with a couple of conversion victories in the early days, although most of those were within state or national forests or other backwoods locations where there was barely any knowledge of the track and where the resulting trail was also marginally recognized or publicized.

Abandonments in urban areas were rarer and the success rate was even worse. In cities it wasn't so much due to landowner opposition or paranoia about outsiders but rather the insatiable hunger for space for cars and trucks. Little-used and abandoned tracks were gobbled up by transportation planners for roads, road widenings, highway construction, busways, parking lots, and storage. The earlier the abandonment, the more likely it was directly given over to cars. In hilly North Arlington, Virginia, the 1935 abandonment of the Great Falls & Old Dominion Railway Company freed up a gloriously graded route past woods and fields, through cuts, and high over ravines. It would have been perfect for cyclists, but it became instead a narrow, fast road with no shoulders and, today, bumper-to-bumper commuter traffic. Moreover, with the construction of houses, driveways, and cul-de-sacs, any chance for converting the

It's Perfect! Who Could Be Against It?

route back to a car-free paradise was eliminated, and cyclists are instead sent on a steep, circuitous labyrinth of backstreets. The road's only remaining hint of its railroad heritage is its name: Old Dominion Drive.

Very wide corridors—outmoded city and suburban freight yards—were also hungrily eyed for cars. Or if too broad for a highway, they were sometimes turned into housing or shopping complexes. Of course trails weren't part of any urban planner's thinking back then. That didn't begin until well into the 1980s or later, and only under pressure from advocacy groups.

By the end of 1975, on the cusp of the congressional passage of the 4R Act, the nation had experienced more than 4,600 track abandonments comprising nearly 70,000 miles. Yet there were only perhaps 160 mostly rural rail-trails in existence, totaling something like 2,400 miles. Not that they weren't attractive and compelling. They were just obscure, hard to find, and unpublicized. Rail-trails were a perfect fit for the environmental movement's recycling philosophy—and Earth Day had already made a big impact—but developing traction for a nationwide rails-to-trails movement was as hard as starting a fully loaded freight train uphill on rain-slicked tracks.

Then a rails-to-trails campaign in Seattle showed the way.

Seattle, starting in 1885, was served from its northeast by the Seattle, Lakeshore & Eastern Railroad, a coal, iron, and timber line from the Cascade Mountains that was created by a dozen city leaders including judge Thomas Burke and businessman Daniel Gilman. The line was soon incorporated into the Northern Pacific Railroad (which later became the Burlington Northern [BN] and even later the BNSF), and the workmanlike route continued until 1971. A few years before its abandonment, community members noticed the line's decline and started talking about saving the land, particularly since the tracks went right through the campus of the University of Washington. In 1970, at a major citywide event where hundreds of participants discussed problems and kicked around solutions for Seattle's future, the idea picked up momentum. The discussants even came up with a historically resonant name—the Burke-Gilman Trail.

Most of Seattle's renowned bicycle and recreation community was thrilled, but the idea wasn't universally endorsed. The tracks bisected a wealthy neighborhood along Lake Washington, and some of the well-connected residents were noisily opposed to creating a "muggers' paradise" behind their houses. Regardless, Seattle mayor Wes Uhlman liked the proposal, even finding himself on a pro-trail march one day when protesters pelted the marchers with tomatoes. The city was also forced to fend off a lawsuit, and Burlington Northern seemed to align with the neighbors when it stated that it could not give priority to land requests by the city or by King County.

Nevertheless, because of Uhlman and others, Washington's U.S. senator Warren Magnuson, powerful chairman of the Commerce Committee, made a last-minute ask of both the Interstate Commerce Commission and Burlington Northern to consider a trail. The ICC had already approved the abandonment, but it found a way to reopen the proceeding and allow the city to intervene. The commission then released an unprecedented ruling that public agencies could be given a first right to negotiate with railroads post-abandonment; with that green light, BN agreed to sit down and talk. Five months later, in 1973, an agreement was reached on 7.9 miles of track in the city; the following year King County bought an additional 4.2 miles in the suburbs.

"It's hard now to believe how controversial the proposal was," Uhlman recalled many years later. "One of the homeowner opponents, a vice president of a large bank, was a personal friend. He had an airplane docked on the water by his house. We both went to Woodland Park Methodist Church, and our children played together. He thought a trail would bring in undesirables. It ended our longtime friendship, and the kids' too. But as soon as the trail finally opened, I put a couple of police on it on bikes, and it worked. We didn't have an incident."

Uhlman continued, "A couple of years ago, I was out and my bodyguard stiffened up. 'There's a man shouting at you,' he said. It was my old friend. He ran up to me and said, 'I owe you an apology, Wes. My next-door neighbor just sold his house for a $50,000 premium because of the trail.'"

It's Perfect! Who Could Be Against It?

The ribbon-cutting on the Burke-Gilman Trail in 1978 was momentous. By virtue of its big-city setting, its route through the largest university in the state, the quality of its management, its high level of usage, and a continuous barrage of coverage by all Seattle's media, the Burke-Gilman became the trail that proved the movement's authenticity. Seattle in 1978 was not yet the trendsetting metropolis it is today, but there were still enough cyclists, recreationists, and soapboxers traveling to and from the region that word of the accomplishment started spreading nationally. In fact one person whose awareness was awakened by the news was this book's author.

The resulting excitement over the fledgling trail prompted an outburst of activity, particularly in communities with relatively strong cycling constituencies who were frustrated by their many roadblocks. It also began to gradually generate articles in early-adopter publications; I wrote my first piece on the subject for *Environmental Action*. At the same time, the enthusiasm generated a few shock waves of concern in the property rights world. It would take almost a decade for these nascent and conflicting seeds to bear fruit as full-scale organizations on both sides of the issue, but people started paying closer attention to old railroad corridors. *Oh, look—a railroad track! Is it shiny—or rusty? Does it look straight and kept up—or a bit crooked and wobbly? I wonder where it goes. Who do you think owns it? Can you tell how old it is by studying any dates on the trash alongside?*

Some of the communities that got an early start, each inventing its own wheel when there was no template or shared experience to learn from, included the Minneapolis suburb of Plymouth; suburban Montgomery County between Philadelphia and Valley Forge; Westwood, California; Copake, New York; Boca Grande, Florida; St. Charles, Illinois; and several towns on Massachusetts's Cape Cod. The last location was particularly significant because of the large number of influential and out-of-state visitors who discovered the trails while summering there. (Also, the co-creator of one of the Cape Cod trails, Barbara Burwell, happened to be the mother of David Burwell, who later co-founded the Rails-to-Trails Conservancy.)

But some opponents began to take the movement more seriously too.

The first group to vehemently shake their heads were supporters of railroading. Some of these people were authentic railroaders, people who knew markets, knew costs and profit factors, and believed that they could make a go of a short-line route where the old main-line railroad had failed economically. Others were sentimentalists who loved the history, romanticism, power, and excitement of old trains, particularly steam-powered locomotives, old boxcars and coaches, and cabooses. The former group received a generally warm reception from the Interstate Commerce Commission. The latter was taken less seriously because of the high cost of running a railroad, but a number of them were nevertheless successful in rescuing old corridors for tourist trains and railroad museums.

In most cases, trail advocates deferred to the wishes and outcry of railroad preservationists. Even those who didn't love railroads saw the logic of continuing the original purpose of the tracks. Moreover the ICC was on the side of continuing rail service. Lastly, the more philosophical of the trail promoters recognized that a new short-line railroad or tourist train was quite likely to fail itself, so the track might well come up for abandonment a second time.

In a few cases trail and rail advocates got locked into an ongoing battle. One of the longest, in both miles and years, occurred in New York, within the Adirondack Mountain Preserve, where a 118-mile route from Lake Placid to the town of Remsen came under contention in 1974; the tourism struggle between those promoting locomotive versus muscle power continues even as this book is being written (although a compromise may finally be coming into focus).

Much more common, however, was opposition by those who didn't care about the old train but simply wanted the disused corridor to evaporate forever. Of many such places, one was the wealthy town of Terrace Park, outside Cincinnati, which held off the state of Ohio for more than twenty years along a key stretch of the proposed Little Miami Trail before finally throwing in the towel. In the Palisades section of Washington DC, powerful neighbors quietly shut down an already funded plan for a trail along a defunct trol-

It's Perfect! Who Could Be Against It?

ley line. Farmers in central Ohio stopped a path that would have connected Pandora and Columbus Grove, with one woman memorably jumping up at a public hearing to explain that it would be impossible to protect trail users from groundhogs. The extension of the Virginia Creeper Trail into North Carolina was prevented when all the neighbors took back the easements the railroad had originally received from their forefathers. The Preston-Snoqualmie Trail in Washington was stopped dead on the border of the Snoqualmie Indian Reservation because it threatened to cross Native American sacred ground. The Guernsey Trail in Ohio was prevented from extending farther east because a neighboring munitions factory made it too dangerous to continue the route. A Union Pacific abandonment along the San Pedro River in extreme southern Arizona would have made a fine riparian conservation path until the U.S. Border Patrol nixed a trail so close to the Mexican boundary.

Mark Ackelson, former president of the Iowa Natural Heritage Foundation, still has regrets over one lost corridor. "The Great Western Trail today runs for 16 miles out of Des Moines, but we could have bought that line all the way to St. Joe, Missouri—175 miles! It went through the beautiful area made famous by the *Bridges of Madison County*, although actually Madison County itself didn't support the project. It was early on in our history and we didn't have the financial or staff resources to pull it off. The corridor is still there, but the ownership is now all broken up. That was a huge regret."

George Bellovics, at the time a young landscape architect for the Illinois Department of Conservation, saw one of the setbacks firsthand. "A tragic early rail-trail loss was the old 15-mile Nickel Plate Rail line segment between Gibson City and Paxton," he said, "not because the route was so beautiful but because it was very well located and also because they had a terrific support group that had gathered all the money necessary to match a federal grant in 1992. All they needed was for Ford County or one of the two endpoint cities to sign on to the grant request. I went to the County Board meeting as the trail guy from the state. The room was filled with trail supporters, but one of the adjacent landowners stood up in opposition and said, 'I don't want no blacks, no Jews, and no homosexuals coming to my town.' The proposal was voted down.

I learned later that some of the landowners wanted the right-of-way for themselves. It's nearly all plowed under now."

It wasn't always self-serving opposition; in Pennsylvania the Public Utility Commission (PUC) required railroads to immediately remove all the bridges on their abandoned lines. The agency was not anti-trail, but its primary job was assuring safe and efficient highways, and many of its old roads twisted dangerously under railroad overpasses. If a bridge removal happened to add hundreds of thousands of dollars to a future trail development—or happened to completely eliminate its possibility—that was unfortunate but not in the PUC's purview. Elsewhere, in numerous places electric utilities had been hungering to find routes for new wires, and they jumped at the chance to buy a rail corridor. They weren't anti-trail—some of them were willing to later share the corridor—but they wanted to be at the head of the line, and with deep pockets, large planning staffs, and teams of real estate lawyers, they could easily outmaneuver any fledgling trail volunteer group and even most city or county governments. Interestingly many utilities are good trail partners as long as they are allowed to remain unfettered in their use of herbicides or in being able to severely prune trees reaching for their wires; rail-trails shared with utilities can be efficient multipurpose facilities but can also be rather low in natural ambience.

Then there were the trail advocates themselves, whose ramblingly broad household wasn't always a happy family. Yes, everyone could agree that auto roads were the problem, but after that, what? Strife occasionally arose between walkers and cyclists: pedestrians were startled by speeding bikes, while cyclists assumed that everyone knew that the rules of the road were to stay right. Worse was animosity between equestrians and the others, with the former knowing that horses are much more skittish than they seem, but many of the latter being annoyed by hoofprint divots and piles of manure.

Worst was the battle between motorized drivers (mostly snowmobilers) and conservationists; motors on the facilities brought up the age-old philosophical debate: "What is a trail, anyway?" Conservationists and the majority of cyclists, feeling that they had already lost streets to cars, were dead-set against giving up another set of corridors to mechanization. But snowmobilers' backs were also

It's Perfect! Who Could Be Against It?

against the wall, since roadways were quickly plowed and salted after each snowstorm, immediately precluding their use. Cross-country skiers were split, some hating the noise and smell, others appreciating that the heavy machines smoothed the deep snow for everyone. The average person felt the struggle was rather a nonissue since (a) they didn't go outside much in the winter anyway and (b) the snowmobile trails became regular people-trails in the six-to-nine other months of the year. (But there was also the sensitive question of motorcycles and dune buggies during the warmer months.) Through much of the rural snowbelt like Minnesota, Wisconsin, New Hampshire, Maine, and Michigan's Upper Peninsula, the snowmobilers did an impressive job of organizing members, building close working relationships with state departments of natural resources, and marching in lockstep with local tourism councils. Only in more urbanized New York and Massachusetts did the stronger pro-conservation element make its anti-motor voice heard. Ironically, in those states, that split held back the early and full flowering of the rails-to-trails movement.

Former U.S. congressman Tom Petri recounted the situation in Wisconsin: "Back when I was in the state senate, there was a fight over some trail legislation. On the one hand were purists who didn't want any motorized uses; on the other was a very substantial snowmobile contingent. After all, in our state, much of the year trails aren't used because of the snow. That gave the snowmobilers quite a bit of momentum and public support. We've got a fair number of people who don't like to bike but who do like to get out in packs on their snow machines and ride from bar to bar in the winter. Frankly, we heard from the chambers of commerce in the north country that there is a stronger economic impact in the winter than in the summer." He laughed. "There may not be more snow travelers than bikers and hikers, but many of the summer folks stay in campgrounds while all the winter folks pay for lodging overnight."

"At the end of the day," Petri concluded, "a deal was struck. Because of the support of the snowmobile users, we were able to pass a law that allowed the DNR to use tax revenue from off-road vehicles for trail acquisition and maintenance. This made a big difference in our acquisition and maintenance budget for both motorized and nonmotorized."

Similar political coalitions were built in Minnesota, Michigan, and other northern states. Later Petri himself led a similar effort in the U.S. Congress.

Gradually the rails-to-trails concept was evolving from a charming, off-beat idea to a realistic public policy issue with all the attendant complexities, supporters and opponents, winners and losers. It was time for increasingly sophisticated approaches, and both sides began to mobilize.

It's Perfect! Who Could Be Against It?

1. Railroad tracks were laid on the toughest, best-designed corridors ever constructed. No modern bicycle or walking trail can match the engineering of these rights-of-way. Courtesy Bill Metzger collection.

2 & 3. The flatter the grade, the faster the train, the less expensive the shipment. Railroads spared no expense when it came to cutting through hills and bridging valleys—to the later benefit of trail users when abandonment came. Courtesy Garrie Rouse (2) and Carol Parker (3).

4. Two brothers enjoying the Illinois Prairie Path. Unlike bike lanes on roadways, rail-trails can play host to unexpected uses. Courtesy Kevin Menke.

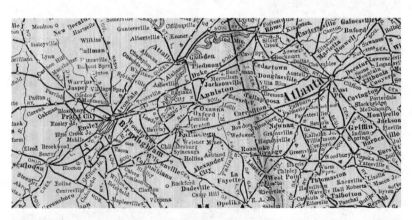

5. Back in 1916, when the U.S. railroad network reached its maximum extent, every city had a web of corridors, and even the smallest hamlet had a least one track. Courtesy Library of Congress, Map Division.

6. From Maine to Oregon, narrow-gauge railroads were less expensive to construct and were often disassembled after the trees ran out. Many rail routes through national forests later became backcountry trails. Courtesy Centennial History of Oregon, 1910.

7. The electric trolley and its longer-distance cousin, the interurban, came onto the scene in the 1890s, just as heavy rail construction was tapering off. Together they added 16,000 miles of off-street track to the rail system. York-Hanover Trolley photo used with permission from York CountyRail Trail Authority.

8. The high wheeler, or penny-farthing, caused a stir in the late 1870s, but that early contraption remained the province of a small group of male speedsters, such as six-day race champion William Martin. Only around 1890, after the development of the modern safety bicycle and the pneumatic tire, did the first real bicycle boom begin. Courtesy Library of Congress, https://www.loc.gov/item/92508479/.

9. Albert A. Pope, the father of U.S. bicycling. Pope built the first bike factory, started numerous bicycle clubs, and was instrumental in forming the League of American Wheelmen. He also funded activism for better roads, which facilitated the rise of the automobile. Courtesy Division of Work and Industry, National Museum of American History, Smithsonian Institution.

10. Ocean Parkway in Brooklyn, New York, was designed by Frederick Law Olmsted as the world's first boulevard with an exclusive bike path. A huge success when it opened in 1895, it also began the century-long debate over on-road and off-road cycling. Courtesy New York City Parks Photo Archive.

11. "You want to do *what* with this?" Only a special kind of visionary can look at an abandoned corridor and imagine it as an alluring natural pathway. Seen here, the Bemis Branch of the Boston & Maine Railroad in Watertown, Massachusetts, before it became a trail. Photo by Craig Della Penna.

12 & 13. Two trailblazers from the 1960s. Chicago naturalist and writer May Theilgaard Watts (*above*) spearheaded the creation of the Illinois Prairie Path, while Waldo Nielsen (*below*), a Rochester, New York, hiker, produced the first published location listing of abandoned corridors. Courtesy Sterling Morton Library, the Morton Arboretum (12), and Maverick Publications (13).

14 & 15. Two behind-the-scenes legislative heroes from the 1970s. Tom Allison (*left*) championed the creation of a rails-to-trails demonstration program in 1976. Pete Raynor (*right*) devised the legal language for railbanking in 1983. More than forty years would pass before their achievements were recognized Courtesy Sharon Nelson (14) and Rails-to-Trails Conservancy, photo by Hung Tran (15).

16. The track that started it all in Congress. The Georgetown Branch B&O Railroad track (overhead) is the corridor that both Tom Allison and Pete Raynor noticed—and started thinking about—when they jogged on the C&O Canal towpath in the 1970s. Today the bridge carries the completed Capital Crescent Trail into Washington DC. Photo by author.

17. California congressman Phil Burton (D), the legislative wizard who steered the National Trails System Act Amendments—with the railbanking provision—through Congress and onto President Reagan's desk. Burton died only two weeks after enactment. Courtesy San Jose State University Special Collections & Archives.

18. John Sam Williamson, one of a group of farmers opposed to the conversion of a 200-mile M-K-T Railroad line into Missouri's Katy Trail in the 1980s. The opponents failed to stop the trail, but they did receive financial compensation. Photo by Phil Schermeister, *National Geographic* magazine.

19. The author (*left*), with his bicycle, and Rails-to-Trails Conservancy president David Burwell, with a borrowed horse, pose for a *People* magazine photograph in 1992. By then, six years after the founding of RTC, there were five hundred rail-trails totaling more than five thousand miles in length. Photo by Robert Trippett.

20. Whether due to a fear of strangers or practical questions of plowing and harvesting, many farmers have opposed rail-trails. This Iowa family blocked the continuity of the Cedar Valley Nature Trail for years until the state arranged a compromise detour. Photo by Phil Schermeister, *National Geographic* magazine.

21. Hundreds of runners and cyclists in 2004 said hello to the Winooski River Trail Bridge and good-bye to nine years of stopgap service by a volunteer ferry (*foreground*). The new deck, near Burlington, Vermont, used the original piers from the former railroad structure. Photo by Brian Costello, courtesy Local Motion.

22. Yes, you *can* have your track and bike it too. The newest movement—shown here on the Ohio-to-Erie Trail near Columbus—is rails-*with*-trails, preserving train service but also providing cyclists a respite from cars on the road. Photo by Willie Karidis, courtesy Rails-to-Trails Conservancy.

23. Minneapolis's Midtown Greenway, part of the nation's most impressive metropolitan trailway system, is the quintessential four-season urban rail-trail. Space is also reserved for a future parallel light-rail trolley. Photo by Carol Parker.

24. New York City needed forty-two years to create a rail-trail, but it finally did it in style. The High Line quickly became the nation's busiest linear park, getting more than seven million visitors a year and generating an estimated $2 billion of economic impact in the vicinity. Photo by Mike Tschappat, courtesy Friends of the High Line

GREAT AMERICAN RAIL-TRAIL™

brought to you by
rails-to-trails
conservancy

EXISTING TRAILS

TRAIL GAPS

25. This cross-country route projected by Rails-to-Trails Conservancy was announced in 2019. Of its 3,773 miles, more than 1,900 were in existence at the time, and 600 more were being planned on known corridors. Courtesy Rails-to-Trails Conservancy.

8

The Movement Gels

ON NOVEMBER 30, 1981, THE UNITED STATES WAS HIT BY THE all-time tsunami of abandonments. Never before or since did a single railroad file for 154 track abandonments on one day. The railroad was Conrail, the huge staggering beast the government had assembled from the wreckage of the Penn Central and four other bankrupt northeastern railroads. Although the Conrail story is ultimately a victory of economic rationalization and governmental planning, that initial shedding of corridors sent shock waves from Massachusetts to Illinois.

Charles Marshall vividly remembers the event. "I was the railroad's commerce counsel at the time, and it was up to me to get the job done," he said. "We had a deadline to file the abandonments, but some highly placed people in the company were against abandoning anything and were fighting a rear-guard action. That's why it all got piled up internally, but November 30 was the statutory last day. We packed up the last of the papers and drove the whole mass from Philadelphia to Washington, using two cars. Human nature cried out to divide the papers between the two vehicles, but we squeezed all the material into one so that if the first broke down we could perform a rescue with the second."

"From the railroading perspective," Marshall added, "I have no regrets about any of those abandonments."

But from the perspective of shippers, small-town mayors, and chambers of commerce, it provoked anguish, and the few rail-trail advocates who existed at that time were also jolted. They had been concerned about the steady drip, drip, drip of defunct corridors, but now it seemed as if a precious resource was being hemorrhaged like a stream bank under a firehose.

And, in fact, it was. In 1977 the Milwaukee Road went into bankruptcy and seven years later abandoned all its holdings from eastern Montana to western Washington. In 1980 the Rock Island was liquidated. That same year the Interstate Commerce Commission made a technical rule modification that greatly increased the number of allowable abandonments; instead of calculating only if a particular line made money, railroads could thenceforth consider whether they could have made *more* money by spending it elsewhere. If so, the track could go. In 1980 the Seaboard System merged with the Chessie System to create csx Transportation, resulting in a slew of redundant lines for castoff. Burlington Northern merged with the Frisco. Two years later the Southern merged with Norfolk & Western, creating the Norfolk Southern, and more overlapping corridors came onto the chopping block. So while there were 134 Class I railroads in the early 1950s, by the mid-1980s there were only twenty-five. And by 2018 that number was down to seven behemoths.

By early 1984 word of the crisis—both the danger and the opportunity—had reached activists working on the national level in Washington DC. Most of them were, broadly speaking, environmentalists, either heartfelt conservationists who wanted to save corridor lands for recreational use or more cerebral optimists who hoped to retain the lines for possible reactivation if and when the nation ever reached peak oil, junked the internal-combustion engine, and needed to utilize an alternative transportation technology.

One of the DC activists was a young, hard-charging lawyer named David Burwell. Burwell had railroads and rail-trails in his blood—literally. Two of his great-grandfathers had been president, at different times, of the same Minnesota railroad—the Duluth, Missabe & Northern, which had been taken over by John D. Rockefeller. And many years later, on Cape Cod, Massachusetts, his mother had spent nearly ten years working to create the Shining Sea Bikeway out of an old New Haven Railroad line near her house. As for himself, David's principal policy interest was opposing unnecessary highways and promoting alternatives to the automobile. His employer, the National Wildlife Federation, was a powerful conservation group made up largely of hunters who wanted to protect

The Movement Gels

habitat in order to make sure there would be enough animals to shoot at. Pro-rail was an ill-fitting combination with pro-hunting, but it had one surprising overlap: concern over abandoned corridors in the agricultural Midwest and Northern Plains. Burwell, as the organization's lawyer, received many letters from places like South Dakota saying that the brush growing up alongside old tracks was the only remaining habitat where game birds like pheasants could breed. Every other square foot was plowed and cultivated, and if the old corridors were lost, the birds would be too. David—an Ivy League blue blood, several blocks from Pennsylvania Avenue and several generations removed from stalking any sort of game— would laugh at the incongruity, but he was also intrigued. Radicals trying to save tracks for bikes was nice, but organized sportsmen— now there was some political heft.

I had met David years earlier, when we were both in our twenties, at Environmental Action, the group that organized the original Earth Day and had gone on to play a major role in opening the federal Highway Trust Fund to transit spending. Curiously, even though he was a couple years older than me, I had been coordinator of the organization and he had come on as an intern. Having gone to law school and served in the Peace Corps, he was delayed breaking into the job market. His internship involved researching and co-writing what became the book *The End of the Road: A Citizen's Guide to Transportation Problemsolving*.

I, like David, had been deeply involved battling the negative effects of automobiles on cities. While David approached it as a lawyer, I had focused more on political organizing for bicycling improvements, car-free parks, and pedestrianized streets. When I first heard about rails-to-trails I was electrified to discover a type of corridor that had never been sullied by the tread of a tire. Giving no thought to any legal niceties or pitfalls, I immediately set out to publicize that, yes, there was something truly new under the sun. The piece I wrote for *Environmental Action* magazine was called "I've Been Walking on the Railroad." I was so enthusiastic that a rule-burdened New York State parks official later referred to me, not admiringly, as a "cheering section," but my word pictures led others to begin enthusing as well.

David, who had studied property law, was less sanguine. "You've got to understand that once these corridors are abandoned," he would say, "they fall apart like a bundle of sticks untied. You're suddenly dealing with dozens of owners, any one of whom can be a roadblock to the whole trail." But David was nothing if not dogged, and when one day in 1984 he overheard a whiff of a reference to some kind of rail corridor preservation statute, he put his legal intern to work investigating. That's when he came upon railbanking, Pete Raynor's two-sentence concept that Representative Phil Burton had tucked into the National Trails System Act Amendments in 1983. Today most people assume that the Rails-to-Trails Conservancy (RTC) lobbied to create the railbanking statute, but it was actually the railbanking law that led to the establishment of the conservancy. The law predated the founding of RTC by two years.

Possibly the most unusual activist to join the early fray in Washington was Jeannette Fitzwilliams, an imposing woman in her seventies with a gruff manner and a harrowing English accent. Even though it was hard to envision her actually out on a trail, she had an impressive activist pedigree with the Virginia Hiking Association, the American Hiking Society, the Potomac Appalachian Trail Club, and the National Trails Council, and she had a truly expansive acceptance of trail users—skiers, snowmobilers, equestrians, bicyclists, off-road "vehiclers," hikers, runners, "wheelchairers." If hoverboards had existed, she would have welcomed them too. Jeannette was unshakably committed to grassroots democracy and was a pugnacious idealist—back in the 1950s when a congressman proposed a 100-foot-wide corridor for the Appalachian Trail, she had countered with the demand for 1,000 feet. Although Jeannette's quirks often pushed squabbles past the boiling point, she would just as frequently prove her worth. Notably, as we saw previously, amid dozens of witnesses at the key 1982 U.S. Senate hearing on trails, she was the only person who publicly blessed rail-trails or whose testimony even mentioned the word "railroad."

Equally idiosyncratic was Charles Montange, a brilliant, misanthropic lawyer from the Midwest who combined a steel-trap mind with a cackle that could almost shatter glass. A Yale Law School graduate, Chuck was severely injured when his bike crossed rail-

The Movement Gels

road tracks at the wrong angle; he returned from the hospital with the motto "Don't get mad, get even." A friend of Burwell's, he was in the process of dissociating from a gold-plated law firm just as Rails-to-Trails Conservancy was being formed, and he offered to provide pro-bono services to the start-up. As with Jeannette, conversations with Chuck could often turn heated and occasionally even tearful, but it was he who conceptualized the legal path forward, not only for the organization but for many individual trails and the entire movement itself. As time went on and he could no longer afford to work without pay, he devised a cryptic fee schedule that seemed to rise for cases on the coasts and drop in his beloved heartland, with advocates in Iowa often getting service for free.

Another young can-do activist, from Ohio, was Ellis Robinson (known back then as Peggy). She began her career as a transportation planner, read and had been influenced by Burwell's *The End of the Road*, and shifted gears into bicycle promotion. Exquisitely adept as an organizer, she put together several large cycling event fund-raisers, got a job at the League of American Bicyclists, and then began turning her attention to building a solid membership base for rails-to-trails. Her successes with direct-mail propelled the organization's growth and consistently confounded the naysayers.

There were also some older seasoned veterans enamored enough with the concept to volunteer as advisors or to serve on a founding board of directors: Doug Costle, the former administrator of the U.S. Environmental Protection Agency under President Jimmy Carter; Bob Cahn, Pulitzer Prize–winning environmental editor for the *Christian Science Monitor* and member of the Council on Environmental Quality; Ed Norton, vice president of the Wilderness Society and later president of the Grand Canyon Trust; and Ambassador Robert Blake, a trustee of the Nature Conservancy.

Under RTC's original concept, an organization wouldn't have been needed. Instead we imagined that a coalition of national conservation, recreation, transportation, health, and historical protection groups would all come together and cooperatively work on the rails-to-trails issue. But that idea rapidly flamed out. Every existing organization was already too busy with its own agenda. Plus we quickly learned that rails-to-trails wasn't as simple as it seemed. But, we wondered, if we did take the plunge to create a freestanding organization, was the rails-to-trails message big enough to attract and retain a paying membership? Most professionals said no. But we were excited about the idea and thought others would be too, so we took the plunge. I wrote a funding proposal, David took it around, and we soon had an auspicious answer. Larry Rockefeller, head of the American Conservation Association, pledged $75,000 if we could match it. It was a fitting start since Larry's father, Laurence S. Rockefeller, was the man who had chaired the federal Outdoor Recreation Resources Review Commission (ORRRC) from 1958 to 1962. ORRRC is often cited as the second-most influential forum for parks and recreation, after the National Park Service itself. The ORRRC report led directly or indirectly to the National Wilderness Act, the National Wild and Scenic Rivers Act, the Land and Water Conservation Fund, and the National Trails System Act.[1] We hoped that getting Larry Rockefeller's imprimatur was a good omen. Plus, we laughed, we would be using oil money to build a post-oil transportation network.

Burwell, who was slated to become RTC president but still worked for the National Wildlife Federation, arranged for his organization to match the pledge, and additional early grants came in from Ski Industries America and the Trust for Public Land. On February 1, 1986, the Rails-to-Trails Conservancy formally opened its doors in an older office building four blocks from the White House. My title was director of programs, and I was the first person on staff.

It wasn't a moment too soon. Railroad tracks were being approved for abandonment almost faster than the Interstate Commerce Commission could print the notification letters. In 1985 alone there were 148 abandonments for a total of 2,343 miles. From famous locations to obscure place-markers, they were everywhere. Ten miles in California not far from San Francisco. Fourteen miles in Iowa, from Council Bluffs to Pacific Junction. Forty-three miles in Alabama and Tennessee, from Florence to Lawrenceburg. Five miles within Jacksonville, Florida. And on and on. The next year, as RTC was building a mailing list and trying to get reporters interested, the flood continued. Thirty-four miles in Iowa from Shell Rock to Oelwein. Twenty-four miles in Florida from Clearwater to Elfers. Five more miles in California, from Santa Monica to Culver City.

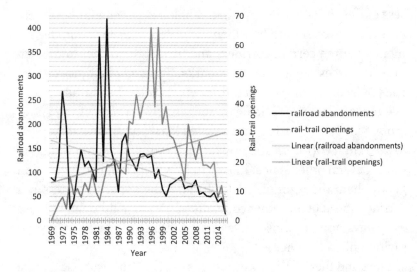

Fig. 5. Railroad abandonments and rail-trail openings per year.
Created by author.

Actually it wasn't in the nick of time. We were late—3,083 miles had been abandoned in 1984, 2,454 the year before, and an all-time record 5,151 in 1982 because of the huge sloughing-off by Conrail. As the torrent poured past, it felt like many nuggets of gold had already fallen through our fingers, and more were slipping by every day. We frantically attempted to notify each community as we heard the news, but there were no systems in place and we didn't have any contacts in the many small towns affected. Plus, even if we reached them, no one out there knew what to do, and we had only a rudimentary sense of the tactics local folks could use to make a trail happen. Worst of all, the old, leisurely Interstate Commerce Commission rules had been rewritten. Now communities had only thirty days to find out about an abandonment notice and file an official protest or a request to save the corridor.

Fortunately not everything was being lost. For starters, there were the nine "demonstration grant" communities that had preceded the founding of the Rails-to-Trails Conservancy; all those projects were making headway and some were even making headlines. Then, too, the fledgling RTC wasn't the only entity trying to put fingers in the dike. The state of Wisconsin, following the success of the Elroy-Sparta Trail, had cobbled together a fairly smooth bureaucratic operation by which the state's transportation department acquired certain corridors and turned them over to the natural resources department for parks. Through that process, by 1985 Wisconsin already had thirteen state-level rail-trails plus a few more local ones. Michigan, too, largely because of the snowmobile lobby in Lansing, had created legal and financial systems to save rural corridors and buy them; by 1985 it had ten state rail-trails. Several other states, mostly in New England, had legislation giving them the right of "first refusal"—the opportunity to buy a corridor ahead of any other company or person—although in those early days none of those states was thinking of anything beyond saving railroad service.

Here and there, local communities—Ojai, California; Gasparilla Island, Florida; Troy, New York; Goodhue County, Minnesota—were enthusiastic enough to take on the challenge and through herculean effort were able to score early victories. But the majority of trail efforts were quashed or defeated. In Nebraska the proposed conversion of a Rock Island corridor from Omaha to Lincoln into the fifty-five-mile Trail of Two Cities was dashed when trail enthusiasts were outbid by speculators. In the end the purchasers' vision never worked out, but the dream of a public pathway was nevertheless killed. In Illinois a spirited group called Northwestern Illinois Recreational Trails was muscled aside by a farmers' group, crushing hopes for a thirty-eight-mile trail from Rock Falls to Earlville. (The farmers had threatened Burlington Northern Railroad with unending legal battles.) On Michigan's Upper Peninsula a beautiful twenty-four-mile stretch along Lake Superior from Marquette to Big Bay was lost when the state's forestry division thought it wouldn't be necessary for industrial access to the trees. (Incidentally the historic Marquette & Huron Mountain Railroad there had served a timber mill that made the original "woody" station wagons for Ford Motor Co.) In Greenville, Georgia, near the center of what would later become the state's filmmaking industry, a short, pretty abandonment was vetoed by cautious county commissioners as too costly. They failed to notice, however, that the property included valuable tracks and ties that could have been sold.

Nevertheless, within the fledgling Rails-to-Trails Conservancy, the slowly gelling movement was stirring excitement—even if the enthusiasm was wildly out of proportion to what the tiny new organization could accomplish. Hope can be a mighty force! During late-night mapping sessions, we would emulate the fantasies of the railroad builders a century and a half before. Washington to Baltimore? *That shouldn't be any problem.* Philadelphia to New York? *Easy, nice and flat, probably all kinds of corridors. Crossing the Hudson is a challenge, but isn't there a walkway on the George Washington Bridge?* Chicago to Detroit? *Oh, everything leads to Chicago—that stretch must be drowning in abandoned routes.* Pittsburgh? *Hmmm . . . those mountains are very steep. Maybe we can find an abandoned tunnel somewhere.* Maine to Florida? *Great idea! It could be an "Appalachian Trail for the Rest of Us!" Or "I-95 without the Cars!"* Seattle to Spokane? *Yes—I think there's already an abandonment the whole way across the state of Washington!* Getting to California? *Now, <u>that</u> will be the ultimate! What about following the old transcontinental railroad route? Are the railroads still using those tracks?*

Burwell, ever curious and irrepressible, learned that, of the hundreds of land grants over the years, those given to the Union Pacific and Central Pacific Railroads back in 1869 were by far the widest—a full 400 feet across. Deciding that that would be plenty of room for locating a trail alongside the rails, he sought meetings with the president of the Union Pacific, the U.S. secretary of transportation, various members of Congress, virtually anyone who would listen. Our strategy would be threefold: first, ask the railroad for a donation of part of their land; second (if that didn't work), get the government to prepare a plan for a trail within that land-grant route; third (if that didn't work either), get Congress to pass a law that any abandonment of the transcontinental corridor would require a 50-foot-wide trail route before any other reversionary laws would kick in. When those ideas raised a host of objections from railroads, ranchers, state departments of transportation, and private-property activists, we regrouped and started investigating other concepts, including the route of the Pony Express through southern Nevada, the Oregon Trail (which, we learned, wasn't a real physical trail), and the Lewis and Clark Trail (which, we learned, was largely a water-based route on the Missouri River).

In sober moments, we sometimes sat back and started thinking about the realities of bicycling across the country on a trail. Pedaling through quaint regions of Amish Pennsylvania or foliage-kissed New England—with granite outcroppings, storybook farms, covered bridges, and romantic towns every few miles—seemed like Nirvana. But what about across the endless, windswept plains of Nebraska, with nary a tree to rest under nor a town to eat in, nor a place to sleep? And Nebraska—just Nebraska—is 422 miles across, the same distance as from the Atlantic Ocean almost to Toledo, Ohio. There are also the endless shrublands of Wyoming, the soybean fields of Iowa, and the cornfields of Illinois, all with just a smattering of towns and small cities to provide services, distraction, nourishment, and entertainment. Might it make more sense to provide a dense network of shorter rail-trails connecting major population centers with higher-profile destinations like the Liberty Bell, Lincoln Memorial, Central Park, Navy Pier, the Golden Gate, Beale Street, Three Rivers Stadium, the French Quarter, the Gateway Arch, and Disneyland? Trails like that might not be as pretty—urban and suburban routes often traversing gritty or boring neighborhoods—but they would serve many more users and could also function as environmental and healthy corridors to escape the congestion and pollution of city streets.

Naturally we solved the dilemma in the way of all idealistic optimists: *We'll do both!* But in reality, in those early days we were completely at the mercy of the timing and location of the abandonments. Long ones that headed in the right direction—like 200 miles across Missouri, alongside the old route of Lewis and Clark—stimulated our enthusiasm about going coast to coast. Short or misshapen ones, with no obvious excitement—Des Moines to Ankeny, Santa Fe to Lamy, West Easton to Old Orchard—caused us to exclaim, hopefully, "Those would be perfect to serve as local connectors!" The great strength of rail corridors—even if also their occasional Achilles' heel—is their immutable solidity and reality. You are either on the corridor or you are not. There are no community-wide "route-finding" sessions as with on-street bikeways or hiking trails through the woods.

No matter how much speculation and dreaming we did in the nighttime, it was the morning mail from the Interstate Commerce

Commission that brought us back to reality—notices of that day's one or two (or three or four) abandonments. We then had to race around, first to our maps and then to our Rolodexes of public officials and trail activists who had told us to notify them if ever something came up. Happily, in those early days of the mid-1980s, the Rails-to-Trails Conservancy was not alone in its efforts. Even though there were many states where the entire weight of advance notification—what we called the Early Warning System—fell on our shoulders, in several others we had partners who were at least as experienced as we were. With them we could share some of the burden: the Iowa Trails Council, the New Jersey Conservation Foundation (NJCF), the Virginia Hiking Association, and the Buckeye Trail Council in Ohio. Later several other statewide rails-to-trails coalitions were formed, and the Rails-to-Trails Conservancy also quickly moved to create state chapters in Ohio, Michigan, Illinois, Pennsylvania, Florida, and Washington State.

The first organization to jump into the fray and attempt a full-fledged formal study was the New Jersey Conservation Foundation. While NJCF attempted to identify every abandoned track in the state, what its condition was, and who owned it, the legal complexities, combined with bankruptcies and mergers, made the task daunting. Identifying a route didn't mean it would automatically become a trail, and many just sat there, gaining no political traction. The process, however, did indirectly lead to the creation of at least one lovely trail when NJCF found an old Central of New Jersey Railroad corridor near the town of High Bridge. At first the organization was outmaneuvered by the Columbia Gas Transmission Co., which took the track for a pipeline route, but the disappointed conservationists decided to regroup and wait. Once the underground pipe was installed, NJCF approached Columbia to donate the regraded surface for public use. The win-win solution resulted in a great recreational amenity and a bit of positive corporate recognition: it's now called the Columbia Trail.

In eastern Iowa, one man, Tom Neenan, launched and then nurtured an almost eight-year effort to create the Cedar Valley Nature Trail. Beginning as chair of the Linn County Conservation Board, then shifting over to found and lead the Iowa Trails Council, Neenan outlasted stiff opposition as he cajoled railroads, encouraged public agencies, and rallied trail enthusiasts to create what has been called the "Elroy-Sparta of Iowa." (Partly because of the impetus from that victory, Iowa today is the unlikely home to more rail-trails than all but six other states.) He worked with strong allies at the well-heeled Iowa Natural Heritage Foundation and the national Rails-to-Trails Conservancy, but Neenan nevertheless endured intense opposition by farmers, ranging from shouting matches and threats at public meetings to midnight bridge torchings. Another time, the Trails Council got approval for a large grant from the Iowa Conservation Commission, only to have the state legislature overrule it, delete the funding, and bar the agency from doing any further work on rail-trails. The Iowa Trails Council demonstrated the outsized impact that a passionate state group—even a small one in an unsupportive state—can have on a citizen-based movement.

Beyond the citizen groups, some states got active too, particularly in the Northeast where the public was truly interested in saving trains. First to act, in 1968, was New Jersey, soon followed by Connecticut and New York. The concept they chose was straightforward: a law simply requiring railroads to offer any abandoned corridor to the state before throwing open the bidding. Then in 1974 a fourth state, Massachusetts, brought its muscle into play. That time it was entirely due to trail advocates, and it happened because of a track on Cape Cod.

In 1968 the New York, New Haven & Hartford Railroad announced the abandonment of the last 11 miles of its route from North Falmouth south to Woods Hole. Two mothers, Joan Kanwisher and Barbara Burwell, had already known of the likely abandonment and had been organizing in favor of public acquisition for a trail they were calling the Shining Sea Bikeway in honor of a Falmouth native, Katherine Lee Bates, who composed the song "America the Beautiful." On April 2, 1969, they secured the town's solid agreement to a purchase, but on the next day came the stunning revelation that the railroad had secretly sold the land to a private individual and that he was unwilling to allow a trail. Five years of expensive and divisive legal wrangling followed, all the way to the state supreme court, before the town finally prevailed. The out-

Table 6. State corridor ownership and right-of-first-refusal laws

	Number of states	Unused corridors owned	Miles
States with right-of-first-refusal law	12	66	1,840
States without right-of-first-refusal law	25	15	422
Data unavailable	13	—	—

Source: Peter Harnik and Tim Balton

come was quadruply momentous: the rail-trail became the first in Massachusetts; the trail became the first in the nation's history to be reassembled by eminent domain (condemnation by the town); the effort was profoundly inspirational to Barbara Burwell's son, David; and the legal struggle led to the passage of the strongest state rail corridor protection legislation in the country.

The legislation was the work of Representative Richard Kendall, a newly elected state legislator whom Kanwisher and Burwell visited early in his tenure. They told him of their near-loss and how important it was to maintain corridor continuity, either for train service to two lumberyards or for a trail. "Fortunately, I was on the Transportation Committee," Kendall recalled years later, "so I submitted a fairly simple bill that said that it was illegal to impede the continuity of any abandoned railroad line. It didn't really deal with the ownership issue, it just said that no one could build anything on a former rail corridor without the express permission of the state secretary of transportation. The town of Falmouth, in my district, was the only place dealing with this issue, and no one voiced any objection to the idea, so it went through without any opposition." Beginner's luck? Perhaps, but also the benefit of being so early in the movement that there was not yet any organization representing adjacent landowners.

The law, known technically as "Chapter 40, Section 54A," is one reason that Massachusetts has saved more miles of abandoned rail lines in public ownership than any other state (see table 7). A closely related reason is the state's "just in case" commitment to corridor continuity. When the bankrupt Penn Central Corpora-

Table 7. State-owned unused corridors by state

State	No. of state-owned unused corridors	Miles of state-owned unused corridors[1]	Right-of-first-refusal law year of passage
New Hampshire	19	339	1990
Massachusetts	15	870	1972
Michigan	15	243	1976
Maryland	12	118	n.a.
Montana	11	n.a.	n.a.
New Jersey	4	68	1968
Vermont	4	105	1988
Maine	4	134	1989
North Carolina	4	83	no state law
Georgia	3	73	1996
Delaware	3	25	n.a.
Minnesota	3	207	no state law
West Virginia	3	41	no state law
Rhode Island	2	8	1976
South Dakota	2	124	n.a.
Texas	2	58	no state law
Oklahoma	1	5	n.a.
District of Columbia	1	4	n.a.
Florida	1	1	n.a.
Ohio	1	11	no state law
Oregon	1	3	no state law
Washington	1	19	no state law[2]
Connecticut	0	0	1969
New York	0	0	1971
Pennsylvania	0	0	1990
Colorado	0	0	2016

Alabama, Arizona, Arkansas, California, Hawaii, Illinois, Iowa, Kansas, Louisiana, Mississippi, Missouri, Nevada, New Mexico, North Dakota, Utah, Virginia, Wisconsin, Wyoming	0	0	no state law
Alaska, Idaho, Indiana, Kentucky, South Carolina, Tennessee	0	0	n.a.
Nebraska	n.a.	n.a.	n.a.
Total	112	2,539	

Source: Peter Harnik and Tim Balton

Note: n.a. indicates no answer to questionnaire.

1 Includes state departments of transportation and departments of natural resources

2 Except in the city of Seattle, by agreement with railroad, 1988

tion put its lines up for sale, Massachusetts was the only state to buy every corridor not purchased by another railroad. Then in the early 2000s the state did it again. Conrail, the principal successor to Penn Central, was sold off to two other railroads, and Massachusetts made sure to purchase all the remaining unclaimed tracks (for $350 million). A study done many years later provides evidence that states with right-of-first-refusal legislation are more likely to acquire abandoned corridors than other states (see table 6). Combined, ten states with first refusal power own more than four times as many miles of unused track as twenty-five states without the law. (The remaining states did not respond to a questionnaire.)

Kendall, incidentally, after four terms in the legislature, was appointed by Governor Michael Dukakis as commissioner of the Massachusetts Department of Environmental Management and later had the honor of adding the prominent Cape Cod Rail-Trail to the state park system.

In other places, however, the state wasn't in the driver's seat. Washington, for instance, was eager to acquire a lengthy abandonment across the top of the beautiful Olympic Peninsula, from Port Angeles to Port Townshend. But with the abandonment already consummated and reversions having kicked in, the remaining corridor looked like "a damn segmented worm," according to Cleve Pinnix, then a recreation deputy at the Department of Natural Resources and later DNR director. "That's what happened before you had rail-banking in place," he said. "We actually had to go back to the legislature, tell them this was Mission Impossible, and give back the acquisition funds they had authorized. And there's nothing an agency hates more than giving back money."[2] In numerous other states, including Kansas, Oklahoma, Louisiana, and Mississippi, the state evinced no interest at all in asserting public rights over those of adjacent landowners.

The rails-to-trails movement was gaining traction, but it was being hamstrung by the legal burden of adjacent property precedents arrayed against it.

9

Fighting for Rights in Court

BY 1986 THE RAILS-TO-TRAILS MOVEMENT WAS PICKING UP steam. That year saw ribbon-cuttings on at least twenty new rail-trails in fourteen states, and there were probably 125 others in some stage of development or in some degree of local agitation. Plus a few of the established trails—the Burke-Gilman, the W&OD, the Illinois Prairie Path, the Elroy-Sparta—were generating regular press coverage and yielding new converts.

Excitement was building, but so was pushback. Few disputes are as visceral as battles over land, and rail-trails were no exception. Advocates saw them as a natural continuation of the old railroad route in a landscape ever more congested with automobiles. In opposition were "adjacents"—neighboring landowners. Not all were opposed, but enough to generate a pack of loud controversies. Some adjacents believed that the land under the tracks was theirs and should be given back when the trains stopped running. Others weren't sure of the ownership but had grown up with ancestral stories of railroad company perfidy and of their grandfather's land being stolen. Some wanted to take down the fence and squeeze in a couple more rows of crops, or square off a field diagonally crossed by the tracks to simplify a plowing operation. Others didn't want outsiders biking, walking, or snowmobiling up and down a track behind their properties. Some were simply riled up by their neighbors' reactions and scared of the unknown.

Generally opponents began with simple direct actions like posting "No Trespassing" signs on the corridor, piling up mounds of tree limbs, dirt, rocks, or manure, or even erecting barbed-wire fences. In one case in Washington, an angry adjacent landowner saw a youthful landscape architect studying the publicly owned corridor, called his friend the local sheriff, and had the young man arrested. Occasionally, if the conflict escalated, a favored and fairly effective tactic was to set a bridge on fire, and many fine wooden railroad crossings were lost in the early days. Some of the most vitriolic struggles ended up in court.

The early lawsuits focused on issues of landownership rights. Which party had which kind of land deed? Whose deed was stronger? What was the precise meaning of "right-of-way" or the scope of an easement under a particular state's laws? How did federal land grants fit into the picture? The problem, in a nutshell, was due to the many ways that railroad companies had acquired their land. Sometimes they had bought it outright (and owned it, in legal parlance, in "fee simple absolute"). But if an owner hadn't wanted to sell a tract of land, the railroad had exercised its right to take it ("condemn" it by eminent domain) and then pay an amount specified by court. But condemnation laws varied by state. In some places the railroad then owned the land; in other places it acquired only a temporary use (an "easement") of the land for as long as trains operated. And to muddy things further, even easements have a range of definitions relating to such factors as underground and overhead rights. There were no generic answers—not by railroad company, not by state, not by original year—which is why each case needed a specific adjudication. Depending on the outcome, some trails were green-lighted, some were blocked, and others emerged limping from the fray—partially allowed, or perhaps allowed only with a miles-long chunk of private land fenced off in the middle.

One early and influential legal decision was handed down in Minnesota in 1983, thanks to the commitment of a legendary conservation attorney there, Samuel H. Morgan. When the Soo Line Railroad abandoned a 10-mile track through bucolic countryside northeast of St. Paul, the state proposed making it into a trail. But several wealthy abutting landowners quickly raised $450,000 to buy the land themselves. Morgan, who was president of the Minnesota Parks Foundation, scrambled to meet with the Soo Line president, using one of his board members to make a connection. The railroad, he discovered, was favorably disposed to its track becoming a trail and agreed to sell it to the state for the same price the neighbors were offering. Morgan helped by pledging an interim purchase until the state could buy him out. But an official appraisal revealed that the track was worth only $442,000, which, under Minnesota law, was the maximum the state could pay. So Morgan stepped up again, making a gift of that extra $8,000. Victory!— but no. The adjacents then filed suit, alleging that they had proper title to the corridor from back when it was first constructed. Eventually the state supreme court delivered a momentous ruling. Yes, many of the deeds were, in fact, reversionary if the corridor ever ceased to be used. But the court found that the corridor was for "public travel," not merely for the operation of trains. Trail use, it ruled, constituted a continuation of that original purpose. The decision was profoundly influential and has since been followed by several high courts in other states. It was also cited later in a U.S. Supreme Court decision.

Something was clearly in the air. The timing of the Minnesota ruling coincided almost exactly with the passage of the railbanking provision that Congressman Burton put into the National Trails System Act Amendments. Even as the railroad industry itself was faltering and evolving, the nation found itself moving to preserve the great resource it contained in already assembled corridors. But the new awareness was colliding with the realities of centuries-old legal precedents regarding landownership. Lawyers quickly became central players, with some of the showdowns concerning individual trails and others dealing with broad policy issues. Many of these confrontations took place in court; some played out in front of the Interstate Commerce Commission and later the Surface Transportation Board.

It was the railbanking law that was the legal game changer, and the Rails-to-Trails Conservancy focused its litigation work on global issues rather than on specific landownership battles. The first major policy skirmish was over a basic interpretation of the new law. Regarding this "bank," we asked, who exactly was the banker?

When the railbanking law was passed, the railroads assumed *they* would decide whether or not to bank a corridor for the future; it seemed obvious to them that they would know better than anyone else whether the route was going to be needed again. This had

Table 8. Earliest railbanking agreements

Date	State	Railroad	Miles	Final outcome	Original endpoints
May 1986	Iowa	Chicago & Northwestern	13	Sauk Rail Trail	Maple River-Carnarvon
January 1987	Vermont	Vermont Railway, Inc.	8	Island Line Rail Trail	Burlington Waterfront
April 1987	Missouri	Missouri-Kansas-Texas	200	Katy Trail State Park	Machens-Sedalia
June 1987	Iowa	Chicago & Northwestern	33	Raccoon River Valley Trail	Waukee-Yale
March 1988	Oklahoma	Missouri Pacific	20	(Trail effort failed)	Kerr McGee-Panama
September 1988	Iowa	Chicago & Northwestern	6	Shell Rock River/Butler County Nature Trail	Clarksville-Shell Rock
October 1988	Iowa	Chicago & Northwestern	34	Three Rivers Trail	Eagle Grove-Rolfe
December 1988	Washington DC/ Maryland	CSX	11	Capital Crescent Trail	Georgetown-Silver Spring
May 1989	Utah	Union Pacific	30	Historic Union Pacific Rail Trail State Park	Echo-Park City
June 1989	Iowa	Iowa Southern	65	Wabash Trace Nature Trail	Council Bluffs-Shenandoah

Source: Rails-to-Trails Conservancy

the effect of quashing railbanking requests since most railroad managements were deep in their own profit-and-loss bubble and couldn't imagine any alternative where a money-losing track would ever be wanted back. In contrast RTC claimed that states and local communities should have just as much right to save a corridor for the future—to put it into a railbank—as the railroad itself. After all, the entity that might one day need it from out of storage might be a different creature entirely. (This is exactly what happened later in Montgomery County, Maryland, where the abandoning railroad,

Fighting for Rights in Court

in 1986, was the csx Corporation while the rejuvenating entity, in 2016, was the Maryland Transit Administration.)

The icc didn't see it that way. Were hikers claiming that rail corridor decisions were too important to leave to the railroads? On appeal, the dc Circuit Court sided with the agency. We had lost our first case. The railroads would be the sole judges of whether their corridors would be preserved upon cessation of active rail service. Soon after, the Connecticut Trust for Historic Preservation brought up the same issue for a track north of New Haven. rtc was a co-petitioner on that one and it, too, was denied. The conservancy's legal record was 0–2.

Next up was a case against the icc brought by the Illinois Commerce Commission. In that one, Illinois, along with rtc and others, charged that certain types of unused tracks were coming up for abandonment so rapidly and so unexpectedly that no one—neither government agencies nor private groups—had time to file a request for railbanking. Trail advocates lost that one too, but this time there was a glimmer of a breakthrough. During the litigation the Interstate Commerce Commission told the court that even though it wasn't *required* to accept a late-filed trail use request, it would voluntarily do so. For practical purposes it was a legal victory for trails—our first.

The most talked-about of all the early specific trail lawsuits played out on the 200-mile-long Missouri-Kansas-Texas Railroad corridor along the Missouri River starting just outside St. Louis. Excitement over this track—at the time the longest proposed rail-trail in the country—ran high on both sides, and even before the lawsuit the corridor had been the scene of intense political jockeying. For one, the "Katy," as it was called, was only the third corridor ever to be voluntarily railbanked. When the trail was finally approved in the closing hours of the 1987 legislative session, a farming couple, Maurice and Jayne Glosemeyer, along with 143 adjacents along the corridor, filed suit. They charged that railbanking was a ruse and that the whole concept was unconstitutional.

While this was unfolding, 1,000 miles to the east, in Burlington, Vermont, another proposed trail had become mired in dispute and was working its way through various cases and appeals.

A Vermont couple with a penchant for litigation, Paul and Priscilla Preseault, had purchased a property alongside a railroad track owned by the state. When two different courts as well as the ICC ruled that the state could lawfully turn it into a trail, the Preseaults, like the Glosemeyers, filed suit against the idea of railbanking, charging that it was an "utter fiction" that corridors would ever be reborn for trains.

By 1989 the U.S. Supreme Court felt the time had come to resolve conflicting rails-to-trails decisions in various circuits. For its official deliberation it chose the case of *Preseault v. ICC*, and on February 21, 1990, in a decision resoundingly endorsing the congressional approach to saving corridors, it ruled unanimously that railbanking was constitutional. At the same time, the court gave aggrieved parties at least a partial remedy for their disappointment. Since the United States already had on the books an important law, known as the Tucker Act, that enables persons to be financially reimbursed by the federal government if any of their property is taken through federal action, the court ruled that adjacent owners with valid deeds could be compensated. Railbanking stood, but adjacents could be paid for their loss. (The federal Tucker Act comes into play even for nonfederal rail-trails since railbanking is decided on the national level by the Interstate Commerce Commission or the Surface Transportation Board [STB].)

For communities all over the country it was a vertical semaphore: the track is clear, proceed! They and their lawyers could take railbanking seriously, even though the Preseaults themselves found their way into court on this issue five more times after their Supreme Court defeat. Before 1990 only a few states and localities had taken the plunge, but now many others were emboldened. New trail efforts mushroomed, and ribbons were cut on completed trails with increasing frequency—about four dozen in 1991, almost one hundred in 1992, perhaps four score more in 1993. The precise trail-by-trail opening dates are often hard to determine, but some high-profile, high-quality, high-use trails came into being soon after the court ruling: the Gateway Trail in Minnesota; the Minuteman Bikeway outside Boston; the Union Pacific Rail-Trail in Park City, Utah; the Withlacoochee Trail between Tampa and

Fighting for Rights in Court

Orlando; the Snohomish County Trail north of Seattle. Great new pathways were opening up, and hundreds of thousands of Americans were discovering the joys of a long, flat, easy-to-use, and car-free trail past fields, through woods, and between towns.

In the following years, thanks to the aggressive leadership of Rails-to-Trails Conservancy's legal team of Charles Montange and Andrea Ferster, and numerous affiliate lawyers often working as volunteers, two more important railbanking principles were established. One was that federal law was preeminent, which put a stop to many state law cases that could tie up potential trail conversions for years. Second was the recognition that states and local governments could also engage in their own mini-railbanking. For instance, the Pennsylvania Supreme Court ruled that a municipality—in this case the hamlet of Buffalo Township—could on its own railbank an abandoned corridor even without an ICC ruling. Then in 2009 that same court went even further, giving the go-ahead to railbanking by a private nonprofit organization, the Allegheny Valley Land Trust, even though the railroad itself did not reserve the right to reactivate the track. The Land Trust promised to return the corridor to rail service if officially requested. In New Hampshire, the state's Supreme Court upheld the government's right to acquire any corridor without reversion to adjacent landowners.

Thus, more than twenty years after RTC's original defeat on the concept of "railbanking for all," the courts had come around to that position. Yes, they were saying, these resources offered numerous future opportunities to the community at large.

In subsequent years railbanking has proved itself the legitimate tool for railroad reactivation that Congress had intended. Railroads have actually applied to reacquire some sections of corridor (and in some cases track has been rebuilt)—for example, 15 miles in Cochise County, Arizona; 22 miles on the Indiana-Illinois border; 26 miles from the outskirts of Tulare to the outskirts of Visalia, California; 121 miles between Wichita Falls and North Abilene, Texas; 16 miles from Cleveland to Hollandale, Mississippi; half a mile in Lincoln, Nebraska; 3 miles in Bethesda, Maryland. Although reactivation is not rampant, the valuable corridor resources remain available if future transportation needs require them.

Table 9. Selected reactivated corridors after railbanking

Corridor	State	Banked	Reactivated	Length (mi.)	Notes
Charleston-Douglas	Arizona	1997	2003	41.5	new railroad company formed
Visalia-Cutler	California	1995	1997	26.0	
Sasser-Albany	Georgia	1997	2003	4.9	new railroad company formed
Spalding-Grangeville	Idaho	2001	2003	52.0	new railroad company formed
Browns-Poseyville	Illinois/Indiana	1998	2005	22.5	new railroad company formed
Wabash Trace	Iowa	1989	1990	0.1	
Napoleonville Branch	Louisiana	1997	2004	4.7	
Cleveland-Hollandale	Mississippi	1999	1999	16.7	
Carondelet Branch	Missouri	1992	1997	0.2	trail allowed alongside reactivated segment
Lincoln Branch	Nebraska	2001	2004	0.4	
Minster–St. Marys	Ohio	1989	1990	10.1	recommenced service on entire line
Midland Valley Branch	Oklahoma	1993	2009	4.7	
Wichita Falls–North Abilene	Texas	1996	1998	121.5	
Echo–Park City	Utah	1989	2005	n.a.	
Pullman-Moscow	Washington/Idaho	1997	2005	0.8	land swap and trail relocation

Source: Rails-to-Trails Conservancy and Peter Harnik

Despite this proof of the concept, opposition did not abate. While RTC was actively promoting and protecting rail-trails, opponents were simultaneously working in the opposite direction. Dozens of lawsuits were filed, although with railbanking being legally enforced, the adversaries' strategy shifted mostly toward compensation payments. Not all the cases were decided in the pro-trail direction. An analysis of the thirty-year win–loss record of Rails-to-Trails Conservancy attorneys, including cases in which RTC filed amicus curiae ("friend of the court") supporting briefs, reveals thirty-four victories and twenty-nine losses. But that overall score masks a truly remarkable record on the major policy-oriented cases. There the success rate was an extraordinary 62 percent. On simpler issues concerning compensation, it was a lower 38 percent.

Many of the anti-trail actions were stimulated by lawyers themselves purely for financial reasons; learning of abandonments, they then reached out to adjacent owners, asking them to sign up for class-action cases that would involve little or no investment on the client's part. (Not only do lawyers get a percentage of a settlement in such cases; they can also recover legal fees from the government. In fifty-five compensation cases decided by the U.S. Court of Claims between 1990 and 2017, the median collective payout to all the landowners was $456,000 while the median payout for attorneys' fees was $378,000.) On the other hand, some cases were brought directly by one of the leading philosophical opponents of rail-trails, the National Association of Reversionary Property Owners (NARPO).

NARPO, despite its countrywide nomenclature, is primarily the vehicle of one individual, Richard Welsh, of Sammamish, Washington, and La Quinta, California. Although details about the organization's structure and finances are sketchy, it has been prolifically active in the legal arena, instituting or participating in numerous petitions at the ICC and STB as well as taking part in lawsuits. Welsh's public activism began in 1977 regarding a boundary dispute over a dock next to his house on Lake Sammamish. Ten years later, when a nearby Burlington Northern abandonment was proposed for a trail, Welsh began by strenuously defending his personal rights and his own backyard, then broadened the effort to advocate for everyone he could find in his position. NARPO itself has no staff and no discernable budget, but it associates itself closely with the national private-property defense community, and it seems to collaborate with several law firms in the Midwest in finding cases to file.

Since Washington is the home of both NARPO and a legally savvy recreational community, the state is a hotbed of both anti- and pro-rail-trail activity. (After Welsh moved out of his lakeside community, the wealthy unincorporated enclave voted to form itself into the new city of Sammamish, in part because of opposition to the rail-trail, although the trail itself survived that maneuver.) By 2018 Washington State had eighty-six successful rail-trails totaling more than 1,000 miles, but NARPO was also particularly active there, having instigated or helped with at least a dozen legal challenges. In one particularly important case in south-central Washington, *Dave v. Rails-to-Trails Conservancy*, landowners sought—but failed to get—compensation from the state of Washington. The court reaffirmed that compensation payments, if any, must come from the federal government.

Trail opponents operate on two levels: At public hearings and in the media they focus broadly on every imaginable negative aspect of the facilities—crime, litter, impact on property value, loss of privacy. In the legal arena they focus on the narrower issue of ownership, claiming to be not so much anti-trail as pro-fairness for adjacent owners. With trails being overwhelmingly popular among the public, NARPO has had more success with the latter strategy than the former. The Supreme Court's *Preseault* decision in 1990 was, of course, a crippling setback for adjacents since it upheld the constitutionality of the railbanking law. But NARPO did score a victory twenty-four years later with a case in Wyoming, *Marvin Brandt Revocable Trust v. United States*. There the Supreme Court ruled that the federal government lacked any interest in rights-of-way that had been acquired by a railroad under an 1875 federal law granting rights-of-way through federal lands. The decision caused a flurry of excitement in the private property world—and a groan of disappointment by rail-trail advocates—but its actual reach has been minor. For one thing, it only affects corridors acquired under the 1875 act, which means only tracks located west of Minnesota, Iowa, and Arkansas, and not even all of them. Moreover, any corridor that is railbanked remains protected. And the particulars of

Fighting for Rights in Court

the case were such that there is doubt as to how many other trails it might affect.

. . .

IN THE BIG PICTURE THERE ARE THREE REASONS FOR TODAY'S intense disagreement about railroad landownership in the West. First, the laws governing the gift of federal and state lands changed over the four decades between 1835 and 1875, as the national sentiment gradually shifted from being strongly pro- to considerably anti-railroad.

Second, there were two completely different kinds of land grants made to railroads. There was the narrow strip—generally 100 or 200 feet wide—upon which the tracks were laid. Then there were the much larger checkerboard properties—usually a mile square, mile after mile on alternate sides—provided as a construction subsidy. The railroads sold off these lands to settlers for the double benefit of raising immediate construction cash and then, later, of having crops and other goods to ship to markets. The essence of these two very different kinds of properties is frequently misunderstood

Third, the actual language used in various legal documents— "easement," "right-of-way," "reverter," "reversion"—was not standardized and had different meanings and implications in different places and at different times. The Supreme Court itself noted on several occasions the confusion surrounding the key phrase "right-of-way" as having two very different meanings: one, a physical route across the land and, the other, a conceptual privilege to utilize someone else's property for certain stated purposes. Later, in the many twentieth-century decisions involving these various lands, some courts rigorously differentiated between the large checkerboard grants and the narrow "rights-of-way." Other courts conflated the two. Although the Supreme Court has spoken about rights-of-way under the 1875 act, opponents continue to challenge railbanking, railroad property rights, and the rights of trails.

One bitter point of contention is whether adjacent landowners should be entitled to compensation when a corridor is railbanked. This topic is sometimes dealt with sweepingly for a broad group of litigants; other times it is resolved so narrowly that it requires parcel-by-parcel analysis of the original deeds to a railroad along a particular track. NARPO and the class-action lawyers in the takings cases claim that between 50 and 80 percent of railroad corridors are owned by abutting property owners who deserve compensation. In contrast Danaya Wright, a law professor and scholar at the University of Florida, has examined thousands of nineteenth-century source deeds and came to the opposite conclusion—that 80 percent of rail corridors are owned free and clear by the railroads. In 2014 Wright wrote:

> Courts . . . walk a fine line between applying standard rules of deed construction . . . that generally favor the railroads and following the anti-railroad precedents and practices that in the past have resulted in windfalls to adjacent landowners who suddenly find their backyards increased by 50 or 100 feet with the discontinuation of railroads. Now that the railroads are selling their property interests to trail groups, state and local governments, and utility companies for other uses such as trails and fiber optics, the always uneasy tension between standard property rules and special railroad exceptions has become even greater.[1]

This vastly different perception helps fuel the current filing of compensation lawsuits over individual corridors, although Wright cheerfully points out that the number of modern legal actions is substantially less than the number filed in the nineteenth century when the corridors were first being assembled. The government's regulatory authority in this area is largely settled, but just as people fought over how much the railroads should pay when they acquired land, people today are fighting over how much the federal government should pay to allow these corridors to continue in use.

Despite the lawsuits, decisions about the large majority of rail-trails are made not in court but through the normal democratic political process—public meetings, plans of action, votes by the duly delegated legislative authority, appropriation of funds, purchase, and development. Despite all the ruckus, by 2018 the number of rail-trails created under the railbanking law was only about

Fighting for Rights in Court

185 (out of more than 2,000 rail-trails total). The collective mileage was just over 4,000 (out of nearly 20,000 miles total).

Railbanking, with its many legalistic controversies, is important, but most trails have been created without bitter litigation. The crucial factor leading to a successful rail-trail has been the building of a strong political base. That is what we will explore in the next chapter.

10

Building the Political Base

LAWYERS WERE IMPORTANT FROM THE BEGINNING, BUT THEY weren't a substitute for the old-fashioned kind of grassroots activism lauded by Margaret Meade when she said, "Never doubt that a small group of thoughtful, committed citizens can change the world; indeed, it's the only thing that ever has." Citizen training, combined with a nationwide publicity campaign, was the genesis of the Rails-to-Trails Conservancy's program.

Step number one was finding out what was happening around the country. In the early days almost every rails-to-trail effort took place in its own political silo, with each group struggling to find a path to success. With a national organization, we could begin to amass data, share stories, and see what lessons could be learned. Gradually patterns from the data began to emerge. Pattern number one was that people loved the idea. Pattern number two was that love was not enough—the majority of early efforts went nowhere. Other patterns were more subtle. One concerned variations in state law: we noticed that states with a legal "right of first refusal" were doing better than those without it. Another pattern concerned railroad companies themselves: some were more amenable to discussing trail creation while others wouldn't even answer the telephone. On the other hand, some patterns were almost inscrutable. We assumed that states with an approved trail plan would be more successful than those without, but we found plan-less states with many trails, and trail-less states with many plans. We also assumed that communities with strong trail advocacy groups would be the places that succeeded. But we found some strong advocates who were winners and others, just as committed, who lost.

Eventually we cracked the code. We learned that if a trail effort contained three ingredients—a formal plan of action, a public agency agreeing to own the facility, and an advocacy organization pushing for approval—it was likely to succeed. Lacking even one of those factors was often enough to prove fatal. We called it the "rails-to-trails triangle": advocacy, planning, and government support. There were occasional exceptions to this rule—a rare government agency determined enough to succeed without an advocacy ally; or, conversely, a particularly strong private group that could operate a lightly used rural trail without government support. But normally the formulation was an uncanny predictor of outcomes, even in battles that dragged out for six, eight, or more years. For instance, Massachusetts's Minuteman Bikeway, which took eighteen years to complete—"17 years of politics and one year of construction," according to Alan McClennen, the stalwart planning director for the town of Arlington—was eventually pushed over the top through the power of the rails-to-trails triangle.

The first leg of the triangle is advocacy. Most rail-trail efforts start with one constituency, whether bicyclists or snowmobilers, prairie-lovers or hunters, equestrians or mothers. To build excitement among their own coterie, that very first promotional message is usually enthusiastic but narrow—"The perfect place to run!" or "Your horse will be smiling!" or "Never worry about your kids in traffic again!" or "Haven't you always wanted to hear the birds chirp?" But a single constituency is rarely enough, particularly when asking the public to spend hundreds of thousands or millions of dollars. When Washington DC's Coalition for the Capital Crescent Trail began, it was led by bicyclists, but by the time it had enough political muscle to win the expenditure of more than $25 million of public funds, it had expanded to thirty-eight organizations representing also walkers, runners, disabled persons, canoeists, roller skaters, conservationists, educators, and outdoor-oriented women.

Some rails-to-trails collaborations, such as between organizations of runners and walkers, are obvious and easy. Some—say, between bicycle and horse organizations—are more challenging but feasible if there is good communication and a willingness to compromise. Others, perhaps between all-terrain vehicle riders and bird-watchers, are essentially impossible. There are happy coalitions where all members enjoy one another, and then there are the somewhat strained alliances born more from need than love. The man who conceived the Walkway Over the Hudson, for example, didn't want to allow bikes, but the effort would never have succeeded without the commitment and muscle of the bicycling community. In some cases (as we'll see later) the coalitions extend beyond even human users to utility entities like sewer districts or fiber-optic companies or even railroads.

At RTC the rails-to-trails triangle rule helped us greatly in our day-to-day organizing and in advice we gave over the telephone.

"We need help," the caller would begin. "You see, we have a railroad, and some of us were gathering around the kitchen table about two years ago, and my aunt said she had an idea. It wasn't really *her* idea, but she said she had heard about it. She's not actually my aunt, she's my—"

"This sounds great, but do you have a written plan for your trail?"

"Um, no, but my aunt—"

"Well, put together a little plan and we'll look it over for you. Name of the trail, the endpoints, who will use it, what its benefits are, who owns the track, who will own the trail, what it might cost. Write it down. Then let's talk."

Or a different call: "We've got an emergency! Our bike group put together a beautiful plan for a rail-trail, the railroad is open to the idea, and we have more than three hundred signed petitions in favor, but the county supervisors are dead-set against it. You've got to turn them around for us!"

"Let's see, you definitely need a managing agency—could it become a state park instead of a county park? Would the state be more amenable?"

"Hey! Interesting idea! That might just work."

One of the classic rails-to-trails efforts took place in Pinellas County, Florida, home to St. Petersburg and Clearwater. Not unlike many other campaigns, the Pinellas Trail grew out of a tragedy— the death on a roadway of a seventeen-year-old bicyclist. His devastated father, Bert Valery Jr., vowed to make cycling safer in the

Building the Political Base

state, so he started speaking widely and joined the county bicycle advisory committee. Three years later csx Corporation announced the abandonment of an old Seaboard Coast Line track that ran the full length of the county a few blocks in from the shore. Valery and the cyclists leaped at the opportunity. Pinellas officials, recognizing the industrial value of the corridor for the densely populated county, had no qualms about acquiring it, but they scoffed at the idea of a bike trail. Their thinking ran more toward light-rail, a busway, or even the kind of overhead monorail so successful at Disney World. But they didn't have the funds for a grandiose project, and a consulting firm confirmed that the county's sprawling pattern of development lacked enough concentrated destination points to justify a transitway.

As competing options failed to gain traction, the cyclists stepped up their campaign. They were bolstered by data showing that, for bikers, Pinellas was the fifth most dangerous county in the second most dangerous state in the country. Floridians were far from leaders in the rails-to-trails movement, but the locals were aided by the arrival of a snowbird, Ernie Foster, a retired corporate executive from Connecticut who loved to bike and knew how to get things done. Under his prodding, a new advocacy group, Pinellas Trail, Inc. (PTI), was created; immediately fund-raising began and a plan was formulated to create a county-managed trail instead of one that would be fragmented between the seven feuding towns it traversed. The effort was strengthened when another snowbird arrived, new county planning assistant Ned Baier. From Minneapolis and Iowa, Baier knew the benefits of trails, and he knew how to plan them. It seemed that the rails-to-trails triangle was coming into focus. There was a plan and an organized group of advocates, but the third leg—a managing agency—was still missing.

By 1988 Pinellas Trail, Inc. had enough capacity to hire Cuma Glennon-Beirne, a crackerjack organizer, publicist, and fund-raiser. In just a year, amid growing enthusiasm for the idea, PTI pulled in two thousand members and an amazing $100,000. Back then, virtually no other local rail-trail organization had that kind of money. PTI could have bought a lot of publicity and even a few water fountains and benches, its organizers knew, but they realized that amount of money wouldn't go very far toward actually developing a 35-mile trail in a thickly settled county. It would require public support, but when Glennon-Beirne approached the county commission chair, she was doused with cold water. "We can't just go and spend a million dollars on *bicycles*," he told her. "You'd need to show us that people really want something like this."

The message was harsh but the timing was fortuitous. A year earlier the state of Florida had for the first time permitted cities and counties to place tax referenda before their citizens, and a "Penny for Pinellas" infrastructure measure—for everything from roads to courthouses—was on the ballot. The sales tax increase was the only hope for funding a bike trail in the fiscally strapped county, but the tax hike was highly controversial. Glennon-Beirne asked: What if PTI worked in favor of the measure, would that change the equation? Yes, pledged county administrator Fred Marquis. If they helped and if the measure passed, he would assure funding for the trail. PTI members plunged into the effort with gusto, giving speeches, doing mailings, distributing flyers and buttons, and leaf-letting on a short stretch of corridor that had been hastily built as a demonstration project. By the time of the election the promotional blitz had many residents under the helpfully mistaken impression that the penny was entirely for the trail rather than mostly for less motivating projects like drainage canals and prisons. It squeaked over the top: out of 135,000 votes, it won by 398.

Marquis, the county administrator, knew who had made the difference and he called Glennon-Beirne. With a victory laugh he said, "I'm telling the engineering department tomorrow that the trail project is the first to come out the chute." The rails-to-trails triangle had locked. Even though the trail itself would require more than twenty years to complete—and after the first 35 miles were finished, new ideas then led to more—the project's validity was proven and never challenged. Today it is the most widely enjoyed rail-trail in the state.

Another example of strong agency support occurred in northern Illinois in 2000. "We were trying to create a trail from Freeport to the Wisconsin line," recalled George Bellovics, state trail coordinator. "The trail was named for Jane Addams, the famous advocate for the poor, who was born in Cedarville. We were met at the public hearing by a group of farmers led by a belligerent out-of-town lawyer who had rounded them up." But the agency had done its due diligence, determining that the track had already been purchased by the South Central Wisconsin Rail Transit Commission, a legislatively created body with the purpose of buying land outside Wisconsin to benefit in-state railroads. "When the lawyer started his bluster," Bellovics said, "I held up the deed and said to the farmers, 'This property is owned in fee by the state of Wisconsin. You can fire this guy right now, save your money and leave the room. On the other hand, if you want to talk to us about how the trail can be most satisfactorily designed, stay and give us your input.' When one of the farmers explained how hard it would be to get his cows across the trail from one field to another, we came up with a whole special gate design for him. It's now a feature of the trail—people come and watch the cows go across."

Sometimes the legs of the triangle take years to click into place. Even when they do, none follow the same script.

In southwest Ohio it was the public agencies and the advocates who took the lead, with the overall plan lagging behind. The Little Miami Trail—the effort we met earlier from the 1978 Rails-to-Trails Demonstration Grant Program—was begun in Cincinnati, but with weak planning leadership from the state, each jurisdiction along the five-county, 78-mile route had to use its own resources to make it happen or to fight off opposition. The trail effort itself was a bit of a fluke. The Little Miami River, which flows into the Ohio River, happened to have a railroad alongside, but the focus of citizen advocates—and their robust group, Little Miami, Inc. (LMI)—was on defending the river against development. When the declining rail line was finally put out of business by a tornado in 1974, LMI's immediate desire was for a tourist train, not a trail. Only when the U.S. Department of the Interior announced its rail-trail grant program did the thinking shift. Fortunately the group was well poised to use its connections and experience, and in short order it lined up more than twenty endorsements from towns and counties along the corridor as well as almost every relevant state official, up to and including Governor James Rhodes. At the same time, Cincinnati attorney Tim Burke went to Washington DC to solicit the assistance of U.S. senators Howard Metzenbaum and John Glenn. When that meeting fortuitously included Chris Delaporte, the visionary and exuberant head of the Bureau of Outdoor Recreation (BOR), Burke convinced him to come to Ohio for a personal tour.

"We wanted to first show it to him from the sky," Burke later recalled. "Bob Teater, our great state director of natural resources at that time, was in the National Guard and he had access to a helicopter. We then got in canoes. We then rode a railroad crew car up and down the corridor. When we arrived in the little town of Morrow, there was a home-cooked lunch from the ladies and we had a performance by the high school band. Delaporte was snowed."

Several months later, when BOR announced its nine grant recipients, the largest chunk—$1 million, 20 percent of the whole pot—went to the Little Miami. That success led to a cascade of other breakthroughs, including a matching million-dollar grant from the state of Ohio. But it turned out that the rails-to-trails triangle hadn't been entirely consummated. There was robust advocacy and government participation, but the third leg—a strong written plan of action—was defective. Instead of cementing the lengthy five-county corridor as a state park under unified design and management, the structure remained vague, necessitating that the route be owned or developed by a confusion of county, local, or even private entities, resulting in, at best, inconsistent maintenance and, at worst, absolute rejection of sections of the trail. Today about two-thirds is identified as a state park, but even that section is technically operated and funded by a series of county and other park agencies under state oversight. Most notoriously the affluent town of Terrace Park, just outside Cincinnati, spent twenty years rejecting every effort to complete the trail through its boundaries. But the small cadre of resisters finally surrendered in 2006 and the bicyclists' victory ride was led by Governor Robert Taft himself.

A place where the triangle really proved itself was in Seattle, on the Burke-Gilman Trail, ten years after its original creation. The Burke-Gilman was already one of the most successful rail-trails in the country and was assumed to be politically invulnerable, but its

Building the Political Base

desirable location along one of Seattle's coveted waterfronts made it enticing to schemes by the wealthy and the stealthy.

In early 1988 Burlington Northern Railroad (BN) quietly sold a three-mile stretch of track to a Montana developer who wanted a place to dock his yacht. The city and the bicycle community had long planned to use the segment as a continuation of the trail. Since there had been no notice and the corridor hadn't even come up for abandonment, the political shock wave was palpable. Recoiling, the railroad first claimed that the track was just a minor "industrial spur" that didn't need to go through normal abandonment procedures. It then said it hadn't known that the city was interested. When the Seattle bike coordinator, Peter Lagerwey, showed the letters he had written to BN about the plan to continue the trail, the railroad countered that he was too junior to count. When Lagerwey also displayed a letter from the mayor, the railroad said that the missive had never been received.

"But on the Sunday morning after the Saturday night sale," Lagerwey recalled, "I went to the affected portion of the corridor, in an industrial area where the tracks had been in the street. When I got there, a two-block section of the rails was gone and the street had been rebuilt. It was done so thoroughly that they had made it impossible to even envision a trail in that space."

The uproar was immediate, particularly since the city at the time was home to Burlington Northern headquarters, and it held the front pages of the Seattle press for two weeks. Mayor Charles Royer bitterly protested; Seattle bicyclists and leaders of area neighborhood groups held a large demonstration at the BN tower, chaining bikes across the building's front door; the state's entire U.S. congressional delegation called for an investigation; a state legislative committee held an oversight hearing; and two organizations filed a petition with the Interstate Commerce Commission, which instituted a formal inquiry. At first the railroad announced the deal was unalterable. But when the mayor assigned Lagerwey to go back to the original deeds and research the old land agreements, the results were startling. "Back at the beginning, no one had believed that any of the tracks would stop being used, so the old promoters felt safe in making all kinds of wild promises in the event of abandonment," Lagerwey said. "Expensive things, like rebuilding street crossings and taking down overpasses." An angry Royer suggested that he might hold the railroad to every one of those written promises.

"At the meeting of all the different sides to begin sorting it out," said Lagerwey, "there were seventeen lawyers—every one of them sworn to secrecy. The newspapers were so keen on the story that they kept calling me at home for quotes, or facts, or just an off-the-record back story. I kept refusing. They would say to me, 'Look, we'll do it this way. We'll tell you the question. Then we'll hang up and call you back. If you pick up the phone on the first ring, it means "yes." If you pick up on the 3rd ring, it means "no."' The whole thing was pretty exciting for a bicycle coordinator."

Eventually the sale was unwound and annulled, and the trail was extended. "And surprisingly, in the end," Lagerwey recounted, "the fiasco turned out to be the single most important event in the history of the Seattle trails movement. The railroad agreed to give the city a right of first refusal on every abandonment from then on, with a guaranteed thirty-foot width and an option to pick up more width as we needed it." A plan plus a strong agency plus an energized citizenry carried the day.

Of course the triangle never just happened on its own. Agency leaders had to be found and cultivated, citizen advocates needed to be trained and educated, and plans required writing. And since almost every trail proposal generates some resistance, advocates needed ammunition to support their case. In many cases the instigators were simply local people who had come across a rail-trail in their travels, were enthralled by the concept, and then incubated it internally until an opportunity suddenly arose where they lived. Other times, an activist from a trail stronghold would move to a new town and become the Johnny Appleseed of the concept. That's what happened when bicyclist Ed McBrayer moved back to his hometown of Atlanta in 1986 after living in the Denver area for a decade. "In Denver I was known as a trail junkie—I just loved them. After I moved back to Atlanta I asked at a bike shop what they would recommend. They said, 'There's a beautiful trail out to Stone Mountain, go out there early next Saturday morning.' Turns out it was a busy two-lane road with no shoulders and six inches to spare on each side. That was their idea of a trail."

Frustrated, McBrayer went down to City Hall to complain. "They were surprised and said to me, 'No one has really ever asked for trails before.' But they also said they were in the process of creating a city master plan and would love to have some trails. That's what led us to developing Atlanta's greenway masterplan," he said. McBrayer went on to co-found the PATH Foundation, a remarkably successful trail planning and construction organization that has physically built 81 miles of rail-trail, and many more miles of other trails, in Georgia and South Carolina. (PATH was originally an acronym for "People of Atlanta for Trails Here" until McBrayer got pushback from non-Atlantans; now the name just speaks for itself across the Southeast.)

In other cases it was the Rails-to-Trails Conservancy that swooped into a community and stirred up the pot.

RTC's first ambitious effort took place in 1988 when it organized exploratory cartography meetings in eight major metropolitan areas. Involving both public agency planners and private citizens who happened to be knowledgeable train buffs, the mapping sessions acted like flashlights in an unexplored cave. In eight metros—New York, Chicago, Philadelphia, Seattle, Boston, St. Louis, Cincinnati, and the Twin Cities—nearly 250 abandoned and likely-to-be-abandoned rail corridors were uncovered. "The nation has definitely not run out of potential trailways," said RTC's research coordinator, Karen-Lee Ryan, at the conclusion. "Even in rapidly developing, densely populated areas there are dozens of beautiful corridors still available."[1]

The movement was proving itself. More than just a nostalgic and esoteric phenomenon, the rail-trail truly had the potential of being impactful. Even better, the very process of asking about corridors could stimulate activism. In New Paltz, New York, Kristen Cole Brown stood up at a public meeting, waved the RTC report in the air and announced excitedly, "Some group down in Washington DC says that we have one of the most promising abandoned rail corridors in the country!" She and her neighbors had been struggling to build interest in the old Wallkill Valley Railroad track through town, and their opposition included the local chamber of commerce, which had other ideas for the corridor. "We had no information. This was before the internet, before e-mail, before even fax machines," Brown said. "When I found out there was a national organization my heart leaped. I called them and they sent me a packet of information about the successes they knew about around the country. It even had testimonials from some chambers of commerce! I asked to make a presentation to our chamber. I was so nervous I couldn't sleep the night before. But when I gave the talk and passed around the information, they got interested and called off their opposition. The chamber president even asked me if I wanted a job." She laughed. "But I think he was kidding." Five years later, a ribbon was cut on the first segment of the Wallkill Valley Rail-Trail.

In Washington State, a young bicycle racer and railroad fan named Fred Wert was alerted by a friend to the RTC cartography meeting, showed up with a remarkable map of his own depicting rail corridors, and left the evening with a job offer from Rails-to-Trails Conservancy. He went on to form a Washington State chapter of the organization, through which he proselytized and provided technical assistance to scores of new trail efforts. And by 2019 Washington State was eighth in the country in rail-trails.

The most remarkable outgrowth of the project occurred in Atlanta, a city that in 1988 infamously had no trails and barely any bikeable streets. As the commercial heart of the Southeast, the "Big Peach" wasn't known for rail abandonments, and RTC didn't know if it would find any. Marianne Fowler, the organization's southern regional coordinator, recalls what happened: "After two public meetings and days spent poring over railroad documents, *nada!*—there were no abandonments in Atlanta. Then, staring at an old railroad map, it emerged like a film image floating into focus in its chemical bath. A hidden ring of rail lines encircled the city's core. They were still sporting trains, but quick research revealed that the tonnage carried on much of the circle was light. It was a pattern that foretold almost certain abandonment. RTC's report identified this Atlanta treasure and alerted the city to catch the pieces as they were indeed abandoned."

Since the government was inexperienced in trail funding and creation, forward motion took place slowly, but later, after a publicity-savvy graduate student named Ryan Gravel wrote his master's thesis on the possibility of a light-rail transit loop on those same tracks, the outline of a massive rail-*with*-trail combination emerged. Several developers seized on the idea of transit-oriented development, while the Trust for Public Land (TPL) dove into the park-and-trail possibilities of what was being called the "Atlanta Beltline." When TPL hired Yale professor Alex Garvin and his former student Jim Schroder to produce a formal plan, they painted a compelling picture of what became arguably the nation's most ambitious center-city trail, rail, park, and real estate mega-development plan—23 miles of trail with nine new and four expanded parks, plus 28,000 housing units and $10 billion in commercial development. Though not yet completed, the Beltline is doing more to stimulate urban walkability and downtown revitalization than any other Atlanta project of the past seventy years.

Every now and then, one or another leg of the rails-to-trails triangle was bolstered or even replaced by the fortunate application of philanthropic support. When the 200-mile-long Missouri-Kansas-Texas ("Katy") rail corridor along the Missouri River in Missouri came up for abandonment, it was a far bigger undertaking than the state's parks department could handle. For one, the department didn't have the money to buy it. For another, there was fierce opposition by hundreds of farmers along the route, which was reflected by rural leaders in the state legislature. Moreover, the state's only successful experience with the complexities of a rails-to-trail conversion was the short eight-mile abandonment in the university town of Columbia, and even that effort was teetering over strong opposition in outlying Boone County. One night, when a long wooden trestle mysteriously burst into flame, the Boone County sheriff shrugged his shoulders and said he thought it was probably due to a lightning strike. On the other hand, there was intense excitement about the opportunity for a car-free trail almost across the state, from St. Louis to Kansas City, with the added bonus that it paralleled the famous route of Meriwether Lewis and William Clark up the Missouri River. This seemed like an opportunity way too good to lose.

Into this fraught situation stepped a wealthy St. Louis couple, Ted and Pat Jones. Pat was a dedicated conservationist who donated several important tracts of land and was affectionately nicknamed the "Prairie Godmother." Ted agreed with her sentiment but came to his appreciation of trails from a different angle. The son of the man who had started the Edward T. Jones Investments firm, Jones had built the business into a powerhouse by concentrating on an unusual niche—opening one-broker offices in hundreds of small places around the country. And he did it in a special way: he actually went to many of the little towns to personally look them over, to judge the level of their economic life, and to check that they had at least a few individuals with enough money to care about investing. When his travels took him to Wisconsin, he had noticed that the towns that had rail-trails showed more vitality than those with defunct and plowed-under railroad tracks. Most impressive to the couple was the beauty of the Elroy-Sparta Trail, which they bicycled on, and the economic impact it had on the area. Another relevant spark: the couple had originally met on a bicycle trip back in the 1940s.

"They had actually called us up way back in 1980 when they heard about a rail abandonment in Mexico, Missouri," said Ron Kucera, longtime deputy director of the state's department of natural resources. "They would have paid to convert that one into a trail, but we decided it wasn't interesting enough for a state park. They understood our response, but they kept their eyes open for other chances."

Like the Katy. Everyone knew that was the big one, and the Joneses immediately offered to pay the railroad's asking price of $200,000—$1,000 a mile. They also pledged an additional $2 million toward the cost of developing the line into a trail. That started the ball rolling; today the Katy Trail is on the list of the "15 best things to do" in Missouri.

A comparable, if unlikely, philanthropic angel appeared at a crucial moment in Washington DC, when a complicated deal to acquire a 3-mile CSX track was on the verge of collapsing. The corridor was located within the C&O Canal National Historical Park, and the National Park Service was desperate to acquire it. But the railroad had good title and there was the threat that a private developer could squeeze a row of houses in a long line through the middle of the park. Not only would the new homeowners, with their million-dollar views of the Potomac River, ruin the ambiance of the park, but they would also block the existing million-dollar views of the wealthy and politically influential residents up the hill behind them. The scene was set for a juicy dogfight.

Between the lobbying of the trail advocates and the concerned residents, Congress quickly perceived the importance of saving the corridor, but csx had gotten a property appraisal for $21 million—$11 million within the national park, plus another $10 million for six more miles in Maryland. The railroad wanted a quick sale, but the Park Service didn't have the money. From behind the curtain stepped Kingdon Gould Jr., a Maryland businessman and conservationist, who offered to buy the whole track and hold it until such time as Congress (and Montgomery County, Maryland) could make an appropriation and buy him out. It put a huge chunk of his money at considerable risk—Congress can be far from a trustworthy partner in situations like that—but the appropriation came through over a two-year period. Chris Brown, a key leader of the effort, later reminisced, "My friends in the hiking community were outraged that we'd been able to get millions for this obscure rail-trail while giants like the Pacific Crest Trail were squeezed for those two years." Today that stretch is the acclaimed Capital Crescent Trail that serves more than a million users a year between Silver Spring, Maryland, and Georgetown in the nation's capital. Kingdon Gould, incidentally, was the great-grandson of Jay Gould, the famous "robber baron" who built up and drove under numerous railroad companies in the wild days of the nineteenth-century stock manipulation—although Kingdon swore until his dying day that his magnanimous action for the trail wasn't taken out of any sense of reparation.

Gould may have backed into his conservation philanthropy, but another organization took on the rail corridor challenge much more frontally. The Trust for Public Land, a San Francisco–based national land conservancy that was founded in 1972 as an offshoot from the Nature Conservancy, dove with relish into corridor acquisition projects. Rail-trails were just a small part of the organization's portfolio, but over a thirty-nine-year period TPL bought and conveyed forty-three rail corridors in twenty states, including those that became the Bizz Johnson Trail in California; the Farmington Canal Trail in Connecticut; the Pinellas Trail in Florida; the Osage Trail in Tulsa; the Chessie Circle Trail in Toledo; the Eastern Promenade in Portland, Maine; the DeQuindre Cut in Detroit; the Santa Fe Rail-Trail in New Mexico; the Three Rivers Greenway in Pittsburgh; and the Iron Goat Trail in Washington State. TPL was the organization that handled the purchase of Kitty Brown's Wallkill Valley corridor in New York. In fact, aside from Rails-to-Trails Conservancy itself, TPL has played a larger role in the movement than any other organization.

At first TPL simply bought corridors from Conrail, Grand Trunk Western, CSX, Union Pacific, and others and transferred them to state and local governments. Over time the organization's role grew to include development. In Los Angeles TPL purchased a 32-acre railyard alongside the Los Angeles River that, in the intervening years, has become a key park in the effort to bring nature and greenery to a concretized spillway that had once even been used for the motorcycle-versus-truck race in the movie *Terminator 2*. In Atlanta TPL was the prime early purchaser of parcels that became the Beltline. In Santa Fe, New Mexico, the organization bought a 50-acre railyard in a complex deal that resulted in a new plaza, a 10-acre park, housing and shops, plus a link to an 18-mile rail-trail to the town of Lamy. Finally, in Chicago, in 2010 the organization put all the pieces together to became a leader of the successful effort to create The 606, a $95-million, six-park amalgam along an abandoned elevated rail line between the city's Wicker Park and Bucktown neighborhoods. The 606, named symbolically after the first three digits of the metropolitan area's zip code, has as its central spine the Bloomingdale Trail, named after the local adjoining street. Regardless of nomenclature challenges, the elegantly designed, 3-mile route quickly became Chicago's most talked about and visited linear park, with 1.5 million annual uses.

Later, seeing TPL's success, Rails-to-Trails Conservancy also decided to try its hand at buying and selling railroad corridors. "We began what we called the Trail Conservancy in 1993 and continued it until 1998," recalled Simon Eristoff, who ran the program.

"We did 16 transactions totaling about 600 miles in length," including the abandonment that became the single longest rail-trail ever, the Cowboy Line across Nebraska. "Making the economics work was tremendously difficult, and there was no way to streamline or automate it—each one required a full-court press," Eristoff continued. "The key was finding a corridor we could get for less than its fully appraised value. Sometimes that meant the railroad would cut the price for a tax benefit or even make a full-fledged donation. In other cases the railroad would sell the line for less than what we could recoup from the salvage value of the tracks, ties, and ballast."

In those cases RTC had to find buyers for the old ties—like landscapers—and for the gravel—like highway departments. "In other cases," Eristoff said, "there was no way we could recoup all our costs but there was a philanthropist who would make up the difference—that was the case in Michigan with the noted supermarket founder Fred Meijer who provided backing for four corridors totaling 125 miles. We hung on for five years, and it was well worth the pain, but it sometimes did take on a certain amount of zaniness."

One of the zanier purchases occurred in Blountstown, Florida, Eristoff recalled. "It involved a line that was owned by the trustee in bankruptcy for Joseph Carmine Bonanno, the former head of a legendary New York crime family," he said. "He had reputedly been using the line to store rail cars of—shall we say—somewhat uncertain provenance. We'd been trying to figure out how to pay for the line, and we couldn't quite make the numbers work. There just wasn't enough money in grants and DOT funding to buy the corridor. Finally, I suggested to Ken Bryan, our Florida director, that he go take a look at the line in person, to see if there might be any steel left that we could sell to make ends meet."

"I was sitting at my desk," Eristoff continued, "when Ken called in on an early cell phone. He had brought a shovel with him, and he was digging in the sand that had blown in over the corridor, looking for rail without success. I heard a big crackle of static on the line. He said, 'Looks like we got some rain coming. That was a bit of lightning.' I'd like to say I told him to get out of there right away, but in truth I encouraged him to keep digging in the storm.

Fortunately, he struck steel before the lightning did. For us it was as good as striking gold. The money from the sale of the tracks enabled us to get the deal done, and later Ken brought me a rail spike he had picked up on the excursion. It still sits on my desk after all these years—a very serviceable paperweight."

Throughout the 1980s, rail-trail advocates learned the ropes, raised their expectations, became more politically savvy, and started tipping the balance in their favor. But a missing ingredient was money. Everywhere, they were hampered by not having access to sufficient government funding.

11

Breaking into the Money Vault

NO RAIL-TRAIL WAS A FREE LUNCH. EVEN IF WAS NOT HELD back by legal conflict or political controversy, each one faced the challenge of funding. Communities needed to purchase corridors, remove debris, repair bridges and tunnels, deck trestles, fabricate handrailings, pave surfaces, erect signs, construct parking lots, establish auto barriers, trim foliage, plant trees, install fencing, and more. In the earliest days there was virtually no "trail money" other than miniscule allotments within the U.S. Forest Service, the National Park Service, and a few state park systems. Some of the very early rail-trails came about only because a railroad walked away from the land, allowing the corridor to revert freely to public ownership in a state park or national forest. In other cases the company was sympathetic enough (or tax-deduction savvy enough) to agree to a donation. The resulting pathways were then developed through the work of volunteers, conservation corps members, or in more than one case the crafty assignment of military service members under the rubric of a "training mission." Volunteers, of course, could not remove tracks, ties, and ballast, but those weighty accoutrements had enough salvage value that the task could be turned over to professionals and done without charge.

Every railroad has a real estate division to buy and sell land. Before the concept of rail-trails gained currency, company agents were limited in their thinking about old corridors, breaking most of them into bite-size pieces that were marketed to adjacent owners, property by property. Until the 1980s, it was only in rare cases that railroads themselves thought about the value of a corridor as a continuous trail. In one notable instance in Cannon Falls, Minnesota, a Chicago & North Western Railroad property official called conser-

vation attorney Samuel Morgan and said, "We are officially abandoning our line along the Cannon River. Both I and my superiors
in Chicago feel that this is too scenic a line to be abandoned with
the right-of-way reverting to abutting property owners."[1] Through
this foresight it became the Cannon Valley Trail.

As the railroading business itself receded, the real estate divisions
became more dominant, some even being spun off with wholly new
names. Southern Pacific's unit melded into Catellus Realty, a powerhouse in California, and Burlington Northern spun off Burlington Resources, which then morphed into, among others, Glacier
Park Real Estate, Trillium Corporation, and Plum Creek Timber.
The latter by itself was a landowning giant with more than six
million acres in nineteen states. Even though the corridors comprised but a small fraction of the railroads' massive checkerboard
holdings, they too had value. Parcels in urbanized locations or at
intersections with roads could command decent prices (or even
eyebrow-raising amounts in places like Washington DC, Miami,
Minneapolis, and Seattle). In other cases railroad real estate agents
were able to bluff adjacent farmers and suburbanites into buying
strips that, in truth, would have been unmarketable to anyone else.
On the other hand, some adjacent owners flatly refused to pay at
all and then gradually encroached their way onto the pathways and
into de facto possession.

Regardless of the specific situations, with most railroads refusing to donate their corridors, it quickly became obvious that money
would be needed to buy them as trails.

Trails are funded in one of two ways: as a "recreation" amenity or
as a "transportation" project. Although in reality the two are seam-
lessly complementary, for many years they were strictly separated
by a perverse philosophical superstition, with recreation programs
prohibiting funding for commuting and transportation appropria-
tions requiring "purposeful" use. At least that was the situation into
the late 1980s. But just as quantum theory upended the idea that
light couldn't be both a particle and a wave, rail-trails challenged
the shibboleth that recreationists couldn't have a goal or that commuters couldn't enjoy exercise. After all, at its heart a rail-trail could
be a narrow park just as well as it could be a slow-speed roadway.

Breaking into the Money Vault

That split cuts two ways. On the one hand, it can suggest where advocates should look for money: either a park agency or a transportation department. On the other hand—for those who already know which bureaucracy happens to have available funding—the choice can shape how a project is defined and branded. In the Boston suburbs which in the 1980s were served by a well-funded state transportation department, an abandoned Boston & Maine track was christened the "Minuteman Bikeway" so that the agency wouldn't think it was being asked to pay for a park. In the Cincinnati suburbs a remarkably similar abandoned Penn Central track was given the nomenclature "Little Miami Scenic Trail State Park" for the opposite reason—the Ohio Department of Natural Resources and the U.S. Department of the Interior weren't permitted to put money into anything that smacked of serving a transportation use.

In the early days the park idea predominated. It was generally assumed that rail-trails should be funded by such sources as the Land and Water Conservation Fund or state park bonds like New York's Environmental Quality, Florida's Preservation 2000, Missouri's Design for Conservation, or California's Community Parklands Act. But the total amount of statutory park funding was relatively small and the line for receiving it very long. In fact almost every time a high-visibility park effort gained widespread public support—Redwoods National Park, for instance, or Cape Cod National Seashore or the Everglades—there was not nearly enough money available through normal land acquisition procedures, and a special appropriation had to be made through Congress. This was even more true on the state level, where state park agencies had so many "regular" facilities to create—pools, picnic pavilions, boat launches, campgrounds, restrooms, docks—that there was rarely budget capacity for a new experiment like a rail-trail. Trail advocates started looking around for other sources, and they inevitably began looking over the fence to the grass-is-greener transportation world.

The first constituents to find a little chink in the "there's no money for rail trails" armor were snowmobilers.

Invented in the early 1960s, the snowmobile almost instantly rocketed to star status in the snowbelt. "For the dreary winter months in the North Country, it was excitement and freedom," explained

Derrick Crandall, the longtime president of the American Recreation Coalition. "The industry mushroomed. By the early 1970s sales reached 600,000 a year. It became so huge that snowmobile clubs in the Midwest replaced the Grange as people's social centers."

However, there were problems. Snowmobilers couldn't travel on plowed roads, so they took off in all directions across privately owned croplands and fields, coming into conflict with farmers and others who didn't like the noise, the smell, the trespassing, and the occasional damage to property. "But the industry did some research," said Crandall. "It learned that not only were trails safer, but that the great majority of snowmobilers actually preferred using them rather than going cross-country. The industry saw a robust trail movement as win-win for everyone."

When Robert Herbst, director of the Minnesota Department of Natural Resources, started looking for a funding stream to buy corridors in 1971, he turned to snowmobiles. Herbst—the visionary rail-trail advocate discussed earlier—collaborated with Crandall on an idea to charge snowmobiles for a license and to then put those fees into a state trails account. The plan garnered the support of the public and even the acquiescence of the snowmobile industry. In addition, thanks to robust lobbying by the snowmobile clubs, the Minnesota legislature allowed their percentage of the state's gas tax receipts to go for trails. By 1991 about twenty other snowbelt states had similar revenue-generating legislation, which may be a factor in the strength of the rails-to-trails movement in the North today. In fact snowmobilers in places like Michigan's Upper Peninsula were so enthusiastic about trails that some of the clubs took it upon themselves to buy and then donate abandoned tracks, bridges, or other facilities that their state governments couldn't afford or weren't able to acquire in time.

In 1978 Congress deregulated the airline industry, making it more affordable for northerners to fly south in the winter. Just then—whether the timing was a coincidence or not—snowmobile sales began to decline. Fortunately in many of the snowbelt states the rails-to-trails movement had already been jump-started (and, of course, the acquired corridors were available to all users during the rest of the year). By 1986, of the barely 250 rail-trails in the

Breaking into the Money Vault

United States, Minnesota had 11, Wisconsin had 23, and Michigan had 25.

But snowmobilers were only a subset of the full trail aficionado universe. The bulk of the activists were walkers, runners, and bicyclists. Cycling activists, in particular, were fixated on a funding source that seemed fairly obvious to them—roadway budgets. For years bike advocates had been rankled by highway departments' claim that they couldn't spend money on freestanding bike trails since roads were funded by gas taxes and bikes didn't use gasoline. Now, with corridors being lost left and right, this was truly a last-chance emergency, and cyclists began to smolder about the money shortage. Until that time it was mostly the transit industry that had been complaining about the highway lobby's "cars-only" mantra. Now cyclists joined the fray.

By the late 1980s the federal interstate highway program was more than thirty years old. It had laid uncounted billions of tons of concrete and had woven the nation together with more than 40,000 miles of interstate highways. But it had also evolved from a popular program of rural connectors to a much more controversial one when it started adding urban dissectors to the network. New inner-city highways were wreaking physical destruction faster than they were generating economic growth, and they were stimulating as much opposition from grassroot activists as they were garnering support from the leadership structure.

A rag-tag group of highway dissidents had gradually been gaining traction. Its progenitors stretched back to 1977 when Washington DC canceled the planned Center Leg Freeway and used the money to partially fund its Metro rail system. It stretched back to 1974 when the Supreme Court upheld Citizens to Preserve Overton Park in its lawsuit to stop construction of Interstate 40 through the central park of Memphis. And back to 1973 when the Highway Action Coalition "busted" open the Highway Trust Fund in Congress, allowing some money to be spent on non-highway projects. And back to 1972 when Boston traded the proposed Southwest Freeway for a new subway line. Dissidents included groups like Movement Against Destruction in Baltimore and Citizens Against Pollution in Chicago. And it stretched back to Jane Jacobs's revolutionary 1961 book, *The Death and Life of Great American Cities*. And even back to a brilliantly prescient article in *The Reporter* magazine in April 1960 entitled "New Roads and Urban Chaos," which called out the disruption of city freeways and exposed the interest-group politics that promoted them. That article was written by a thirty-three-year-old academic named Daniel Patrick Moynihan.

By 1991 Moynihan was a U.S. senator from New York and the second-highest-ranking Democrat on the Environment and Public Works Committee, the entity designing the next version of the federal highway law. It had taken half a lifetime, but Moynihan was finally in a position to challenge the "highway boys" and put his ideas into practice. While Moynihan was the brightest star in that firmament, other luminaries were lining up as well. The ranking Republican on the committee, Senator John Chafee of Rhode Island, was also deeply skeptical of ceaseless highway construction and strongly committed to environmental protection. Meanwhile the grassroots groups—including environmentalists, historic preservationists, architects, landscape architects, supporters of scenic roads, advocates for inner cities, foes of billboards, bicyclists, and defenders of pedestrians—had coalesced into an entity called the Surface Transportation Policy Project (STPP). Under the leadership of environmentalist Jessica Tuchman Matthews, STPP tapped into the support of four deep-pocketed foundations and quickly produced an alternative transportation policy manifesto, *Acting in the National Interest*, which was widely distributed to Congress and beyond.

Moynihan introduced his bill on April 25, 1991. It picked up many of STPP's ideas, and the new paradigm was signaled even by its title: the Surface Transportation *Efficiency* Act. Emblematically, it said that Congress would now be paying attention to travel effectiveness, not just the number of car lanes built. In more powerful symbolism, the bill was co-sponsored by four senators, two from the East and two from the West, two Republicans and two Democrats. Bolstered by strong supporting testimony, a broad grassroots lobbying effort by dozens of local and state organizations, a wide-ranging outpouring of editorial support from urban newspapers, and of course the close attention of Moynihan's and Chafee's staffs, the bill rewrote transportation policy. Specifically it mandated much more coordination with other agencies and conformity with environmental requirements. It also contained for the first time a set-aside account to pay for "Enhancement" projects to mitigate some of the negative impacts of highway construction. The enhancements could be chosen as on a Chinese menu—a bicycle/pedestrian project or billboard removal or historic railroad station preservation or scenic highway protection or roadside archaeology or landscaping, and more. One of the identified enhancement categories was titled "Preservation of Abandoned Railway Corridors (Including the Conversion and Use Thereof for Pedestrian or Bicycle Trails)." The bill passed the full Senate, 91–7, on June 19.

The House of Representatives got started a month later, but when Representative Norm Mineta (D-CA) introduced his version of the bill, the name he gave it was even more revolutionary: the *Intermodal* Surface Transportation Efficiency Act. (With the acronym ISTEA, it was referred to as "ice-tea.") On October 23 the House passed it, 343–83, and the two bills were sent to conference to iron out their differences.

The enhancements portion represented only 2.4 percent of the total ISTEA authorization, but in a six-year, $98.6-billion bill, that still came to an eye-popping $2.39 billion. No previous trails or bicycling program had ever come close to a budget figure that began with a *b*. Finally there was a highway bill that truly had some non-auto jewels worth lobbying for, and there was an outpouring of grassroots support from cyclists, trail advocates, walkers, and many others.

"Local rail-to-trail and bicycle interests were very important to our success," said Sarah Campbell, the first director of STPP. "You had lots of bike and trail people who had worked for a very long time trying and mostly failing to get things done. They knew how important this was and they were fired up. They pushed very hard to bring in people from around the country, to deliver letters and telegrams, and to meet with politicians in the home districts. Candidly, the transit industry was not as strong an ally as we had hoped, but the bicyclists made up for it."

"Enhancements were only the tail on a much bigger dog," said Carol Werner, director of the Environment and Energy Study Institute and an STPP co-founder, "but they were a great way to organize local support. The categories were specific and sounded so much more exciting than that generic old word 'planning.'"

Another STPP board member, architect Robert Peck, said, "We conceptualized enhancements to be like the government's 'one percent for art' program—a small fraction to be used to embellish roadways or make up for the destruction they cause. I remember sitting down at my computer one night and saying to myself, 'Okay, what would *you* want this money to be spent on?'" But when he was honest with himself, Peck's thought was more negative: "When the highway boys find this section we're going to be squashed like a bug." Sarah Campbell agreed: "We put Enhancements in as a stalking horse. We never thought we would get it."

The stalking horse had strutted in, but there was still a hurdle. The two bills had to be reconciled—had to be brought into exact conformity with each other. "That was a fascinating dance," said Jean Lauver, committee staffer for Senator Chafee. "Senators Moynihan and Chafee were deeply committed to the policy questions—how were future transportation decisions going to be made? They didn't care as much about the actual dollars. In contrast, the House members very much wanted to fund specific highway projects in their districts. The highway lobbyists didn't like the Enhancement idea at all—they saw it as a theft of their road money—but they knew that both lead senators, one from each party, really cared about those alternative programs. If the new ideas were shot down, the overall funding for precious road projects could be cut too. It was the perfect basis for a compromise to move forward."

David Burwell was among the most active in building the STPP coalition, even while he was leading the fledgling Rails-to-Trails Conservancy and trying to stave off a severe financial downturn there. Ironically as the enhancements list was being drawn up, he was reluctant to specifically name rail-trails as one of the particular programs that could receive funding.

"David didn't want to appear opportunistic for his particular interest," said Marianne Fowler, longtime lobbyist for Rails-to-Trails Conservancy. "He didn't want to undermine his credibility representing the broader voice of transportation reform." Fortunately the nationwide clamor for rail-trails was by then so strong that the category rose to the top on its own merit. Even though bicycle projects had already been slotted for funding, rail-trails were also added as a specific possible category. ISTEA was ratified by both houses and signed by President George H. W. Bush on December 18, 1991.

The impact of ISTEA on the rails-to-trails movement is impossible to overstate. Between 1992 and 2018 that law and the subsequent highway renewal acts that grew out of it—laws with ever more esoteric names such as Transportation Equity Act for the 21st Century (1998), Safe, Accountable, Flexible, Efficient Transportation Equity Act: A Legacy for Users (2005), Moving Ahead for Progress in the 21st Century Act (2012), and Fixing America's Surface Transportation Act (2016)—resulted in more than 1,500 "Enhancement"-type rail-trail grants totaling more than $820 million for rail-trail projects. Combined with the required matching gifts from states, localities, and private entities, the total came to more than $1.1 billion.

And there were even many dollars more. Enhancements comprised the highest-visibility of the alternative programs, but ISTEA also created two other pots of money—one primarily for rural areas and one mostly urban.

The rural program, the Recreational Trails Program, found its way into the law through a completely different political route. For many years motorized trail users—snowmobilers, off-road vehicle riders, and motorcyclists—had been frustrated that there was no specific source of federal money they could call their own. They were envious that the recreational boating community had managed to get some motorboat fuel tax money out of the Highway Trust Fund, and they wanted the same treatment. Their effort gained momentum in the mid-1980s with support from the report of President Reagan's Commission on Americans Outdoors. By the time the next highway bill came up, they had a champion, Senator Steve Symms of Idaho. The highway lobby was opposed to any frittering of its traditional funds, but it in fact had a greater fear of transit projects (which would siphon off much more money), and at least the Symms initiative enshrined the concept of the user paying. "At the very end of the deliberations," said Derrick Crandall, who was involved in the negotiations, "the highway boys made the decision to allow motorized trail users into the tent." There were other political hurdles, and the program limped along for several years at a funding level of only $15 million. "Properly estimated," Crandall noted, "the actual amount of gas used by motorized trail vehicles would justify a program of about $300 million a year." Later, another Idahoan, Senator Dirk Kempthorne, led bipartisan efforts to substantially increase the program's funding.

The idea of motors on trails has always been controversial, due to conflicting attitudes toward noise, fumes, speed, wildlife impacts, and danger on narrow pathways, so the political dance around this program was classic. Going in, the environmental groups opposed the idea while the motorized trail interests felt that any trail funded with gasoline tax money would have to allow motors. With that split likely to doom any success, a compromise was crafted, unifying the motorized users and most of the bicycle and hiking groups (but not strong conservation organizations like the Sierra Club) behind the idea that gas taxes could be used to fund trails, even if some of the facilities prohibited motors. To cement the deal, the law carefully mandated that each state establish a broad-based advisory committee and that the state distribute funds by a formula—30 percent for motorized trails, 30 percent for nonmotorized trails, and 40 percent for hybrid facilities that could serve everyone. The fragile compromise held, and between 1993 and 2018, the Recreational Trails Program delivered nearly $200 million to mostly backcountry rail-trails.

The urban program, which was another one of Senator Moynihan's lasting legacies, was even bigger. It attempted to deal with two major problems afflicting crowded places (such as New York City, the source of most of Moynihan's votes): air pollution and traffic tie-ups. It was entitled the Congestion Mitigation and Air Quality Improvement Program, and it marked only the second time that Congress tried to force government planners to promote transportation projects that had less rather than more impact on the environment. (The first time was through the Clean Air Act of 1990.) Known as CMAQ, the program was mostly used for mass transit, but it also had the surprising effect of funding hundreds of trails.

"The Senator wanted to bring a definitive end to the highway-construction-dominated structure of the federal program," said Roy Kienitz, one of Moynihan's top aides at the time. "He had the theme but it had never been done before so the methods had to be experimental. We decided to make the larger part of the program eligible to all uses, not just highways, and also to segregate a portion of the money for non-highway approaches. We hoped we could force the existing bureaucracy to do some rethinking, and also force a conversation that could create a constituency where none had existed before."

Jean Lauver, the committee staffer from across the aisle, agreed. "I remember Senator Moynihan lecturing us on numerous occasions how the Interstate System had ruined New York City and its neighborhoods," she said. "To him there was justice in directing highway money to address issues like congestion and air quality. This approach was also an easy sell for my boss—Senator Chafee had a long involvement with and commitment to the Clean Air Act, as did some other Republicans on the committee." (The political geography was also fortuitous in the House of Representatives. The radical CMAQ provision could easily have been killed, but the chairman of the House committee was Representative Robert Roe whose northern New Jersey district had the same environmental problems as New York, so he left it untouched.)

Over the ensuing years the CMAQ program pumped more than an estimated $550 million into metropolitan-area rail-trails. Among the high-recipient states between 1999 and 2018 were Washington, California, Massachusetts, Pennsylvania, Illinois, and Ohio. Ironically the largest of the support grants went not to a New York City project but to one in Chicago. Thanks to a favorable smile from Mayor Rahm Emmanuel, the Bloomingdale Trail—which provides the central spine for Chicago's "606" park grouping previously discussed—received record-breaking CMAQ grants in 2014 and 2017 totaling just under $50 million.

Passage of the 1991 transportation law was a high-water political achievement of the coalition that included the young rail-trail movement, and it demonstrated not only that trails were popular but that support for them was bipartisan. (ISTEA, like the two pre-

Table 10. Funding for rail-trails

Year	Enhancement rail-trail projects	CMAQ projects	Rec trail program rail-trail projects	Total projects	Enhancement rail-trail dollars	CMAQ dollars	Rec trail program rail-trail dollars	Total dollars
1992	38			38	$32.0			$32.0
1993	114		14	128	$88.8		$0.5	$89.3
1994	174			174	$114.6			$114.6
1995	160			160	$88.2			$88.2
1996	168		37	205	$86.0		$2.0	$88.0
1997	110		32	142	$59.7		$2.1	$61.8
1998	117		26	143	$61.0		$1.6	$62.6
1999	172	2	50	224	$138.1	$0.7	$5.0	$143.8
2000	172	14	70	256	$119.9	$7.4	$5.8	$133.1
2001	137	7	55	199	$106.5	$3.4	$4.0	$113.9
2002	154	26	51	231	$114.9	$16.5	$5.5	$136.9
2003	112	16	52	180	$132.5	$5.9	$5.8	$144.2
2004	106	19	42	167	$86.3	$9.9	$2.6	$98.8
2005	76	22	50	148	$83.8	$17.2	$4.9	$105.9
2006	131	20	48	199	$110.4	$11.9	$3.0	$125.3
2007	95	27	76	198	$85.0	$18.5	$14.3	$117.8
2008	81	12	53	146	$56.6	$12.4	$7.8	$76.8
2009	121	22	69	212	$108.4	$29.1	$14.5	$152.0
2010	115	20	67	202	$112.1	$16.0	$7.5	$135.6
2011	52	24	89	165	$50.4	$33.8	$15.1	$99.3
2012	76	27	59	162	$84.7	$34.7	$9.9	$129.3
2013	73	21	72	166	$64.2	$30.6	$21.6	$116.4
2014	106	31	61	198	$102.6	$89.8	$13.3	$205.7
2015	57	26	47	130	$49.5	$53.6	$8.8	$111.9
2016	61	35	45	141	$53.1	$36.2	$15.7	$105.0
2017	39	29	57	125	$40.5	$77.8	$13.0	$131.3
2018	27	29	58	114	$35.3	$56.4	$13.6	$105.3
Total	2,844	429	1,280	4,553	$2,265.1	$561.8	$197.9	$3,024.8

Notes: All figures are estimates, and all dollar figures are in millions; a 2004 entry in Massachusetts ($123,456,789) and a 2017 entry in California ($96,386,000) have been removed as questionable outliers. Created in 2020 by author.

ceding pro-trail laws, was spearheaded by Democratic legislators and signed by a Republican president.) During the 1992 presidential race—when a publicity contest was launched to achieve the creation of the 500th rail-trail in time for the 500th anniversary of the arrival of Christopher Columbus, on October 12—efforts were made by local groups to involve both President George H. W. Bush and candidate Bill Clinton. The president even made Rails-to-Trails Conservancy one of his "thousand points of light" in his wide-ranging program to celebrate America's greatness.

Opening the ISTEA spigot led to a flowering of the movement, as we will see in coming chapters. But the political landscape was far from settled. Many old-school highway lobbyists were committed to ensuring that the "Enhancements" victory was a onetime-only fluke. Knowing that the act was scheduled for renewal six years later, they began strategizing the program's elimination. For rail-trails the counterattack would come on two fronts—from highway interests that wanted to build roads and from adjacent opponents who wanted to prevent public pathways. Trail advocates had to learn quickly to play defense.

The first counterattack was launched in 1997 when freshman representative Jim Ryun (R-KS) introduced the Railway Abandonment Clarification Act. Ryun was an unusual leader for an anti-trails bill since he happened to be a world-class runner, the first high-schooler to surpass the four-minute mile, and a medal-winner in three different Olympics. But with the backing of the American Farm Bureau and the National Association of Reversionary Property Owners, Ryun sought to rewrite the railbanking law so that it would not preempt state laws covering abandonments. After the bill was pulled on a technicality, Ryun slightly rewrote it and tried again the following year. Only a vigorous campaign by Rails-to-Trails Conservancy and support by a bevy of Republican politicians sent the measure down to defeat. In the next two years Representative Ryun tried twice more, seeking further compensation to adjacent owners and failing both times.

Meanwhile in the Senate another Kansas Republican was pursuing a different tack, attempting to turn off the money spigot for

bicycle facilities and trails. Senator Sam Brownback, using deliberations over reauthorization of the transportation bill, proposed
that states be allowed to opt entirely out of using their enhancement funds. When that idea garnered little support, he offered a
different amendment that required every local government through
which a rail-trail would pass to affirmatively approve the proposal
before it could move forward. In a close call, the measure passed
the Senate, but thanks to a power-play by Senator Chafee, it did not
survive in the House-Senate Conference Committee.

But the closest call came in 2003 when Representative Ernest
Istook (r-ok) introduced an amendment to the transportation
department appropriation that eliminated all federal funding for
rail-trails.

"It was in his own subcommittee, it was a surprise move, and he
got it through," recalled rtc vice president Marianne Fowler. "He
did it again in the full committee. For us the measure would have
been catastrophic. Literally our only hope was to defeat it through a
floor vote in the full House, but that kind of thing just about never
works. Everyone told us to drop the idea, even our closest allies in
Congress. But our back was against the wall."

Fowler, rtc, the League of American Bicyclists, and other groups
under the rubric of the "Enhancements Coalition" sprang into
high gear. Since the House that year was controlled by the Republicans, Fowler knew that any effort to mobilize Democrats would
be a waste of time and might even be counterproductive. Fortunately there were several Republicans who passionately supported
trails. And there were others who were on the fence, not wanting
to speak up loudly but also knowing that the trails in their districts
were popular with both users and trailside businesses. Fowler convinced pro-trail Democrats to sit back and keep an invisible profile.
She then arranged to get a letter of support from Linda Armstrong
Kelly, the mother of Lance Armstrong, the then-superstar of bicycle racing—a Texan from a rock-ribbed Republican family—which
rtc distributed to all members of Congress. Fowler then recruited
an impeccable champion—Representative Tom Petri (r-wi), chair
of the Highways Subcommittee of the Transportation and Infrastructure Committee, who had strong conservative credentials but

also the confidence of both bicyclists and snowmobilers—to introduce the amendment stripping out the Istook provision. The vote on the floor started out very close, but as members saw which way the winds were blowing more and more of them went back and switched their votes from "nay" to "yea." By the time the bell rang, the amendment had passed smashingly, 327–90.

"Not only was it a great victory," Fowler said, "but the vote was so lopsided that it inoculated the trails program against attack for the next few years. For a while it made trails politically untouchable."

The reality was that, even though landowner opposition had been slowly growing more sophisticated, there had been a much larger countervailing surge throughout the nation in favor of public health and healthy living. Everywhere, doctors were promoting physical activity and people were on the lookout for all kinds of places they could walk, run, bike, and skate. Rail-trails, no longer obscure outlying locations, were proving themselves an integral part of the health and recreation infrastructure. Even Ray LaHood, a former Republican congressman who was appointed U.S. secretary of transportation by President Obama, recognized the restorative powers of rail-trails. "This program has probably done more for America's health than anything else we've built," he said, speaking of his department's involvement with the movement. (LaHood, who had earlier helped create the Rock Island Trail in Illinois, was given a "Rail-Trail Hero" award by Rails-to-Trails Conservancy.)

It was the new rallying slogan "active transportation" that marked the shift in bicycle promotion from the old emphases on environmental sustainability and energy conservation to health maintenance and fitness celebration. The pleasantly ambiguous definition—something like "every travel mode that revs up your heart rate"—seems to have been coined in England, picked up by the League of American Bicyclists in the 1990s, and then aggressively adopted by Rails-to-Trails Conservancy after 2000. Even though the general public was often unsure about the meaning, the phrase provided the triple benefit of lumping most trail users into one category, gaining the political high ground of championing health, and qualifying for funding under the guidelines of the major public health agencies and private health charities. Historian James Longhurst reports the phrase started showing up in public discourse in 2000 and by 2015 had surpassed the previous ambiguous phrase—"alternative transportation"—in its number of uses. It was one in a string of attempts to unseat the automobile from its domination of transportation terminology.

RTC's legislative winning streak lasted for ten more years, not stumbling until 2012. In that year's transportation funding battle over what was then called "MAP-21," Representative John Mica (R-FL), chair of the Transportation Committee, moved to eliminate the Enhancements program to give local transportation agencies more discretion over which projects would be funded—roads or such alternatives as trails. With the decline in the quality of infrastructure throughout the United States, Americans' frustration with bad roads seemed to have finally pushed past their love of trails. Although opposed by Representative Petri, the measure passed. As a result even though strongly pro-trail communities maintained their spending on bicycling facilities, others found themselves outmaneuvered by the traditional road lobby. Trail advocates would have to regroup and form even broader political coalitions to keep the movement growing.

But we jump ahead. In 1991 the Mica amendment was still more than two decades in the future, by which time rail-trails were utilizing a broad multitude of funding sources that partially mitigated the setback in Washington. Moreover, in 2020, just as this book was going to press, Congress was on the verge of creating a massive new funding program, the Great American Outdoors Act, to fund all kinds of new parks and park renovations—including rail-trails. Once again, the rails-to-trails movement had shown its ability to maneuver adeptly between the worlds of transportation and recreation.

Breaking into the Money Vault

12

City Trail, Country Trail

ON OCTOBER 12, 1992, RAILS-TO-TRAILS CONSERVANCY announced with a flourish the opening of the nation's 500th rail-trail, a competition timed to coincide with the 500th anniversary of the landing of Christopher Columbus in the Americas. The winner was the Minuteman Bikeway, running from Cambridge, Massachusetts, through Arlington, Lexington, and Bedford—the trail we met earlier when we learned what can go wrong if one side of the rails-to-trails triangle is missing. Although not everyone agreed that the joyous celebration in Arlington made up for the eighteen-year wait, there was no denying that the contest champion had beaten out a raft of other rail-trail efforts that were also breathlessly heading for that Columbus Day finish line—the Harlem Valley Rail-Trail in Dutchess County, New York; the Banks-Vernonia Trail in Washington County, Oregon; the Frisco Greenway Trail in Jasper County, Missouri; the Historic Union Pacific Rail-Trail in Summit County, Utah; the General James A. Van Fleet Trail in Lake County, Florida; and at least three dozen others. It was the dawning of a new era, not only because the advocates had become more sophisticated but because the ISTEA funding spigot was beginning to open—$25 million in 1992, $60 million in 1993, almost $70 million in 1994. It wouldn't be a uniform flow, but in the first fifteen years it would put $875 million into rail-trails around the country. And with that many trails, the diversity in the field became noticeable.

Gertrude Stein may have said, "A rose is a rose is a rose," but she wouldn't have said that about a rail-trail. There are enough variations in trails to make even the hundredth outing special. And a key aspect in the distinctiveness stems from the question, "Why was this trail created?" Or maybe even, "What *problem* does this trail solve?" It turns out that a paramount factor relates to the surrounding context—specifically, is it urban or rural? In urban areas the problem is dangerous roadways. In rural areas, it's economic stagnation. Two very different motivations.

A paradigm for a city rail-trail is the Capital Crescent Trail, from Washington DC to Silver Spring, Maryland. A country paradigm, 300 miles away, is the Virginia Creeper Trail, from Abingdon to White Top, Virginia.

Even though every trail has its own unique birth story, the tale of the Capital Crescent is emblematic of the transportation basis for urban facilities. As discussed previously, the Capital Crescent in the late 1970s was still the lightly used Georgetown Branch railroad track, the corridor that Pete Raynor and Tom Allison each independently eyed while jogging on the nearby C&O Canal towpath, the track that stimulated their imaginations about saving rails for trails. In 1986 Kingdon Gould had stepped in with a multi-million-dollar purchase to save it for public agency acquisition. By 2018 it was an 11-mile trail firmly entrenched as an important piece of the Washington area's transportation and recreation infrastructure and visited more than a million times per year. Most notably, in gridlocked Washington it was the route of choice of about a thousand rush-hour users every workday.

For much of the twentieth century, Washington DC actually had two rail corridors running parallel to the Potomac River. Both were ultimately abandoned. The first to go down, in 1968, was a trolley line that had served the Glen Echo Amusement Park in suburban Maryland. By the late 1970s those tracks were gone, but the corridor through the lovely, leafy neighborhood overlooking the river was still relatively intact, and some bridges remained. The city had come up with the idea of turning it into a trail. I was an official with the Washington Area Bicyclist Association at the time, and I heard about it but was told to keep the plan fairly quiet. It was controversial, but there was more than $600,000 in the budget and we were told that everything was programmed to move ahead. Unfortunately the process was far from transparent. Before we knew it, the well-heeled neighborhood had found out and then quietly but quickly killed the idea. They also made sure the money was thoroughly redirected.

We were political neophytes and we were furious. Why hadn't

we been warned about the opposition? This had been a once-in-a-lifetime opportunity! We could have turned out a multitude of pro-trail troops! We swore many oaths. The final one was "Never again."

Then, surprisingly, a few years later the other route went under. This was the Georgetown Branch, a track so obscure that few knew it existed. It had been built in the 1890s when the B&O Railroad briefly had the grandiose idea of crossing the Potomac River upstream and outflanking the powerful Pennsylvania Railroad's downtown bridge. (After that plan fizzled and the track became a stub in Georgetown, its few moments of fame came in the 1910s when it was utilized to transport the limestone blocks to construct the Lincoln Memorial.) By the 1980s it was a money-losing remnant of the CSX system; most Washingtonians were unaware that it had any traffic. The trains, about one a week operating mostly after midnight, brought coal deliveries to a minor power plant. The railroad shifted the delivery to trucks and was seeking permission to abandon the track.

Amazingly, part of the route was almost identical to the one that we had lost three years earlier, a bit closer to the river and down an embankment. From the perspective of bicyclists it was actually superior; instead of terminating at a defunct amusement park, it curved through the two most important urban nodes of Montgomery County. Moreover, using bridges and tunnels, it avoided almost every high-trafficked avenue along the way.

We had said "never again," and here it was, "again." It was also the very moment that the Rails-to-Trails Conservancy was being formed, so it provided a real-life, local-level test of the highfaluting national rhetoric we were generating. After determining that the railroad did actually own the land and that it had no intention of donating it, we knew that our effort would have to be every bit as public as the previous one was quiet. I took a look at the curving route on a map and excitedly said, "This could be a Bicycle Beltway!" But to be honest it was only half a belt. It really looked much more like a semi-circle. I thought: *Well, how about a Capital Crescent?* We formed an advocacy group, the Coalition for the Capital Crescent Trail. CCCT eventually grew to include three dozen local organizations, including runners, walkers, conservationists, and many others, but always the driving force behind it was the bicycle community. It was the bicyclists more than anyone who felt that this was literally Washington's now-or-never moment to create a gentle, smooth, car-free, 11-mile route without even the danger of cross traffic.

Typical of almost any effort in the nation's capital, there was a Rubik's cube of bureaucracies that could either help or stymie us: the Interstate Commerce Commission, Federal Railroad Administration, Army Corps of Engineers, National Park Service, DC Department of Transportation, Maryland Department of Transportation, Montgomery County Department of Transportation, Montgomery County Parks. And, in truth, while each of those agencies had strong parochial curiosity about the now-defunct track, none had the least interest in converting it into a bike trail. Then we learned that the railroad had set the price for its property at $84 million. (Fortunately this turned out to be a bargaining ploy.)

The hurdles against success were very high, and we didn't have a high-profile national supporter the way the C&O Canal National Park effort had Supreme Court justice William Douglas back in the 1950s and '60s. But there were still some fortuitous factors in our favor. One was that the National Park Service desperately opposed any development within its canal park. Another was that the group of neighbors—the ones who had killed the Glen Echo Trail—didn't want their views blocked. Third, Montgomery County's transportation department had visions of eventually using part of the corridor for mass transit. Fourth, there was already an example of a rail-trail across the Potomac in Virginia—the Washington & Old Dominion Trail—that had been generating political enthusiasm among the cyclists and runners. Fifth, the ICC had recently finalized its rules on using the new railbanking provision allowing a corridor to be saved for possible future rail reactivation, and the two lawyers most knowledgeable about it, Chuck Montange and David Burwell, lived nearby and were itching to try it out.

After numerous public meetings, rallies, lobbying campaigns, volunteer work outings, lawsuits, fund-raising campaigns, and deals cut with politicians, corporations, and agencies, the corridor was saved and the Capital Crescent was gradually constructed. The full story of the trail (including a legal battle in which sole-

Table 11. Usership of selected urban area rail-trails

Trail name	Urban area	State	Length (miles)	Year opened	Annual use
The High Line	New York	New York	2	2009	7,200,000
Washington & Old Dominion Railroad Park	Washington DC	Virginia	45	1974	2,000,000
Bloomingdale Trail/The 606	Chicago	Illinois	3	2015	1,500,000
Fred Marquis Pinellas Trail	St. Petersburg/ Clearwater	Florida	49	1990	1,500,000
Katy Trail	Dallas	Texas	4	2000	1,290,000
Midtown Greenway	Minneapolis	Minnesota	6	2000	1,250,000
Capital Crescent Trail	Washington DC	DC/Maryland	11	1996	1,200,000
Burke-Gilman Trail	Seattle	Washington	19	1978	1,140,000
Shelby Farms Greenline	Memphis	Tennessee	11	2010	930,000
Cady Way Trail	Orlando/ Winter Park	Florida	7	1994	880,000
Clovis Old Town Trail	Clovis/Fresno	California	6	2000	875,000
Three Rivers Heritage Trail	Pittsburgh	Pennsylvania	24	1996	820,000
Cedar Lake Trail	Minneapolis	Minnesota	9	1995	500,000

Source: Rails-to-Trails Conservancy and Peter Harnik

practitioner Chuck Montange defeated the Columbia Country Club whose membership included 400 lawyers) would be as long as this book. And it would continue up to the present day, since the Capital Crescent is located in one of Washington's premier power-and-growth sectors and the route is under continual assault by interests who want to use or encroach upon it. Suffice it to repeat that the driving force behind the idea was the bicycling community, from commuters to recreationalists, and even to young families taking children out to learn on their training wheels.

The story was very different in southwestern Virginia. In 1977 in that mountainous and impoverished Appalachian area, bicycling was a minor issue and calls to tackle traffic congestion would have been laughably inconceivable. When the Norfolk & Western Railroad (N&W) petitioned for the abandonment of its Virginia Creeper line in Virginia and North Carolina, the response in the small city of Abingdon and the hamlets of Damascus and White Top was not excitement but fear—fear that it meant another economic catastrophe following the recent shutdown of the area's lumber mills. The public's first reaction was a wall of opposition that delayed the abandonment for five years. Initially the locals wanted to maintain freight and passenger service. When that dream proved hopeless, they shifted their desire to a tourist railroad. But for such a rarely visited area that, too, was unrealistic. Meanwhile N&W was impatient to salvage its tracks, ties, and the one hundred bridges and trestles along the 32-mile route.

Just at that moment, Dave Brillhart, a Washington County planning commissioner, read about an abandoned track "somewhere out in Iowa or Wisconsin" that had been turned into a trail. Fellow commissioner French Moore Jr. pricked up his ears when he heard that, as did a couple of creative staffers at Abingdon's adjoining Jefferson National Forest. (About half the route ran through the recreation-oriented national forest, which already contained a piece of the Appalachian Trail.) But the rail-trail concept was a new idea in a place that preferred old ways, and opposition was widespread. Of the opponents, half wanted the land for themselves while the rest feared undesirables walking or off-roading through backyard fields and woods. Because of a difference in state laws dating back over a century, the 25-mile portion of the route in North Carolina had only been an easement and was slated to revert back to adjacent landowners at the moment of abandonment. Learning that fact, adjacents in Virginia wanted the same treatment. But Virginia law was different, and the N&W had no intention of giving away something it truly owned. So the adjacent farmers agitated for more time to try and raise the money to buy their individual segments.

On the other side of the issue, French, who was by that time mayor of Abingdon, led trail advocates in *their* search for money and for political support. He was particularly aware of the importance of the major trestles in that mountainous region; if the trestles weren't saved the corridor would be almost worthless. He assembled five or six people, including Rick Boucher, the local state senator, on a legal committee to deal with the railroad and to handle a lawsuit by one of the adjacent farm families. He then convinced the Tennessee Valley Authority to pay for the purchase of materials for bridge decking and guardrails, and he prevailed upon the local Job Corps center to provide free labor. It was trail building in the tradition of barn raising.

In the beginning it was hard, remembered French's wife, Maryanne. "The hearings were vicious. I came home in tears after some of them. My husband, who was also a dentist, lost some of his patients over his advocacy of the trail."

"French Moore was a very farsighted man with good ideas," Boucher recalled. "The trail was really his innovation and he did all the coordinating." Boucher himself was later elected to Congress and used his position to help get a million-dollar grant to improve the trail. He was also so impressed by the benefits of the Virginia Creeper that he later worked with Norfolk Southern Railroad and Virginia governor Gerald Baliles to arrange a donation of an even longer track in the area to create the New River Rail-Trail.

Now that it's open, the Virginia Creeper is one of the most remarkable rail-trails in the country. Its remote backwoods location should generate almost no usership at all, yet it is so bustling that signs warn, "Keep to the Right," "Pull off Trail if Stopped," and "Ride with Caution." With up to 250,000 users a year, it almost certainly has the highest user-to-resident ratio of any trail in the nation. (Damascus, the only real town along the way, has a population of 800; if not for the trail its population might be close to zero.)

There are three factors in the Creeper's popularity: its lovely setting with ferns, trickling waterfalls, and curtains of rhododendrons; its steady downhill grade that delights visitors; and its conscious bike- and trail-oriented tourist economy. Small towns all over the country have trails nearby, but most chambers of commerce ignore them. In Abingdon and Damascus the resource is celebrated and promoted. First to do so was one enterprising woman, Phoebe Cartwright, who recognized the challenge of ascending the upper por-

Table 12. Economic impact of selected rural rail-trails

Trail name	State	Miles	Year opened	Percent users nonlocal	Annual economic impact
Clarion–Little Toby Trail	Pennsylvania	18	1997	40	$900,000
Virginia Creeper Trail	Virginia	33	1987	53	$2,500,000
Pine Creek Rail Trail	Pennsylvania	62	1998	69	$3,600,000
Torrey Brown Trail	Maryland	20	1984	4	$5,300,000
Katy Trail State Park	Missouri	240	1996	n.a.	$8,200,000

Source: Peter Harnik and Tim Balton

tion of the Creeper. In 1992 she started Blue Blaze Shuttle, offering rides to the high point at White Top. By 2018 eight companies were providing bicycle shuttles with trailers (and rental bikes, if needed), so there's now no need to pedal the 15 miles up the 2- and 3-percent grade hills. Coming down is like whitewater rafting without getting wet, all speedy fun and no work (other than squeezing brake levers and bouncing over the bumps). To be honest, 2- and 3-percent hills are not steep by hiking or mountain-biking standards (and several trail reviews note that "the ride up is better" since slower-moving visitors have a chance to enjoy sights, sounds, smells, and companionship), but it was those grades that pushed the old steam trains to the limits of their power (hence the name "Creeper"), and it's the descent that lures visitors from all over the Southeast and beyond.

Once the visitors arrive, it's up to the local communities to make their stay fun and profitable. Damascus, named by the website Budget Travel one of the "Coolest Small Towns in America," also hosts an annual reunion for Appalachian Trail hikers. "The trail is our economic engine," says Aaron Sizemore, town manager of Damascus. "It's the biggest one we've got. It's the thing that keeps us going." Farther down the valley, touristy Abingdon is able to support a live theater and a twenty-square-block historic district. Kevin Worley, director

City Trail, Country Trail

of Abingdon Parks and Recreation Department concurs. "They come to do the Creeper, then come in to do other things in town."

Not all rural trails can hit the trifecta of fun, popularity, and economic vitality. Many trail managers report annual usership levels of 20,000, 15,000, or even fewer. Iowa's Heart of Iowa Nature Trail gets about 26,000 uses, which translates into an annual average of about six persons per hour, spread over a 26-mile trail. It's about the same for New Jersey's Paulinskill Valley Trail and a bit lower for Vermont's Lamoille Valley Rail-Trail. Among the very low on a user-per-mile basis is Maine's Down East Sunrise Trail. A total of 14,300 annual uses on the 87-mile-long trail means that some stretches get as little as one visitor every two days. Of course, it runs for mile after mile through very low-population regions and past very occasional towns with little or no services to offer, compounding the chicken-and-egg situation of "not much to do" and "not many people to sell services to."

As for the financial equation, country trails are less costly to build and maintain on an absolute basis, but city trails do better when measured per user since they are so much busier and thus generate income to nearby businesses.

Of course for some people the great attraction of rural trails is that very solitude, whether to savor the natural environment or for simply the relief of getting away from a surfeit of bicyclists, walkers, dogs, and others who make using some urban trails almost as challenging as being on a street. And for folks like my wife and me, who enjoy riding side by side and talking, there's nothing like a peaceful rural rail-trail with only the occasional walker or cyclist—or fisherman or photographer—to provide the perfect natural getaway. It's almost the rail-trail equivalent of a wilderness area. But for most rural communities looking for ways to keep their economies above water, the message is that most country trails still have room for a great deal of development, promotion, and publicity.

• • •

THERE IS ONE OTHER KIND OF RURAL RAIL-TRAIL, THE TRAIL built on federal land—land owned by the National Park Service, the U.S. Forest Service, or the Bureau of Land Management. To the

Table 13. Urban and rural trails compared

Item (per mile)	Urban area	Rural area
Average annual usership	26,000	2,800
Average development cost (excl. acquisition)	$307,000	$75,000
Average development cost per user	$12	$27
Average annual maintenance cost	$7,000	$1,700
Average annual maintenance cost per user	$0.27	$0.61

Source: Peter Harnik and Tim Balton, 2019
Note: based on 283 rail-trails

casual user, these ownership technicalities may be entirely invisible, but at the time of creation the difference can be stark. In fact rail-trails built on federal land often seem to violate the "rule" of the rails-to-trails triangle. Or more accurately, because of the power of these agencies, the triangle becomes distorted. The California mountains provide a particularly illuminating place to study the divergent fates of two such trail efforts.

One is the abandoned track of the old Yosemite Valley Railroad, famous for taking tourists up to Yosemite National Park and bringing gold down from the mountains. Abandoned in 1946, the route parallels the Wild and Scenic Merced River for more than 26 miles. With four million visitors a year to the national park—not to mention severe auto traffic management problems in the congested valley—it's hard to imagine a more high-profile candidate for a world-class transportation-and-recreation rail-trail, yet for more than thirty-five years the idea has been unable to gain traction.

The corridor crosses the lands of all three agencies, and there is a plan from 1988 that ties together the efforts of each of them, but it hasn't been effective. The National Park Service is preoccupied with bigger issues inside Yosemite, the Forest Service has little interest (or even awareness) of a route so far from any of its ranger stations, and the Bureau of Land Management (which is enthusiastic about the concept) has no funding. Meanwhile, with the old train line in an ecologically volatile region, it has been subject to destructive natural assaults including fire, rock slides, flooding,

City Trail, Country Trail

and general overgrowth, becoming less and less usable—or even findable—every year. There are other threats, including small private inholdings, possible patches of toxic contamination, and an area with periodic inundation behind a major dam, but the largest challenge is finding agency leaders to take up the task.

An excellent model exists only 200 miles to the northeast. Westwood, California, deep in the Susan River Valley of the Sierra Nevada Mountains not far from the Nevada border, was home to a huge lumber mill and a branch line of the Southern Pacific Railroad. The mill closed in 1956 and the railroad followed suit in 1978. Of the 25 scenic miles between Westwood and the small town of Susanville, fourteen reverted to the federal government. The dominant of the two federal agencies, the Forest Service, wasn't much interested in a trail, but a Bureau of Land Management manager named Mark Morse was. The visionary Morse pushed relentlessly until the Forest Service finally suggested that he take charge of the whole idea. Morse then turned his attention to the rest of the route—the intervening parts on private land—working for ten years to arrange a land swap with a timber company for six of the miles, and trying to negotiate with Southern Pacific Railroad for the 4.5 miles it still owned. When those talks broke down in classic fashion—Southern Pacific claiming a high value for its many bridges, trestles, and tunnels and the government deeming the structures so risky that it didn't want to pay anything for them—Morse asked for negotiating assistance from the Trust for Public Land. TPL attorney Harriet Burgess came through with a canny accommodation: While leaving the authentic railroad bridges for actual trail use, why not calculate the theoretical cost of building all new pedestrian-scale bridges and then using that number as a compromise figure? That worked. Burgess also helped by bringing into the conversations the local congressman, Harold "Bizz" Johnson.

The Bureau of Land Management is by far the largest landowner in the United States, about three times larger than the National Park Service, but its holdings are less glamorous, and it is traditionally accorded low status when it comes to funding. In 1978, despite submitting numerous grant requests from its holdings, BLM was only awarded two. One was for the trail in Westwood. In appreciation, a few years later that trail was named for Bizz Johnson.

Mark Morse was the political schemer behind the work; Stan Bales, a young part-time employee from the East, was the day-to-day man who made the trail happen on the ground. Bales cut his outdoor chops in the White Mountains of New Hampshire, went to college to study biology and outdoor recreation at the University of Utah ("I didn't want to go to Colorado like everyone else"), then started getting seasonal work with the BLM. When he heard about the corridor, he was intrigued. The older staffers were much less interested. "They told me," he recalled later, 'You're in recreation, you go work on it.'" Bales did just that, with gusto, getting bridges redecked and handrailed, organizing festivals, even arranging for a foot race that now serves as a qualifying event for the Boston Marathon. (Conveniently, the Bizz Johnson is almost the same length as an official marathon, though few marathons include the novelty of an 816-foot-long rock tunnel and a 70-foot-high trestle.)

I first met Bales in 1986 just as we were getting the Rails-to-Trails Conservancy started. He had already opened his trail for public use and gave me and my wife a bike tour, with our son in a child seat. I was impressed not only by the beauty of the accomplishment but also by Bales's upbeat, can-do attitude in a remote, low-income part of the country. (Lassen County, the size of Connecticut, is above 4,000 feet in elevation and has only 30,000 residents. The distance from Susanville to the nearest highway is 65 miles, and the county is so undeveloped that it has only seven stoplights.) When we organized the first national rails-to-trails conference, near Chicago, I invited Bales to be a speaker and his presentation was profoundly motivational. Then, on a field trip to Iowa's Heritage Trail, the motivation reciprocated. Bales was astonished to come upon a beautifully restored old depot, and he was inspired to try something similar. Seven years later the Lassen Land and Trails Trust had acquired and restored the Susanville Depot. Bales also led the effort to reconstruct a trestle that had been partially burned in an accident. Turned down for funding for ten straight years, he nevertheless kept all the paperwork up to date and was able to land $1.6

million for the "shovel-ready" project after passage of the American Recovery and Reinvestment Act in 2009.

There aren't many public land managers with the commitment and time to put into projects as tough as a rail-trail, but when they emerge, so can an outstanding public-land trail.

13

Bridges and Tunnels

A BRIDGE IS USUALLY THE MOST MEMORABLE FEATURE OF A rail-trail. A bridge can also be a major headache and a source of paralyzing fear to a trail manager. I've been on 182 rail-trails (not that I'm counting), and while many of the thousands of miles are a blur in my recall, nearly all the major bridges stick out. They offer panoramic views of broad rivers, steep valleys, urban neighborhoods, farm fields, distant mountains, or even just traffic-clogged highways with drivers below wishing they were out on the trail. They can also be works of beauty in and of themselves, or, if not always beauty, at least marvelous engineering, or at the very least astonishing relics of rusting industrial might. But they can also be structurally unstable and covered with peeling lead-based paint. Over roads they can be too constricting for large trucks passing under them. They can be a place from which items fall or are thrown. They can be enticing targets for vandalism and arson.

The strongest and most authentic bridges are the ones built by the railroads themselves. Even though most had only tracks and ties, with large leg-swallowing gaps in between, and many also didn't have side railings, those aren't insurmountably expensive problems when a trail conversion occurs. Sometimes decking can even be decently handled by competent volunteers using donated lumber. More costly is removing lead paint, creosote, and other toxic substances, and repairing weakened supporting members caused by storms, washouts, earth movement, or wear and tear. Worst is the dilemma of replacing a bridge that is fully missing. It took the folks who created the Illinois Prairie Path five tries to rebuild the span over the east branch of the DuPage River. The first bridge, constructed from wood as a training project by the Illinois National Guard, was dismantled by vandals. Then Sierra Club members took the unfastened timbers and reframed them into a new low-water crossing, only to have it wash away in a flood. Re-created by the DuPage County Forest Preserve District, the third bridge was burned by an arsonist—as was the fourth. Finally, the trail's support organization raised funds for an all-steel bridge and erected it above the one hundred–year flood line.

The nation's two greatest rail-trail bridges—in Minneapolis and in Poughkeepsie, New York—could hardly be more different. The former, looking like something from the Roman Empire, is the Stone Arch Bridge, a weighty, spectacular, curving, twenty-three-arch span constructed across the Mississippi River in 1883 and a beloved icon of its city. The latter, built in 1889, is now called the Walkway Over the Hudson—a lacy, steel cantilever structure held aloft by seven pillar stilts that is literally the tallest structure between New York City and Albany and provides a sweeping vista from the Catskill Mountains to the Berkshires. The stories of the two bridges' deliverance could hardly be more different.

In Minneapolis today, bicyclists and walkers can have fun fanta-sizing that the Stone Arch Bridge was erected for their pleasure as they grandly pedal or stroll high above the Mississippi. Of course, it wasn't. It was built by James J. Hill for what became his Great Northern Railway, and it was part of the story of Minneapolis's rise as the nation's milling capital. By 1978 the successor railroad, Bur-lington Northern, had reordered its routes and stopped using the bridge. The timing also coincided with a reversal in fortune for Minneapolis's downtown riverfront, with gutted mill buildings, acres of parking lots, and homeless camps on Hennepin Island. The structure was saved by its official historic status and the pos-sibility that it could be used for light-rail, but nothing happened. Then, in 1988, under prodding from the Minnesota Historical Soci-ety, the legislature created the St. Anthony Falls Heritage Board to plan an office, residential, and tourism rebirth of the falls area. The board decided that visitors would need a loop path on both sides of the river and that the Stone Arch Bridge would be perfect. Through deft lobbying, the bridge was transferred from the county rail authority to the state department of transportation, freeing it up for possibilities other than light-rail. Three years later, when Congress passed ISTEA, money was available for renovation, and the political stars aligned. Two Jims coalesced to land a major grant—Jim Pederson, a former state legislator, wrote an "Enhancement" application that hit the sweet spot of rail-trail and historic preservation, and Jim Oberstar, the congressman, brought home the $2.8-million earmark.

"This was a unique project," explained former National Park Service supervisory ranger Dave Wiggins. "The bridge was not only a stunning icon but it had the added protection of a Historic Preservation designation, which raised the bar on ever getting permission to tear it down. Also, the Minnesota Historical Society is an unusually influential entity—it is actually nine years older than the state of Minnesota itself. And the National Park Service has a presence on the upper Mississippi River, so we were able to consult with and help the local agencies. Finally, the state department of transportation was supportive and willing to take responsibility for the bridge."

"At the end of the day," Wiggins said, "the trail was part of an extremely successful preservation and revitalization effort, with $500 million of public investment generating more than $1.5 billion of private investment. And, with all the users and their 'eyes down from the bridge' plus the new downtown housing, Hennepin Island itself has also become safer and a better park."

The New York story was considerably wilder. The Poughkeepsie bridge during World War II had carried up to 3,500 freight and passenger cars per day and was so militarily vital that it had round-the-clock protection by the U.S. Army. But it steadily lost traffic after the war, finally going out of service after a train's spark lit a billowing blaze in its creosoted ties in 1974. (The bankrupt Penn Central had laid off the bridge's watchman and hadn't maintained the emergency water pipes, and the firefighters' hoses down at river level couldn't reach the 212-foot-high deck.) But unlike in Minnesota, no New York state or local agency wanted to touch it. The blaze didn't affect its structural integrity, but the Coast Guard ruled it a navigational hazard and demanded demolition. The railroad (which by then was Conrail) couldn't afford the approximately $10 million

Table 14. Extraordinary rail-trail bridges

Bridge	State	Crosses over	Length (ft)	Height (ft)
Walkway Over the Hudson	New York	Hudson River	6,768	212
Harahan Bridge	Tennessee-Arkansas	Mississippi River	4,973	n.a.
Beverly Bridge	Washington	Columbia River	3,200	n.a.
High Trestle Trail Bridge	Iowa	Des Moines River	2,526	130
Big Four Bridge	Kentucky-Indiana	Ohio River	2,525	n.a.
High Bridge Trail	Virginia	Appomattox River	2,440	125
Stone Arch Bridge	Minnesota	Mississippi River	2,100	n.a
Kinzua Bridge	Pennsylvania	Kinzua Creek	2,053	301
Salisbury Viaduct	Pennsylvania	Casselman River	1,900	n.a.
MKT Boonville Railroad Bridge	Missouri	Missouri River	1,615	n.a.
Cowboy Trail Trestle	Nebraska	Niobrara River	1,320	148
Paulinskill Viaduct	New Jersey	Paulins Kill River	1,100	115

Note: n.a. indicates "not available"

to take the bridge down, and it scrambled to get it off the books by finding a buyer (for $1) who hoped to make money on cross-river fiber-optic leases. But that didn't work out, and the bridge continued to deteriorate, with pieces falling onto roads below and into the river. Fines were being assessed for nonfunctioning navigational lights, and unpaid property tax bills piled up.

Meanwhile, far below, in the city of Poughkeepsie, in the shadow of the structure, a thirty-two-year-old dairy-farmer-turned-carpenter-and-handyman named William Sepe had a vision. He thought the bridge would be perfect for walkers. Actually, in the most formative stage of his thinking, he believed it would be a great place for parents to enjoy the view while keeping an eye on their children in a new playground he was also working to create. Moreover he was adamant that he didn't want any government funding in the effort.

Sepe is the kind of visionary who gives pause even to visionaries. And if I'm not mistaken, I was the first out-of-state person he called, in 1990.

"Hello, Rails-to-Trails?" he said. "How do you convert a railroad bridge to a walking path? I've got one that crosses the Hudson River, it's about a mile long and it's been sitting there abandoned since 1974."

"Wow, really?" I said. I knew that there were precious few non-auto crossings of the Hudson River and that nearby trail networks were extending from both New England and Pennsylvania. "That's great! Do you have support from your congressman and senators?"

"No, I haven't told them. The government has too many other things on its plate. I think we can do it the same way they renovated the Statue of Liberty, with everyone contributing a few dollars. I've calculated that if every registered voter on either side, in Dutchess and Ulster Counties, contributes 20 dollars, we'd have about 4 million dollars a year."

We went on a few more minutes, with each exchange more surreal than the one before—no, he didn't know who owned the bridge, no he didn't have an advocacy organization, no they didn't have permission to go out on it, they just clambered up the side of the cliff and gingerly walked out on the open ties.

I distinctly remember ending the call with a rueful laugh and an announcement to my colleagues in the office: "I just got off the phone with a guy who will *never* get his trail built."

Shirley Anson and her husband, Butch, were part of the gang who joined Sepe in his challenge. "It's unbelievable that one person could drag so many people into an effort like this," Shirley reminisced several years later. "It was exciting, it was so big, and it was fun." Butch recounted one of many adventures. "The company was being fined $1,000 a day by the Coast Guard for not having functioning navigation lights. My son rappelled with a rope off the bridge to check each of the bulbs. I discovered that it wasn't a power problem—the power on the bridge was still on—but one of the wires had rubbed so long against a railing that its insulation had worn off and it had shorted. We strung up new wiring and got the lights working again."

Well, my prediction was right, but fortunately I was wrong. The Walkway Over the Hudson did open to the public, nineteen years later, with a triumphal ribbon-cutting attended by 24,000 celebrants. But Sepe wasn't one of the revelers. He had resigned from the effort. When it moved from his idealistic, libertarian fantasy into the realm of dry governmental reality—including federal, state, local, and foundation funding and, ultimately, management under the New York State Office of Parks, Recreation and Historic Preservation—he had become disillusioned. In fact Sepe, the man who had clambered hundreds of times across terrifyingly unprotected open decking and who had landed reams of media coverage all the way to the *New York Times* (under the headline "Worthless Bridge. Priceless View"), announced that he would neither attend the opening nor ever personally cross the finished bridge. It was sad and ironic, but it didn't make the campaign any less legendary.

One of the men who had been turned on to the Walkway by Sepe, local attorney Fred Schaeffer, picked up the reins of the faltering effort in 2004. His ideas were a bit different: he was avidly pro-bicycle, while Sepe wanted to ban bikes from the Walkway Over the Hudson, and he thought the bridge could become a national attraction while Sepe wanted to create it only for local appreciation. But, like Sepe, Schaeffer knew the number one job was to build awareness of this wonder in Poughkeepsie. He arranged to get the temporary decking made slightly safer, and he personally took hundreds of people, week after week, up there for the view. He also gave scores of slide showings to every organization he could find. And he started looking for some serious financial and technical support, such as a structural study. "The report was golden," Schaeffer said. "Only one percent of the steel needed replacement. They told us it's one of the greatest structures ever built." Then, through his congressman, Schaeffer got a federal grant. Gradually the public's perception of the project started shifting from "impossible" to "maybe there's a very slight chance."

"There were ten miracles that led to the creation of the Walkway," Schaeffer likes to say, and he plans to write a book detailing them all. Without stealing his story, here are two. Number one occurred on February 12, 1993, in six-degree weather with ice on the Hudson, when Schaeffer brought Rob Dyson, heir to a Wall Street fortune and president of a major foundation, up on the Walkway deck. Dyson instantly fell in love with the project and, over the years, ended up donating more than $20 million to it. Number two happened in 2003 when Schaeffer was looking through an old picture postcard collection on eBay. The postcard that Schaeffer saw, from 1909, celebrated a proposed bridge in New York City that would honor the 300th anniversary of Henry Hudson's exploratory voyage up the Hudson River. Schaeffer had an inspiration. Here it was now nearly the *400th* anniversary—was anyone looking for an official Hudson River memorial project this time around? He added the postcard to his slide show.

Schaeffer didn't know it, but New York State actually *did* have a commission to celebrate the river's quadricentennial, and the commission was stymied in its efforts. By this time interest in the Walkway had built to such a pitch that Rob Dyson's foundation decided to make a $2-million gift—half to inspect the structure and the rest to design the pathway on top—and the local congressman was able to get a sizable ISTEA earmark for the effort too.

Dyson met with Governor Eliot Spitzer; Schaeffer met with the director of state parks. It was decided that if the local group would handle all the repair and construction work, New York would accept the Walkway as a gift and operate it. Then the Quadricentennial Commission named the Walkway its primary legacy project. With the politics in alignment, money started flowing—$5 million from Washington, $20 million from Albany, $13.5 million from foundations and the local community. Even csx (which had replaced Conrail) helped out with some land donations, thanks to a request from Senator Chuck Schumer. The workers—including some men specially trained in Colorado to rappel over the edge of the structure—began their work, and the bridge opened on time for the quadricentennial in 2009.

Bridge stories could certainly fill this book. Another hulking edifice, one that spans the Missouri River between St. Louis and Kansas City, is the rusting Boonville Bridge, the iconic structure

Bridges and Tunnels

on the Katy Trail. A technological marvel when built, it was the world's largest lift bridge, regularly raised for river traffic and lowered for train crossings, but the mechanism was by the end of the 20th century so rusted that it had to be locked in the raised position. As with the Walkway, the Coast Guard considered it a hazard and, citing a regulation governing abandoned and unused bridges, wanted it removed. The state seemed to agree; during negotiations over railbanking, the bridge had been exempted. A few years later Union Pacific decided to dismantle the bridge and re-erect it elsewhere. Railfans, historical preservationists, and the city of Boonville rose up in protest, and when Republican governor Matt Blount gave the go-ahead, he was immediately sued by his own attorney general, Democrat Jay Nixon. The suit was eventually thrown out, but the process took a year, and during that time Nixon himself ran for governor and was elected.

Once in the governor's mansion Nixon wanted to unwind the Blount decision, but the state hadn't broken any laws when it modified the original contract, and the railroad was anxious to move ahead with its project. There also appeared to be no recourse at the federal Surface Transportation Board, since all statutory time limits had run out. But RTC lawyer Chuck Montange had an idea. Back in 1986, he recalled, the STB had placed one final requirement on the abandonment—that a historic study had to be carried out before the bridge could ever be taken down. Had that been done? No! Governor Nixon added the argument to the state's legal complaint, it was accepted, and the entire Katy abandonment proceeding was reopened in Washington. It was only a delay, not a reprieve, but it bought the state time to arrange for Union Pacific to receive a federal grant to build a brand-new bridge downstream and leave the old one where it was. The two sides then renegotiated the railbanking agreement, this time including the Boonville Bridge.

But that's not all. The center span is still locked in the raised position and the Coast Guard still wants the whole structure removed. Though the bridge can't be traversed from shore to shore, a vigorous fund-raising campaign has allowed one-third of the span—the portion jutting from the southern shore—to be repaired, cleaned, painted, and used as a tourist attraction. Now folks can stroll out from Boonville for the view (and occasionally for a unique wedding), legally changing the bridge's status from "abandoned" to "utilized." Thus, as the bridge serves the walkers, the walkers save the bridge.

Memorable bridge stories don't require massive crossings of world-famous rivers. There's also little Marley Creek in Maryland. When the Anne Arundel County Parks Department was planning the Baltimore and Annapolis Trail in 1989, it knew a bridge was needed over the 90-foot-wide, 35-foot-deep valley. The original wooden span had been removed years before. So when Jack Keene, county construction chief, stumbled across a small notice in a preservation magazine that Polk County, Missouri, had a one-hundred-year-old, single-lane, through-truss bridge available for reuse, he leaped to his feet. Any jurisdiction that could utilize it in a unique project could get it—for free. The bridge was already disassembled and catalogued; the only cost would be transportation from Missouri. Keene and his trail manager, Dave Dionne, submitted an application.

"The bridge arrived on the back of an 18-wheeler," said Dionne, "looking like a huge version of a child's erector set. We got it only seven weeks before the grand opening of the trail." Keene and Dionne carefully worked out reassembly plans with their subcontractor, a company named High Steel, but something went wrong. During erection, a temporary anchor was removed too early from under the almost-complete bridge, and the whole structure slid down into the ravine landing in Marley Creek, hopelessly twisted. Fortunately no worker was injured, but the local newspaper had a field day. And the next day's postmortem by engineers and lawyers promised to be highly unpleasant.

"There were about 50 of us at the meeting," Dionne said. "I had no great expectations beyond posturing, blame casting and bickering. Then, at exactly noon, a man walked down the aisle to the front of the room, introduced himself as the president of High Steel and told us he was there to buy his company's reputation back. He was alone—no lawyers, no one to hand him documents. He said that High Steel had been erecting buildings and bridges for more than one hundred years and had never before dropped a piece of steel on a job. He made us a guarantee that the company would have an exact replica bridge in time for opening day."

High Steel carried through on the promise, buying highway girders to fit the footings, reusing the one salvageable remaining steel support, and fabricating the rest of the bridge as a copy of the original. "The trail opened right on schedule," Dionne said, "and the B&A Trail today has one of the strongest bridges in America over Marley Creek."

Bridges can also be Achilles' heels. As we've seen, wooden crossings are susceptible to torching, either by trail opponents or simply by vandals and pranksters, so trail lovers in Iowa have spent many an hour devising strategies to guard their bridges. "On the Wabash Trace Nature Trail," said Mark Ackelson of the Iowa Natural Heritage Foundation, "we came up with the idea of assigning each of the seventy-two bridges to the stewardship of a local person. That helped a lot. On the Heritage Trail out of Dubuque there was a spate of bridge burnings that were extremely demoralizing—there were even situations where fire chiefs would take a suspiciously long time to get to the fire or not even try to put it out. But then an old railroader came forward and taught us how to effectively rebuild burnt bridges. It turns out the railroads had this very same problem."

"And then," Ackelson continued, "there was the time the folks on Heritage Trail gave a local private investigator a couple of cases of beer in return for sitting in a local bar and mentioning in a low voice to all the patrons, 'I'm here to find out who it is that's burning the bridges.' The fires stopped immediately."

Some of the removals aren't illegal: many states *require* abandoning railroads to take out their bridges. It's an understandable rule for highway engineers but pernicious for trail users, and many a cyclist gliding along a smooth, flat trail unaccountably finds herself suddenly descending a stiff slope—or even a flight of steps—down to a roadway, only to have to wait for a break in the traffic and then climb back up the other side. The only silver lining to that frustration is the mini-thought, *Thank you, railroad! If it weren't for your engineering the whole day would be like that.*

Since bridge removal laws are hard to defeat or circumvent, the challenge is what to do next. Weak advocacy groups live with the inconvenience year after year. Stronger ones find funding to purchase a new replacement bridge, as the folks on Pennsylvania's Cumberland Valley Rail-Trail did after twelve years of lobbying. (In many cases the replacement will be one of those arching, clean-looking, prefab structures of rust-colored Corten steel—attractive and perfectly functional, even if it does silently scream, "Not a Railroad Bridge!" No railroad bridge is *ever* arched.) The very strongest and most creative of the trail groups look around for an authentic old replacement bridge and arrange for it to be moved. This is what would have happened at Marley Creek if disaster had not struck. And it's what *did* happen near Meyersdale, Pennsylvania, after a road was widened, threatening the demise of a prim, century-old iron Bollman truss bridge. Soon after, when the state decided to eliminate an inconvenient concrete arch bridge on the nearby Great Allegheny Passage rail-trail, the locals remembered the orphaned Bollman bridge and had it moved to the trail as a replacement. Amazingly, according to historian Bill Metzger, that replacement marked the *second* time in its life the bridge was relocated. Now, on the entire 150-mile Great Allegheny Passage, it stands as its most historic structure.[1]

In car-dominated Memphis, where nondrivers had no way to cross the Mississippi River, bicyclists for years had enviously eyed the massive steel Union Pacific Railroad Harahan Bridge. Although still a heavily traveled main line, it had a protected and unused service way cantilevered alongside the tracks. It would have made the perfect connector from Tennessee to Arkansas, but the railroad vehemently refused to give permission. Then, one day, Memphis's legendary environmental lawyer Charles Newman happened to be studying an old lawsuit and discovered that the service ways were actually owned by Shelby County, Tennessee, and Crittendon County, Arkansas. No one had known. Legally the railroad was powerless to prohibit their use. It then turned out that Union Pacific's president, Jim Young, was a bicyclist and loved the idea of using them. Today the railroad bridge is not only a key part of the bike system but also plays host to thousands of pedestrian sightseers who walk out, day and night, to watch the boat traffic as well as to enjoy the view and the hourly "Mighty Light" show. The old bridge has also picked up the hip new moniker "Big River Crossing."

In Washington State, the 2,200-foot-long Beverly Bridge represented the most visible of many obstacles to the completion of the long-stymied Palouse-to-Cascades State Park Trail. Abandoned by the Milwaukee Road in 1980 and then damaged by fire, the massive crossing was deemed too expensive to either repair or tear down. As with the span in Poughkeepsie, it was partly protected through the National Register of Historic Places, but still it just sat there, fenced off, for more than thirty years while cyclists were told to head north for the next bike-friendly bridge—135 miles away. The impasse was finally broken when BNSF Railroad (the old Burlington Northern, renamed after its merger with the Santa Fe) sought permission to remove three other historic structures farther downriver. A quick-thinking trail advocate, Mark Borleske, suggested that, as a mitigation measure for those losses, the railroad should pay to study the cost of refurbishing its old Beverly Bridge. Conducting that analysis broke the logjam, and then the unified lobbying effort of cyclists, equestrians, trail advocates, historic preservationists, and even the owner of a nearby fruit orchard looking for a way to get workers across the river successfully persuaded Governor Jay Inslee to put a major restoration item into his 2019 budget.

Perhaps the most heroic bridge saga took place in Vermont at the crossing of the Winooski River, a few miles north of Burlington. This involved the Burlington Greenway, the trail previously discussed that was given the green light in 1990 by the U.S. Supreme Court in the pivotal railbanking case of *Preseault v. ICC*. A few years after the first part of the trail was constructed, bicyclists naturally wanted to keep going north, but the large truss railroad bridge across the Winooski had been removed down to its abutments. When trail advocates sought government funding for a replacement bridge, they were strenuously opposed by some politically powerful residents of Colchester, the town on the other side, who were fearful of Burlington riffraff biking through. "This highly vocal group preferred to use the Winooski River as a moat," wrote Rick Sharpe in his lively history of the battle.[2]

Events then spun wildly forward. A boat captain named Brian Costello, who was initially recruited to pick up trash on the evolving trail, became intrigued with the route and started speculating about the possibility of ferry service across the Winooski. Then Governor Howard Dean was invited to a ribbon-cutting ceremony on the newest section of the trail. Dean knew the corridor—he had been involved many years earlier and had even resigned from his church when it joined the lawsuit against the trail. (Alex Beam, a columnist for the Boston *Globe*, later wrote, "Henry VIII abandoned a great religion because he wanted a better wife. Howard Dean abandoned Henry VIII's new religion because he wanted . . . bike access.")[3] When Dean, at the ceremony, heard of Costello's idea, he enthusiastically told him, "I hear you have a plan to operate a bike ferry across the river. Get it on my desk by Monday," so that he could try to provide some state funding.[4] There hadn't been a plan, but there was by the end of the weekend, and sure enough, money did appear. However, when Colchester opponents heard about it, they got the grant turned down. The cyclists responded by forming a new nonprofit, Burlington Bikeways, Inc., to accept the funding. By the summer of 2001 a small four-bike ferry was crossing the Winooski, asking a donation of $1 per ride. The service was spectacularly successful, graduating to larger boats and, over a three-year period, transporting 40,000 people across the river. It succeeded in another way too. As the people of Colchester realized that trail users were not criminals, they dropped their opposition to a bridge, and the state was finally able to erect a grand new span across the river. The nonprofit then changed its name to Local Motion, shifted its ferry service to a different gap in the trail farther north, and expanded into the largest bicycle advocacy group in the state.

• • •

THEN THERE ARE TUNNELS. RARER THAN BRIDGES, THEY TOO provide memorable interludes for users but often head-shaking conversation pieces for managers. Even without the mythic and harrowing experiences of nineteenth-century Chinese laborers on the Central Pacific Railroad in the Sierra Nevada or Irish immigrants boring the Hoosac Tunnel through the Berkshire Mountains in Massachusetts, there are still plenty of gripping tunnel stories within the rail-trail oeuvre. For instance, there is the Cli-

Table 15. Extraordinary rail-trail tunnels

Tunnel	Rail-trail	State	Crosses under	Length (ft)	Notes
Snoqualmie Tunnel	Palouse-to-Cascades Trail	Washington	Snoqualmie Pass	11,896	Completed 1914
Taft Tunnel	Route of the Hiawatha	Montana–Idaho	Roland Summit	8,771	One of 11 tunnels
Tunnel No. 3	Elroy-Sparta State Trail	Wisconsin	Summit Ridge	3,810	Longest of 3 tunnels on the trail
Big Savage Tunnel	Great Allegheny Passage	Pennsylvania	Big Savage Mountain	3,295	Longest of 5 tunnels on the trail
Tunnel No. 6	North Bend State Trail	West Virginia	(unnamed)	2,297	Longest of 13 tunnels on the trail

max Tunnel, alongside Redbank Creek through the steep Appalachian Mountains in Pennsylvania.

"We built much of the Redbank Trail with volunteers," said Ron Steffey, former director of the Allegheny Valley Land Trust (AVLT) north of Pittsburgh, "but when we wanted to open up a 328-foot, caved-in tunnel, that was something we needed professionals for. We went to the Pennsylvania Department of Transportation. When they said they weren't interested, we showed them that the corridor was railbanked for possible reactivation of rail service, and they agreed that it could be useful to rehab the tunnel."

With the support of local transportation officials, AVLT received federal seed money to get started. Then the state department of conservation and natural resources realized that others were investing in the project, so it decided to help too. But the funding still wasn't enough to finish.

"We asked if we could get started with the money we had," Steffey said. "We thought that even if we couldn't open the entire tunnel, going halfway in would still be very interesting for tourists. They laughed and said no, they couldn't fund something that didn't go all the way through the hill. But soon after, we found the Kinzua Bridge, a Pennsylvania state park. This is a former railroad bridge that had been partially knocked down by a tornado. It doesn't go 'all the way' across the valley anymore, yet the state took over ownership and opened an observation site where it stops. That gave them pause! Eventually they agreed with our logic and allocated the funds. We used our many volunteer hours as the required financial match. Then, one grant led to the next, and the full tunnel finally got opened in 2018."

Not surprisingly, a trail with myriad tunnels is in West Virginia. The North Bend Rail-Trail, between Clarksburg and Parkersburg, now has ten of them, the longest almost half a mile, but back when it was still a main line of the B&O Railroad, it had twenty-two. In some places the locomotive would be entering one tunnel while the caboose was still in the previous one. When Mark Twain rode on it, he called it "the Appalachian Subway."

There is even a tube story from generally flat Texas. When Andy Sansom was a student at Texas Tech in the 1960s, he heard rumors that his state had railroad tunnels. "For real?" he wondered. With encouragement from his advisor, Sansom scoured the records and discovered that, yes, five tunnels had actually been dug. Years later, after he became director of Texas Parks and Wildlife, he had the satisfaction of purchasing three of them as state parks—two on trails and one in a natural area protected as bat habitat. (Number four is privately owned, and number five is partially submerged by a reservoir.) As a matter of fact, Texas rail tunnels seem perfect for bats—the 630-foot Clarity Tunnel on the Caprock Canyons State Park Trailway is home to half a million of them every year between April and October.

14

Sharing the Corridor

YOU'VE PROBABLY NEVER GIVEN MUCH THOUGHT TO TROUT
Lake on Michigan's Upper Peninsula, but Jonathan Macks had.
Back in the 1970s the town's Soo Line railroad corridor was in shaky
economic shape, so when Macks, a lawyer for Michigan Bell Telephone, learned that the Soo desired to abandon the track—along
with almost two hundred more miles in the area—he jumped at
the chance. Michigan Bell wanted to lay fiber-optic lines throughout
the Upper Peninsula, and those old corridors were the perfect way
of keeping down the cost of traversing that rough countryside. The
25-mile route north from St. Ignace passed through the Hiawatha
National Forest, and the U.S. Forest Service was also interested in
it for a snowmobile trail, but Bell muscled the agency aside and
bought the land from the railroad to construct its underground
grid. Michigan Bell did the same thing on several hundred more
miles of rail corridor in the Upper Peninsula, some abandoned,
some still active. Finally, in 2001 the company recognized that it
could reduce its carrying costs and provide Michigan with a great
trail system if it would turn the land over to the state department
of natural resources (DNR) and simply retain an easement for its
underground wires. Macks, the lawyer, was particularly enthusiastic since he happened to also be a board member of the Michigan chapter of Rails-to-Trails Conservancy. He arranged for his
company to partially sell and partially donate its lands. "It was a
classic win-win deal," said Roger Storm, DNR trailway acquisition
specialist. "In fact, of our 487 miles of rail-trails in the Upper Peninsula, about 160 miles came from Bell, and they've gifted us two
hundred more miles if and when railroads stop running on those
tracks. Everyone saves money by sharing these facilities."

Something similar happened in upstate New York when the Highland Rotary Club tried to create a trail on an already publicly owned abandoned New Haven Railroad track running east from New Paltz. The club members had been introduced to the joys of rail-trail walking by another community farther upstate, but they were reluctant to launch a campaign that could burden local taxpayers. Soon after, Rotarian (and town board member) Ray Costantino heard that a company was looking to cross the Hudson River with its high-speed internet cable, so he pursued the chance for a partnership using the abandoned corridor. The town negotiated an underground easement payment, which then served as a match for what eventually became several million dollars of state, county, and private transportation grants for the creation of the Hudson Valley Rail-Trail.

People are only part of the rail-trail story. The other part is commerce. We've already seen how, back in 1978, Baltimore County executive Ted Venetoulis leaped for the opportunity to buy the Northern Central Railroad corridor because of its potential use for a fiber-optic cable. The headlines were all garnered by the political tug-of-war over human use on the trail, but the key factor in the decision to move forward was the route's value as future subsurface industrial infrastructure.

The trail that is probably the country's most multifaceted economic-recreational complex is the w&od—the Washington and Old Dominion Railroad Regional Park in the Virginia suburbs of Washington dc. At ground level the w&od annually has two million human, canine, and equine users. Overhead is a 230-kilovolt powerline serving most of northern Virginia. Underground are Verizon and at&t fiber-optic lines supplying business and residential service to hundreds of thousands of users.

We've already touched on the w&od, one of the original nine "demonstration grant" trails selected by the Interior Department back in 1978, and also the trail so influential with members of Congress and their staffs. When the 53-mile-long w&od Railroad ceased running in 1968, it had been partly nudged into bankruptcy by the state of Virginia, which wanted a short part of the route for a new highway into Washington. The corridor was diverse and exciting, from urban, historic Alexandria almost all the way to the wilds of the Appalachian Trail in the Blue Ridge Mountains; as soon as the tracks were removed, people started walking on the path. The first written trail proposal was produced in 1973 by a remarkable junior high school student in Falls Church, Virginia, Dana Gumb Jr., and fortunately there was an equally young, aggressive park agency in place that saw the potential. It was the Northern Virginia Regional Park Authority (now called Nova Parks), formed just over a decade earlier by three counties and three cities specifically because they felt their region wasn't getting enough attention from the state park system. The track, coincidentally, was aligned so that it traversed five of the agency's six member jurisdictions.

However, before Nova Parks could do anything, the Virginia Electric Power Company (now Dominion Energy) pounced on the corridor, bought everything the state didn't need, and erected high-tension electric lines on it. To the eyes of trail lovers, the towers were dishearteningly unsightly, but the action did save the corridor from dismemberment and even helped minimize encroachment by adjoining neighbors. (The company maintained control with mowers, herbicide sprayers, and lawyers.) The area was the fast-changing, highly contested region that included Tysons Corner and Dulles International Airport, so once the wires were up, Dominion was happy to offload management of the land under them and escape the headaches of the surrounding development pressures. Despite the steep $3.6-million asking price, Nova Parks took the plunge and bought the corridor, giving the power company a permanent easement for its lines. Key to taking the risk was Nova Parks's hope that it could lease underground rights along the route. That worked out better than imagined, as the area became a world center of internet storage, switching, and transmission, with the need for large amounts of fiber-optic cabling.

The trail grew over time to become one of the best in the country. It runs through lovely natural areas as well as through bustling suburban downtowns, resulting in a dynamic mix of purposeful and recreational users. For most of its 45 miles it contains two separate treadways—one paved and flat for thin-tired bikes, the other crushed gravel and undulating along the edge of the old corridor for horses, runners, and mountain bikes. It crosses over babbling streams as well as roaring highways, and drops beneath some roads too, in friendly, open underpasses. It has excellent signage, regularly spaced rest areas (some with air pumps and bike tools), and no litter. Even though it is well used, you can set a cadence and pedal evenly for miles. It's the kind of trail that users dream of.

Part of the w&od's success is due to its substantial budget and adequate staffing. Trash is collected, pavement repaired, vegetation mowed, trees trimmed, benches fixed, signs replaced, callboxes checked, and crime, if it occurs, investigated. That budget has been made possible, in part, by the trail's corporate lease income.

Of course, even beneficial relationships have their share of behind-the-scenes rough edges. Dominion, among the most powerful companies in Virginia and accustomed to getting its way, was surprised by the sometimes dogged aggressiveness of its trail mate. First up were a couple of battles over trees. Nova Parks suggested a written memo regarding vegetation management, but Dominion dismissed that by saying that an "advance patrol" of its experts would mark all offending trees before the felling crew arrived. Soon after, Bill Dickinson, chairman of the parks board, happened to be out on the trail and came upon a crew removing a large tree. When he asked if that tree had been marked by the patrol, the crew leader said he didn't know anything about patrols. "I make the decision and cut down any tree I want," he said to the surprised Dickinson. Shortly thereafter, a memorandum was agreed to.

Several years later Dominion announced a planned extension of its electric line farther out on the corridor, which would have necessitated the removal of 26,000 trees. The company was legally allowed to deforest, but it still needed a permit from the state. The loud protest launched by conservationists was quietly assisted by the park agency.

"I think I wore out several printers making posters," chuckled Paul McCray, who was manager of the trail at the time. "They merely said, '26,000.' Of course, I did it after hours, on my own time. We put them up on trees all along the corridor. Responding to the outpouring of outrage, a company vice president finally agreed to take a van ride along the route with the Save the Trail group. What he saw, which included a particularly scenic stretch known as The Cathedral, shook him up. 'We have to make this stop,' he said. 'We have to look at an alternative.' We had won," said McCray.

Next, Dominion unexpectedly strung a fiber-optic cable along the top of its towers and leased it to a communications company. Most park agencies would have only grumbled about the competition with its business plan, but Nova Parks went to court. The agency had a small local law firm against Dominion's powerful legal team in the state capital, but it was twice victorious (the second time in the state supreme court), and today it is the park authority that receives the more than $1 million a year from two fiber-optic licenses plus a water line and other commercial users. "Plus, AT&T likes being alongside a managed trail," added McCray. "It provides them with more security against line damage. They know we have very tight control over our path and also that we own the right-of-way under every road crossing."

Because of the many development pressures alongside the W&OD, Nova Parks has had to adopt some of the most stringent trail protection policies of any agency in the country. "Not only do we have fees for leasing any of our land; we've also banned any new at-grade road crossings—every new road has to go over or under the W&OD," said McCray. "Developers were shocked, but we had to do it—the crossings were ruining the trail. Even for subsurface entities, we require them to *bore* under the trail rather than dig a trench. For too long we had people tell us, 'we'll do 100 percent compaction after we dig the trench,' and then not do it. Until we cracked down, each crossing became a bump or a drop for people riding on the trail."

Because the W&OD is more than just a recreation amenity, Nova Parks has grown to become a powerful player in its region. In the early days, when a citizen group launched a campaign to fund a new W&OD bridge, Virginia secretary of transportation John Milliken gave a speech at the groundbreaking and jokingly asked the crowd for spare change contributions. He even took off his yellow hard hat and passed it around. By 2019 that approach was a distant memory. The latest bridge was funded through a high-level political agreement utilizing some of the automobile toll revenue generated on nearby Interstate 66.

• • •

OF ALL THE POSSIBLE SHARED USES ON A CORRIDOR, THE MOST dramatic is with a railroad itself. Called "rails-with-trails" or "rails-and-trails," it is a concept that flies in the face of everything the railroad industry stated publicly for two centuries, yet it's a rapidly growing phenomenon that can meet many needs. A 2017 study by the Rails-to-Trails Conservancy documented nearly three hundred different places in the United States where live rails run alongside a trail, for a total of nearly eight hundred miles. (The trails actually cover more than 4,000 miles, but many of them adjoin live tracks for only a portion of the way.)

Railroad opposition to the idea of rails-with-trails can be summed up straightforwardly in one word: safety. Or, more precisely, liability. Around five hundred track trespassers are killed by trains every year. (It's a sobering number but a big improvement from the past; in the year 1907, 5,612 were killed.) Of course, this lumps together a wide range of causes, including suicide, but the industry's simple position is that people should stay away from tracks—no ifs, ands, or buts. In fact one railroad rule of thumb calls for a foot of separation for each mile per hour of train speed. In contrast, advocates for rails-with-trails bring up a more subtle concept: might lonely, isolated railroad tracks constitute an attractive nuisance, while placing well-designed and well-used trails alongside them actually make them safer?

To understand the debate, it is important to clarify the loose label "rail-with-trail," which covers a wide spectrum of situations. There are former two-track corridors where one of the tracks has been removed, with its old graded treadway turned into a trail. There are tracked corridors where the trail is developed in the swale or shoulder area to the side, still on railroad property. Then there are corridors where the parallel trail is located even farther away—50 or 100 feet from the edge, beyond the property owned by the railroad. This last arrangement is more common, even if it can lower the trail quality by eliminating most of the smooth grade and the

Table 16. States with the most rails-with-trails

State	No. rails-with-trails
California	40
Illinois	21
Washington	20
Ohio	19
Pennsylvania	19
Wisconsin	17
Michigan	14
Indiana	13
Colorado	10
New York	9
Iowa	8
Minnesota	8
Oregon	8

street-separation benefits of old railroads (resulting in not much more than a regular bikeway in view of a railroad track). Nevertheless it can be remarkably successful. A particularly felicitous example is the Green Bay Trail through the northern suburbs of Chicago. Constructed on the defunct Chicago, North Shore & Milwaukee interurban, it directly adjoins (but is separate from) a Union Pacific main line. By being so close to the active train corridor, the trail is protected from the interruptions of block-by-block street crossings; for most of the route there is less than one at-grade crossing per mile. Moreover, since the UP track serves Metra commuters, the trail also provides seamless linkage between bikes and trains, with trailside stations in towns like Glencoe, Winnetka, and Wilmette.

The safety debate is multifaceted and includes issues of fencing as well as of the frequency and speed of the trains involved. Most facilities have some kind of separation between track and trail, although some rely on grade separation or thick vegetation, and a few are barrier-free, simply assuming sensible behavior. In many rails-with-trails situations, only a few slow-moving trains pass by per week, substantially reducing the risk. All these topics were explored in detail in the 2017 RTC study, which also pointedly noted that there was only a single reported train-related fatality on a rail-with-trail facility over a twenty-year period.

To cyclists the rails-with-trails controversy is ironic. Obviously, biking alongside an occasional train, which is effectively locked onto its track, is much safer than riding on a roadway with streams of unconstrained automobiles—even on a road that might have painted bicycle lanes. Yet the number of streets with bike lanes is growing while most railroads continue to staunchly oppose rails-with-trails.

"Keep in mind that safety is not the same thing as liability," explained Charlie Marshall, the retired Conrail counsel. "Safety is relatively measurable. Liability is a game of deep pockets based on tort law. In Chicago once, a fellow urinated on the third rail of a Chicago Transit Authority track. Six hundred volts of electricity flowed back up the stream and electrocuted him. His family sued the agency and won. Yes, there were warning signs but the signs were not in Spanish."

Former Seattle bicycle coordinator Peter Lagerwey understands the railroads' position, and he says that it doesn't bother his city. "BNSF Railroad has a policy that it will never allow rails-with-trails," he told me in 2017. "We have no problem with that. If we want a trail alongside one of their tracks, we buy the space along the track and then move the fence over. It becomes their track and our trail."

After all, danger comes from all directions and all technologies, and rails-with-trails can afford some safety benefits in unexpected ways. Most important is providing a pathway that has few or no cross streets. These are where most accidents happen, and one outstanding benefit of the average rail-with-trail is that it eliminates many grade crossings.

Another benefit is that constructing a rail-with-rail offers cyclists and other users many more opportunities for a route with true purpose. Traditional rail-trail placement is relatively rare and almost whimsical—a route comes into existence where a track happened to be abandoned. If it doesn't serve a useful or attractive destination, there's nothing that can be done about it. It would be wonderful if Philadelphia's Schuylkill Trail would go to the Liberty Bell or if New York's High Line would go to Times Square, but they simply don't—the rail routes never did. But if, say, Chicago could somehow squeeze a trail alongside one of the many currently in-use tracks that go to and through the core of downtown, it could serve a million or more people who now must utilize one of the on-road—and more dangerous—bike lanes downtown.

Rail-with-trail argument number three flips the situation on its head. It posits that any new rail line merits having a trail constructed alongside it. This is a rarer circumstance, since few new rail corridors are being built, but it is a possible harbinger of the future. It was occurring in the late 2010s in both Montgomery County, Maryland, and Marin County, California. In Maryland, thirty years after purchasing the abandoned Georgetown Branch from csx Railroad, the state was finally ready to use a portion of the track to revive rail service—not as the original freight line but as a new light-rail transit route. This was the same corridor as the popular Capital Crescent Trail, but it was on the eastern three miles. The county had attempted to dampen public interest in that portion by refusing to pave it with asphalt or even to brand it with the Capital Crescent name. Nevertheless, during the many interim years of planning, the Georgetown Branch section had been used by thousands of residents who made no real distinction between it and the official Capital Crescent. So, when Montgomery County started talking about a transitway taking up the full width of the right-of-way, cyclists and others arose in protest. One subset sought to stop the train entirely, but the majority of protesters were willing to countenance it if a bike/hike trail would be constructed alongside. Because the right-of-way is narrow, the trade-offs, such as tree removal, were painful, but the county's strong commitment to both trail and transit resulted in the two being squeezed into the space. In fact the forces pushing for political compromise were so powerful that the county even agreed to tear down a major office building and redevelop its site in order to construct two subsurface tunnels, one for trains and one for the trail.

In hilly Marin County, bicyclists had long bemoaned the fact that they had no feasible north–south route between Mill Valley and San Rafael. The flat parts of the area were impassably developed with highways and housing, and the undeveloped parts of the county were devilishly steep. There was an old Northwestern Pacific railroad corridor, which included a 1,100-foot tunnel through the worst of the inclines, but the unstable, wood-supported bore had partially caved in and was deemed far too expensive to repair just for cyclists. But when Marin County began developing its SMART light-rail system on the old line, creative engineers determined that the tunnel could be split in two with a protective center wall, half for trail and half for train. Suddenly there was the basis for a political partnership. Two not-quite-strong-enough-on-their-own constituencies—transit advocates and the Marin County Bicycle Coalition—found common cause and mounted a lobbying effort that put them over the top on the $360-million project.

While most railroad companies are skeptical, a few have gone against the grain, touting the *benefits* of the rail-and-trail opportunity. In Cumberland, Maryland, the first 11 miles of the Great Allegheny Passage lie directly alongside the Scenic Western Maryland Railroad, which runs tourist excursions on steam and diesel trains. Most people ride both ways, but the railroad is happy to also offer tourists the option of bringing along a bike (or renting one) and returning on two wheels. The corridor is remarkable in several ways. Not only is it steep by railroad standards (an average grade of 2.3 percent, guaranteeing that every cyclist who takes the train up has an easy, exciting roll back down to Cumberland), but it also offers no physical fence or barrier between rail and trail. This greatly preserves the visual purity of the Blue Ridge mountain vistas for both train riders and trail users. There is also an unfenced, 900-foot-long rock tunnel (for which one trail guide helpfully notes, "It's recommended to avoid entering the tunnel with the noisy and smoky train; the locomotive emerging from the tunnel makes a better photo anyway").

A few years back, John Sayler, the longtime former proprietor of the Trail Inn in Frostburg, Maryland, told me how the innovation came about. "I retired from the board of the trail council, and two weeks later I was invited onto the board of the railroad. I suggested that they add on a railcar to carry bicycles. The company accountant ran the numbers and said it would cost them $75 more per trip and that they'd need to raise the price of the excursion. I said no, I think we will more than make up for that in new busi-

Sharing the Corridor

ness. They tried it, adding a car, and advertising it as "Train Up, Bike Down" service. In the first year, 2,200 people did it."

There is a similar train-and-trail program on the Lehigh Valley Trail, in eastern Pennsylvania, where the Delaware & Northern Railroad gets 150,000 tourists a year, 10,000 of whom come with a bike and pedal their way down. The safety record has been perfect at both locations, possibly aided by the fact that the trains move slowly and the companies run excursions only a few times per week. In fact most cyclists never see a train on the track. On the other hand, outside Kansas City, the Gary L. Haller Trail parallels for 5 miles a BNSF track with more than thirty trains a day traveling at speeds in excess of 50 miles an hour, and there the trail-related casualty rate has also been zero.

One of the most unique rails-with-trails efforts took place on the Armstrong Trail in western Pennsylvania. It involved the Allegheny Valley Land Trust discussed earlier, the organization that won the landmark legal decision allowing private railbanking of a corridor. Not long after AVLT agreed to buy its 52-mile Conrail corridor under a railbanking condition, a coal company filed a request to reactivate service on the southern 9 miles. The loss of what was to have been a connection to Pittsburgh was regrettable, but this was, after all, the underlying purpose of railbanking. When AVLT had the corridor appraised, it came to $1.25 million. The land trust made one last stab at saving its trail continuity by offering the railroad a deal—full price for the full corridor, or only $1 if it set aside 30 feet for a trail alongside the track. Unfortunately it didn't work. For logistical reasons the railroad preferred to shell out the higher number rather than risk having trail users near its tracks. However, the very offer demonstrates the lengths that some trail advocates will go to for a path alongside a rail line, and there is hope that when the coal mine is exhausted the Armstrong Trail use may finally link directly to Pittsburgh.

Railroads continue to resist most rail-with-trail proposals, which is why a majority of rails-with-trails are created by public agencies rather than by railroad companies themselves. Of 105 rails-with-trails whose landowners were identified by Rails-to-Trails Conservancy, only nine were railroad companies; the others were cities, counties, states, special transit authorities, electric utilities, and departments of transportation. In 2008, in Virginia, canoeists and bicyclists launched a major legislative push to finally bring a resolution to their problems with recalcitrant railroads. (The boaters got involved because they needed to cross a track to reach the James River, and the railroad kept having them arrested when they did.) They knew that Virginia—like virtually every other state—has a "recreational use statute" that protects landowners from lawsuits if they freely allow people to traverse their property for such activities as hiking, fishing, cross-country skiing, or hunting and if there was an injury. They got the law amended to make it explicitly clear that the recreational statute covered railroads too, if they allowed a trail on their land.

"Yes, we got the law passed, but nothing came of it," said Champe Burnley of the Richmond Area Bicycle Association. "The railroads had been using the liability argument to push us away, but when we fixed that problem they still didn't relent. They still said no."

Kelly Pack, director of trail development at Rails-to-Trails Conservancy, believes the answer lies in incentivizing the railroads to do more. "It could be using a carrot or using a stick," she said, "or both. But we have to hold the railroads accountable to be better community partners. Many states bend over backward to help railroads get things they need and it's only right for us to ask them for some trail space in return."

Burnley agreed. "The state of Virginia gave csx Railroad $100 million to upgrade a major railyard in Richmond so that trains could get through there faster and more easily. They want to build for future high-speed rail. Would it have been too much to add on a bike trail?"

But not everyone is so glum. Tom Sexton, director of the Northeast Office of Rails-to-Trails Conservancy, thinks the government can play a positive role. Sexton recalled a time when he accompanied the Pennsylvania secretary of transportation to a meeting where a railroad company and an adjoining trail group were feuding. He said, "The secretary came in, reminded the participants that both of them had funding requests sitting on his desk, told them that there would be no money if the dispute weren't resolved, and announced that he had another meeting to go to and would be back in two hours. When he returned, a compromise had been reached and everyone was smiling. It was pretty impressive."

15

Full Throttle Ahead

BY 1991, WITH THE SUPREME COURT BLESSING THE LEGALITY of railbanking and Congress approving money for trails as transportation, Rails-to-Trails Conservancy itself was in full swing. With a staff (plus interns) of about thirty, a budget of about $2 million, and a spiffy new office on 16th Street in Washington, the organization was trying to settle into a regimen of tightly interconnected activities. My division closely monitored railroad abandonment notices; alerted public officials and activists in the affected states, counties, and communities; produced printed materials to explain the benefits of rail-trails and the steps needed to create them; maintained communication with the Interstate Commerce Commission staff, the National Park Service, and, wherever possible, the railroads themselves; and worked with local newspapers, TV, and radio stations to spread the good news and try to counteract negative innuendo. We published a newsletter, traveled widely to small communities around the country, and spoke at hundreds of formal and informal gatherings. We maintained a comprehensive national database that we could draw upon every time someone asked for information to bolster a contention or an argument—whether for economic, environmental, health, or safety reasons. If and when a trail proposal became so controversial that it ended up in court, we connected the advocates (or the town leaders) with our legal division, either for advice or for full-fledged representation. Meanwhile other RTC divisions were working to build membership, write funding proposals, organize trail tours, explore partnerships, and advocate in Congress and the state legislatures. At the top of the pyramid was indefatigable David Burwell, churning out blizzards of memos, generating a flood of new ideas, seeking to meet with everyone, ravenous for the mission, always looking over the next hill and around the next bend, never satisfied.

He was also an extraordinary fund-raiser. "David once asked me to call a New York foundation executive to set up a meeting," said Karin Cicelski, Burwell's longtime administrative assistant. "The man said no. No meeting and there would be no money. David told me to call him back. I did, and he again said no. David told me call him again. It took me three days to get up the courage. The man said, 'You again?! Listen, just to get you to stop calling, tell David he gets 20 minutes and no money.' After the meeting David thanked me. 'He gave me an hour and $50,000,' he said."

Although Burwell loved taking on new challenges more than solving recurring ones, and though he often struggled to maintain a smoothly functioning management regimen in the organization, he was an eternal optimist. "If I ever gave him some bad financial news," recalled Connie McGuire, one of RTC's finance directors, "he would say, 'Well, all facts are friendly!' And it would usually work out."

Meanwhile the movement itself was developing a strong momentum. In the decade between January 1992 and December 2001, 179 notable rail-trails opened along with about 600 others. They included the Chief Ladiga Trail in Alabama, 33 enchanting miles through farms, forests, and wilderness in northeastern Alabama, midway between Birmingham and Atlanta; the Pumpkinvine Trail in northern Indiana's Amish country, not far from South Bend, created by Amish leaders themselves in a state notoriously unfriendly to rail corridor preservation; the White Pine Trail in Michigan, a 93-mile tour de force through lush farmland and over rivers on a former Pennsylvania Railroad line that once ran all the way from Little Traverse Bay to Cincinnati; the Harlem Valley Trail along the New York–Connecticut border, 17 miles through rock cuts and alongside ponds on a route that back in the Blizzard of 1888 featured the crash of a five-locomotive plow train into an immovable mountain of wedged snow and ice at 40 miles per hour; the 27-mile-long Paulinskill Valley Trail in the wilds of northern New Jersey, including the magnificent seven-arch 1910 Hainesburg Trestle, the world's largest reinforced concrete structure built to that time; the American Tobacco Trail running south out of Durham, North Carolina; Pennsylvania's picturesque Lebanon Valley Trail, an effort spearheaded by John Wengert, a prominent dairy farmer who learned the ropes of the trail business as a young intern at Rails-to-Trails Conservancy; the Hank Aaron State Trail in Milwaukee; and the Pine Creek Trail, 62 miles through the rugged and pristine "Grand Canyon of Pennsylvania."

And the stories we kept hearing: When Virginia transportation secretary John Milliken and his wife went to the deep Appalachian town of Abingdon in 1994 to check out a trail, a huge sign-of-the-times banner draped on the general store gave them a double take. It said: "GUNS. VIDEOS. BICYCLES." Up in Lexington, Massachusetts, in 1993, when teacher Steven Levy asked his fourth-grade class, "What is the biggest change in your town since you were born?" the children agreed it was the Minuteman Trail and then embarked on a nine-month group research project to write up the whole story. The eighty-page document was so authoritative that it was reprinted twenty-five years later at the trail's quarter-century commemoration ceremony. In Minnesota, when farmers adjacent to a portion of the Luce Line Rail-Trail convinced the state legislature to override the department of natural resources and give them back 38 miles of the already-purchased corridor, DNR pointed out that federal regulations forbade the loss of parkland and used that rule to buy a different track for a new trail.

And it wasn't just anecdotal. Statistics backed our claims. When Greater Philadelphia's regional planning organization in 1997 published its *Abandoned Railroad Inventory and Policy Plan*, it analyzed the status of sixty-eight abandoned tracks in New Jersey and eastern Pennsylvania. It found that as of that year eighteen had become routes for utility lines; eleven had become or were planned to turn into roads or driveways; seven were slated for reactivation to rail; five had been developed for housing or shopping—and twenty-seven had become trails.

States in the Northeast, upper Midwest, and Pacific Northwest have done the best in creating trails from their original stock of rail lines, with New Hampshire being the standout leader on a percentage basis. But in fact the number of rail-trail stories was mul-

Table 17. Miles of rail-trail vs. miles of original rail, by state

State	Miles rail, 1916	Miles rail-trail, 2016	Percent converted
New Hampshire	1,252	558	44.6
Rhode Island	203	78	38.6
District of Columbia	37	12	32.7
Michigan	8,876	2,442	27.5
Wisconsin	7,694	1,889	24.6
Minnesota	9,153	2,104	23.0
Connecticut	1,000	211	21.1
Washington	5,698	1,072	18.8
Massachusetts	2,133	390	18.3
Maine	2,263	400	17.7
Pennsylvania	11,635	1,925	16.5
Idaho	2,873	462	16.1
Florida	5,280	812	15.4
West Virginia	3,974	566	14.2
New Jersey	2,338	327	14.0
New York	8,493	1,152	13.6
Maryland	1,428	187	13.1
California	8,441	1,051	12.4
Vermont	1,073	130	12.1
Ohio	9,121	986	10.8
Oregon	3,067	311	10.1
Delaware	335	32	9.6
Iowa	9,946	865	8.7
Virginia	4,799	408	8.5
Illinois	12,742	1,027	8.1
Utah	2,137	153	7.2
Nebraska	6,169	431	7.0
Indiana	7,475	463	6.2
Colorado	5,702	323	5.7
Missouri	8,270	433	5.2
Montana	4,848	236	4.9
Nevada	2,318	98	4.2

Full Throttle Ahead

South Carolina	3,724	143	3.8
South Dakota	4,279	147	3.4
Tennessee	4,091	136	3.3
Kansas	9,345	287	3.1
Arizona	2,410	73	3.0
Wyoming	1,906	52	2.7
Georgia	7,482	197	2.6
Mississippi	4,439	110	2.5
Louisiana	5,603	134	2.4
North Carolina	5,537	118	2.1
Texas	15,867	301	1.9
Alabama	5,495	87	1.6
Kentucky	3,836	54	1.4
Arkansas	5,294	73	1.4
New Mexico	3,040	31	1.0
Oklahoma	6,454	52	0.8
North Dakota	5,275	36	0.7
Total U.S.	254,850	23,562	9.2

tiplying so exponentially that by the early 2000s a dart thrown at a map of the United States would seemingly reveal a rail-trail story almost wherever it landed.

One such story was in Kittaning, Pennsylvania, about forty miles northeast of Pittsburgh, where Ron Steffey grew up. Steffey got a degree in mining engineering at Penn State and rose to the position of assistant foreman at a coal company, but his life took a turn when his foot was mangled in a mine roof collapse in 2002. During recovery, on crutches, unable to drive, threatened with the possible loss of the foot, and severely depressed, he one day hobbled over to a bicycle, put his crutches in the basket, and gingerly began pedaling. He was in first gear and barely moving, but he realized he could do it. At first his doctor strenuously objected, but he then realized that biking might provide enough blood flow to save the foot. So Steffey hobbled out the door and started riding on the still-being-developed Armstrong Trail.

The 30-mile-long Armstrong Trail—the trail previously discussed that was established through private railbanking by the Allegheny Valley Land Trust—had taken more than a decade to wrestle through the legal system. It was a great victory, but then AVLT realized there would be no leadership from Armstrong County and that the land trust would have to build the facility itself. The recovering Steffey watched the work being done. "They were using professional contractors, but I had enough engineering background to see design flaws and poor practices in the building and surfacing," Steffey said. "And I kept calling them out." Finally the land trust's president, tired of the criticism, suggested that Steffey join the group himself and help. Steffey arranged to get a funded position through AmeriCorps, and within a year the former miner became full-time executive director of the trail group.

AVLT is proud of its ability to contain costs. "Because we're way out in the country, we have a lot of guys who know how to use construction equipment," Steffey said, "and many of them are so committed that they'll volunteer after work. We started out with a 'Buck a Foot' fund-raising campaign," he said. "A triaxle truck carries 23 tons of limestone screenings at about $20 per ton—that's $460. If we tailgate a truckload and spread it on thinly, it covers 460 feet. That's a buck a foot. This makes a barebones but rideable surface. People got excited and brought in more people and funds. We've since come back, doubled the thickness and made the trail wider. Our end cost with limestone is about $4 per linear foot. We get four times the mileage out of every dollar we raise, public or private. The state really appreciates that."

A different dart thrown into the middle of the map, in Minneapolis, would have pierced the Midtown Greenway, probably the most game-changing of all the nation's urban bike trails. When George Puzak came across the wide, below-grade but trash-filled corridor stretching from the Mississippi River to Lake of the Isles, he had a vision. He then introduced his find to bicyclist and organizer Tim Springer and the two of them conjured up a trail conception that even in recreation-crazed Minneapolis was breathtaking. The corridor had already been purchased and banked by the regional rail authority for a future light-rail route, but Springer and Puzak thought it was wide enough for the new train *and* a generous trail. It was so thoroughly separated from cross traffic that it had the potential of becoming a virtual bike superhighway. As of mid-2020 construction of the light-rail hadn't begun, but the trail was getting about 1.5 million uses a year. The greenway is plowed of snow in the winter, it features its own café and bike shop, and it has helped spawn a housing and retail resurgence in its formerly struggling neighborhood.

If the dart landed in Missouri, it would have revealed steady and rapid progress on the lengthy Katy Trail, which the state was opening to the public at a breakneck pace—55 miles in 1990, 46 miles in 1991, 39 more miles in 1992. Then, when the Missouri River catastrophically flooded in both 1993 and 1995, the Katy Trail became the first rail-trail ever to be approved for reconstruction funding from the Federal Emergency Management Agency. Despite a few raised eyebrows, the decision set a national precedent. (Meanwhile, the vitriol between advocates and opponents was dissipating; one leading trail foe decided to allow scouts to camp on his land, while the grandchildren of the lawsuit-filing Glosemeyers opened up a lemonade stand alongside the trail.)

The dart, if it dipped farther south, would have poked into a *different* Katy Trail, a shorter but busier one, in downtown Dallas. ("Katy," which is the hyper-abbreviation of the initials of the old Missouri-Kansas-Texas Railroad without the *M*, made such an impact on folks in the southern plains that there are now at least five different Katy Trails, not to mention the classic song by Taj Mahal, "She Caught the Katy [Left Me a Mule to Ride].") The trail in Dallas, created out of a 3.5-mile piece of leftover track from construction of the DART light-rail system in the 1990s, was at first staunchly opposed by neighbors but soon became the most popular trail in the city. It helped change Dallas's attitude toward non-automotive travel, and it spurred many proposals for extension and expansion both toward the Trinity River and, in the other direction, to White Rock Lake.

A dart curving to the left might have landed on Ojai, California, up the hill from Ventura, where a coalition of equestrians, park professionals, cyclists, and even adjoining neighbors came together to

Table 18. Rail-trails by state

State	Number	Mileage
Pennsylvania	186	2,097
Michigan	130	2,462
California	128	1,059
New York	111	1,161
Ohio	100	1,000
Wisconsin	99	1,894
Iowa	89	884
Washington	86	1,085
Illinois	83	1,030
Minnesota	78	2,123
New Hampshire	75	558
Indiana	70	463
Massachusetts	69	404
West Virginia	68	567
Florida	55	816
New Jersey	52	328
Virginia	48	412
Colorado	42	323
Maryland	37	338
Maine	33	400
Texas	33	301
Tennessee	33	139
North Carolina	32	120
Georgia	28	197
Connecticut	27	220
Nebraska	25	431
South Carolina	25	143
Idaho	24	462
Kansas	23	296
Alabama	23	92
Missouri	22	441
Oregon	21	311
Arkansas	21	73
Montana	20	239

Vermont	18	130
Kentucky	17	54
Utah	15	154
Mississippi	13	110
Arizona	13	73
South Dakota	10	161
Rhode Island	10	78
Oklahoma	10	55
New Mexico	9	33
Louisiana	7	134
Nevada	6	100
Delaware	6	37
Wyoming	5	52
Alaska	5	47
North Dakota	5	36
Hawaii	3	17
District of Columbia	3	12

Source: Rails-to-Trails Conservancy, 2019

create a two-tread facility—asphalt for bikes, wood chips for horses—separated by a handsome wood rail fence. The facility, taken on by a park agency without county tax funding, was financially supported through the lease of valuable underground utility rights.

The torrid pace of growth was, of course, aided by the Rails-to-Trails Conservancy, not only through its technical assistance but also through plain old tourism promotion. Initially RTC got involved with creating guidebooks so people could find the trails. Then with the growth of the internet it moved into computer-based trail-describing and trail-locating technology. The website, Traillink.com, became a one-stop information spot with every rail-trail in the country listed, mapped, photographed, explained, and rated. "We started in 2000 with maybe 30,000 visitors a month," said Frederick Schaedtler, senior director of technology marketing, "and by now it's up to seven-and-a-half million a year. It revolutionized both the movement and the organization." RTC provides the service for free but asks users to register, and an impressive number of the visitors then become members or contribute to keep the movement going.

Then, in 2009, in Manhattan, something unprecedented happened. The first section of the High Line opened.

• • •

NEW YORK CITY CAME VERY LATE TO THE RAILS-TO-TRAILS MOVEment. The rail-trail idea took root in the rural Midwest and gradually picked up steam in places like Pennsylvania, Virginia, and Washington State, so it didn't easily break through the Big Apple's cosmopolitan media institutions. Even though in 1966 it was a New Yorker—Waldo Nielsen—who had started walking the rails around Rochester, upstate New York is as alien to New York City folk as Ohio or Iowa. And even though the *New York Times* did give sporadic attention to rails-to-trails over the years, it was mostly as something exotic, quaint, and far distant. As for the city's railroad tracks, they were generally located in the outer boroughs and were still in some kind of use. And New York's bicycle advocates were primarily focused on trying to get better access to the streets.

Meanwhile there was one hulking monstrosity looming over the avenues and through the vertical canyons of Lower Manhattan. Called the West Side Elevated Line, it was a foreboding railroad trestle that operated from 1934 until 1980, primarily bringing animal carcasses to the famous and fetid Meatpacking District. Eventually meatpacking moved out of Manhattan, and Conrail— soon replaced by csx—found itself stuck with the abandoned line. There then began a multiyear slugfest between residents, building owners, shopkeepers, real estate developers, the city, and the railroad—not over *whether* the steel monster should be torn down but over who would pay the $30 million that demolition would cost. Not "too big to fail," this one was "too big to derail." So there it sat, year after year, gathering dust, rust, and pigeon guano, with occasional visits from hobos and teenage daredevils. Gradually, in the late 1990s a few people started noticing that the structure's surface was actually starting to sprout bushes, flowers, and even trees— that it was begetting a strange, primeval beauty. Two of those people, Robert Hammond and Joshua David, began to think that the structure could be worth saving and turning into a kind of park, similar to something that had earlier been created in Paris, the Promenade Plantée. They called it the High Line. The outgoing mayor, Rudolph Giuliani, was not interested and actually signed a demolition order, but the incoming mayor, Michael Bloomberg, loved parks, was intrigued, and countermanded the teardown. In fact Bloomberg and his planning director, Amanda Burden, devised a special overlay rezoning—changing it from light industrial to commercial-and-residential, with density shifted away from the rail canyon itself—to accomplish two goals: protect the views of (and from) the structure and increase the potential profitability of any redevelopment in the then-undervalued (at least by Manhattan standards) neighborhood.

The full story of the High Line's evolution, complete with its parade of corporate titans, glittering celebrities, and star landscape architects, is too long for this book. Suffice it to say that the High Line's timing and location, plus brilliant marketing, allowed for a vast influx of neighborhood investment, a prodigious amount of public funding and private philanthropy, and a level of design opulence and excellence never before seen with any rail-trail. The trail—although the High Line is far too elegant for anyone to refer to it as a "trail"—also catapulted to an unparalleled level of usership: more than seven million people a year by 2018, on a mile-and-a-half-long route. With bicycles and roller skates banned from the facility, the High Line has become New York's premier spot for walking and people-watching (and foreign language–listening), with sumptuous architectural, horticultural, historic, and artistic surprises every few steps. There is even a place where the Empire State Building suddenly pops into view and then, with a 180-degree swivel of the head, so does the Statue of Liberty.

New York had done it again. The city, after almost pointedly ignoring a bicycle-oriented (or at least an active-motion-oriented) movement that grabbed the public's imagination everywhere else, had reinvented the rail-trail. As redefined by the High Line, the rail-trail became a passive (rather than an active) urban park loaded with beautiful objects and plantings (and people) to look at while one slowly, aimlessly moved above the earth. Even though one *did*, of course, walk, it was not done briskly—only with the kinds of back-ups and interruptions that are found in, say, a crowded museum or a busy zoo. Today the High Line not only fails to provide traditional high-aerobic rail-trail "exercise"; it is actually one of the few trails where one might consider dressing up before attending.

The effect was electrifying. New Yorkers went from being clueless and uninterested about rail-trails to being proud and even smug: "Oh, you mean like the High Line?" And it wasn't only New Yorkers. Much of the rest of the country rapidly found out too. Since the High Line was both unprecedented and free, tourists were eager to flock there. (About one-third of the visitors are from New York City, one-third from the rest of the United States, and one-third from overseas.) Within five years it had become the city's ninth most visited attraction. Moreover its economic effect was almost beyond belief—a reported $2 billion in economic impact in the nearby area in a few short years, and a bolstering of the city's property tax revenue by an estimated $900 million over a twenty-year period. It wasn't all the High Line's doing—there were a number of other factors playing into the old neighborhood's resurgence—but the rail-trail was a major trigger.

The High Line set off a group of other cities on a search for outmoded elevated structures that they could rescue, clean up, lavish money on, and repurpose as parks. It was a particularly thrilling development for the Northeast and Midwest—finally a realm where the Rust Belt had a natural advantage! Three cities—Chicago, Philadelphia, and St. Louis—soon found possibilities and got to work trying to re-create the magic. Advocates in the outer New York borough of Queens were also energized to propose a similar elevated rail-trail they dubbed the "Queensway." Many other cities came up short but then tried "High Line Lite" concepts, grabbing any overhead structure they could find and attempting to brand it like New York's. In Washington DC, for instance, a group that was working to build a new pedestrian bridge across the Anacostia River started describing the effort as "like the High Line," even though there was no previous structure there that was being recycled or had served a railroad.

The Chicago effort moved the fastest. This was the almost-three-mile-long Bloomingdale Trail within the multi-park "606" project discussed earlier. The Windy City, which is famously competitive with New York (and every other place), was still on a psychological high in the mid-2000s because of the spectacular success of world-renowned Millennium Park downtown near Lake Michigan. When the High Line started shifting the nation's park buzz back to New York, Chicagoans bristled at the notion that the Bloomingdale was an effort to copy their rival. And they were right. Even though it seemed similar—raised above the ground, with bridges over every cross street—the Bloomingdale Trail was really more like a traditional transportation facility, with a smooth and fast surface for running and biking. Their rebuttal was reinforced by the fact that $50 million of the Bloomingdale funding came from a federal bicycle/pedestrian program specifically aimed at reducing traffic congestion and air pollution, something that the High Line doesn't strive for. In fact the commuter-oriented Bloomingdale Trail is open twenty-four hours a day, while the High Line closes at night.

But, in another way, the Bloomingdale Trail *was* like the High Line: it was created by a city that was looking not necessarily just for more connections, but for more actual parkland. "Just when I moved to Chicago," said Ben Helphand, a leader of the Friends of the Bloomingdale Trail, "the city started the Logan Square Open Space Plan. Of all Chicago's neighborhoods, Logan Square had the second-lowest amount of open space in the city. The city held a community meeting and it just jumped out at us—creating this new park would constitute 85 percent of the open space in the whole neighborhood." Gaining parkland for "under-parked" Chicago was also the reason that the Trust for Public Land threw itself into the project. (Ultimately TPL acquired and developed six access plazas along with the old rail line itself.) Significantly, as in New York, the Bloomingdale Trail was given a much higher level of landscape design attention than the average rail-trail—more like a garden than like a bikeway.

Of course New York– and Chicago-level excitement also entailed New York– and Chicago-level prices—$95 million for the latter and $260 million for the former. (And that was just for development, not acquisition, since both properties had been donated.) In forty years the movement had come a long way from the $12,000 "deal of the century" Elroy-Sparta Trail. Even though there were still many reasonably priced backcountry trail efforts going on, nationally rail-trails were moving into the mainstream of the nation's park-development efforts.

So—now that some of the jewels were sparklingly set into place—perhaps it was time to revisit the idea of using old corridors to cross the entire country.

16

Filling the Gaps

THE PENDULUM-LIKE TOPIC OF LENGTH VERSUS INTERCON-
nectivity has occupied the Rails-to-Trails Conservancy almost from
the beginning. Both goals have true appeal: the vision of "the rainbow ever over the horizon"—a trail ultimately extending from coast
to coast—or that of the "twenty-first century ecological city"—a
densely patterned trail network within each metropolitan area that
allows meaningful numbers of people to quickly access a trail and
then safely and healthfully get everywhere without using a car.

In the organization's early days, the principal concern was length.
Our elevator speech usually ended with, ". . . and maybe one day
we'll even be able to ride off-road from coast to coast!" It was an
echo of the original pied piper song of the transcontinental railroad,
and it provoked some of that same excitement (if also some conde-
scending skepticism from non-bicyclists). Everywhere we looked,
we believed we could see for miles and miles. RTC was the earliest promoter of what is now becoming the East Coast Greenway
(first conceived as from Boston to Washington, later expanded to
reach from Maine to Florida). It also was first on board with such
concepts as the Grand Illinois Trail, the Discover Michigan Trail,
and the Cross-Ohio Trail from Cincinnati to Cleveland. The steady
nationwide growth in mileage seemed to bear out the hope for success, even as the realities of routing, lack of rail corridor density
outside the East and Midwest, and the great distances in the West
gave pause to those doing the actual planning of a cross-country
rail-trail route. (There was actually another coast-to-coast effort
under way at the same time, led by the American Hiking Society. Christened the American Discovery Trail [ADT], it was laid out
from Point Reyes, California, to Cape Henlopen, Delaware, but

large distances of the ADT are on lightly used roads and streets, and even sidewalks. Of the 80 percent of the route on trails, many of those miles are on steep or rugged mountain paths that cannot be cycled or traversed by casual walkers.) So, gradually, in the face of the challenges, alternative visions gained momentum.

Keith Laughlin, who arrived at RTC six years after I left and who served as president from 2001 to 2019, explained the evolution of the organization's mission: "Until 2004, the creation of the cross-country trail was a major theme of ours. At that time, the board of directors came to the realization that large stretches of this trail would pass through extremely lightly populated parts of the country, so they shifted gears from length to proximity. They decided to liquidate our ownership of all the remaining rail corridors, and instructed us to shift from building new trails to making the network more usable by filling gaps. The new goal became that every American should be within three miles of a trail."

After plunging through a good deal of computerized mapping analysis, Laughlin said, "we were happy to discover and determine that 45 percent of all Americans *already* lived within three miles of a trail! In fact, in doing this analysis, we learned that there were nine metropolitan areas with such a large number of trails that over 90 *percent* of their residents lived within three miles of a trail."

But the research also yielded some discomfiting findings. Even in those metros with the highest percentage of residents near trails, the number of people utilizing what was by then called "active transportation" (walking as well as bicycles and other human-powered vehicles) was still very low.

"The answer, we came to believe, is that actually people had less need of *proximity* and more need of *connectivity*," Laughlin said. "Thus was born the campaign known as 'TrailNation,' an effort to provide extreme connectivity, starting within eight metropolitan statistical areas—Miami, Philadelphia, Baltimore, Washington DC, Cleveland, Pittsburgh, Milwaukee, California's Bay Area, and Brownsville, Texas."

Inevitably the effort to assure "extreme connectivity" in urban areas moved RTC in the direction of the broader active transportation community—specifically working to provide facilities like bike

Filling the Gaps

lanes on roadways and better sidewalks alongside them. It was good for that movement in general, since RTC brought considerable lobbying strength to the funding battles in Congress, but it also moved the organization somewhat away from its original focus on rail corridors. Even though lobbying for more money for biking and walking projects had many benefits, it also meant that there weren't quite as many internal resources available for organizing the grassroots movements and consulting on local rail-trail campaigns, efforts that had already been relatively difficult to carry out and to pay for.

After more than a decade, the irresistible lure of the transcontinental trail returned to the fore. In 2018, just as Laughlin was moving toward retirement, the RTC pendulum swung back again. The next year, with a splashy set of Facebook Live announcements strung out coast to coast, the organization returned to the cross-country trail concept, this time rebranding the focus as the "Great American Rail-Trail," from Washington DC to Washington State.

The trail that did the most to give a sense of reality to crossing the country is the Great Allegheny Passage, 140 miles from Pittsburgh to Cumberland, Maryland (and then, through a seamless connection with the C&O Canal towpath, another 184 miles to Washington DC). There are several longer, east–west trails—the Cowboy Trail in Nebraska, the Katy Trail in Missouri, the Palouse-to-Cascades Trail in Washington State—but the GAP, as it's known, had many features that made it rise to the top. For one, it had the benefit of two iconic endpoints, Pittsburgh and DC, separated by many miles of visually captivating countryside. The ascent up and over the mountains seems rugged on the map, but since it follows rail-trails it can provide bragging rights to people of even average physical strength. The route is filled with interesting old industrial history, and it follows the original path of the railroads' struggle to surmount the Appalachian Mountains back in the 1840s and '50s. More significant, the GAP was the first effort to pull together all the elements necessary to achieve widespread political, promotional, and economic success. It took thirty-eight years, cost about $80 million, and is a tale worth recounting.

My first introduction to the effort was in late 1986 when I got a phone call from Hank Parke at the chamber of commerce in Somerset, Pennsylvania. I had never gotten a call from a chamber of commerce before, so I was both intrigued and skeptical. Chambers didn't usually promote environmental projects, but Hank said that they had an idea for a rail-trail from Confluence to Connellsville, and could we help? I joked that maybe it could be called the Con-Con Trail, but when I did a little research, I began to perceive how remarkable this corridor through the Appalachian Mountains could be. (I remembered reading that cross-country bike racers would complain that, of their whole superhuman journey from the Pacific Ocean to the Atlantic, climbing the steep West Virginia and Pennsylvania roads was the most grueling part.) Using the valleys of the Potomac, Casselman, Youghiogheny, and Monongahela Rivers, it was a recreational paradise, but it was also a history lesson: in the 1870s the route offered so much economic potential that two different railroads had built on opposite sides of the rivers. Eventually, through bankruptcies and mergers, both lines came under the ownership of the Chessie system, which finally abandoned one of them in 1967. Trail users today can watch and listen to heavy freight trains chugging up and down the other side of the valleys and even catch Amtrak's *Capitol Limited* on its daily run in each direction.

But making a trail would be a heavy lift for five postindustrial Appalachian counties in Pennsylvania and Maryland. The challenges were similar to those we've already learned of, though more extreme: multiple political jurisdictions, almost no local public money, a scarcity of planning expertise, lots of skepticism, recalcitrant railroads, a dearth of advocates, fear of chemical contamination, fear of liability, fear of the unknown. Fortunately the pro-trail forces had some unusually strong resources to call upon: a Pennsylvania governor—Tom Ridge—who was an enthusiastic bicyclist and even led rides around the state; other local politicians who were well positioned in Washington and Harrisburg; supportive federal programs aimed at reviving Appalachia; a handful of very seasoned private foundations; and a long history of overcoming adversity. Most important they had a corridor that many felt was crying out to become a trail.

The first track to come up for abandonment, in 1967, was the 116-mile Western Maryland Railway corridor from Hancock, Maryland, to Connellsville, Pennsylvania. This was many years before the railbanking law, but the railroad had clean ownership of much of the land. Abandonment was fiercely opposed by economic interests, so the process dragged out for nearly a decade, during which some planning was able to take place. Maryland decided the continuous corridor was too important to lose, even without an immediate use in mind, and bought it. (Years later one part was leased to a tourist train operator and another part became a bike trail.) The state of Pennsylvania was unwilling to do the same, but the prominent Western Pennsylvania Conservancy stepped up. In 1975 Conservancy president Joshua Whetzel organized a "final train ride" excursion for two carloads of conservationists, railroaders, government officials, and members of the press and then fronted $800,000 for the purchase itself.

The most spectacular section of the route is around the town of Ohiopyle, where the powerful Youghiogheny River froths its way through thick forests and over ancient rocks while falling as much as 120 feet per mile. It was already a whitewater rafter's paradise, and the Conservancy thought it could be the same for trail users. After spearheading a campaign for a new Ohiopyle State Park, it sold 17.5 miles of the corridor as its nucleus. By 1986 the first 11 miles had been surfaced with crushed limestone and, under the name Youghiogheny River Trail, it was drawing 80,000 users per year.

That's when Hank Parke called me. Although he lived in the next county, he had cycled on the trail and was exhilarated to realize that the same track continued all the way to his town of Somerset. At the same time, downriver, in the other direction, walkers, runners, and bicyclists in Pittsburgh, led by Mayor Tom Murphy, were developing a full-fledged, multi-river greenway system to redefine their formerly polluted city. The railroad track that could bring the route into Pittsburgh wasn't abandoned yet, but it was teetering financially. With the writing on the wall, several localized trail advocacy groups sprang up.

The Pittsburgh area was once a wealthy city, and one residue of that past wealth is a large and active "old money" foundation community. By the late 1980s the foundations were being besieged by seven separate groups requesting trail funding. Enter Linda McKenna Boxx, a savvy political organizer from nearby Latrobe, Pennsylvania, who had a family foundation as well as ties to

Map 1. The Washington DC to Pittsburgh Trail. This initial leg of a trail across the United States combines a canal towpath and several rail-trails to cover the first 328 miles heading west. Map by Bill Metzger.

people in the philanthropic community. She took it upon herself to hammer together a unified effort and a continuous trail.

Boxx recalled, "The foundations said, 'We can't sort this all out—how about if you guys get together as a group and decide who's going to ask for how much and for what purpose?' They wanted one vision and one name. But it took awhile to get there."

The area was so historically and culturally rich that the trove of available themes seemed overwhelming. There was river hydrology and colonial history, industrial manufacturing and ecological succession, Native American artifacts and geological processes, labor union strife and, of course, great feats of railroading. When the superintendent of the Potomac River National Heritage Trail suggested that the group collect its thoughts by undertaking an interpretive study, the participants came up with 150 items to explore. The disunity was exacerbated by the steep countryside that reinforced tribalism and hampered inter-group communication.

Boxx worked tirelessly to cajole the participants, and they eventually agreed to unify into two groups: the Allegheny Trails Alliance, for advocacy, and the Regional Trail Corporation, for landownership. That structure allowed fund-raising to proceed, and when the Pittsburgh and Lake Erie Railroad finally abandoned its 40-mile corridor in 1990, the Regional Trail Corporation bought it.

"My best quality was being the mother of boys," Boxx later said. "I understand active people who don't like meetings. I sat them all down. They were all completely bought in to the concept, but things kept getting lost in translation when they would go back to their members. There was so much jealousy and suspicion! I worked on it every week for 20 years."

Another key participant was Dave Mankamyer, chair of the Somerset County Commission. A farmer, Mankamyer was also a conservationist concerned about the pollution of the Casselman River, and he was also a service station operator interested in promoting tourism. It was Mankamyer who presided over the key emotional meeting when Boxx led advocates in favor of a unified trail against those who wanted to pull the county out of the project. After hours of listening, Mankamyer said, "I think we're going to go with her."

"It was the defining moment," Boxx said. "There was no way we could get the whole trail without Somerset County, and there was no way that impoverished county would be able to pull off this huge undertaking on its own."

But toughest was unifying the name.

"We had so many names floating around—Steel Valley, Steel Heritage, Three Rivers, Youghiogheny North, Youghiogheny South, Allegheny Highlands, Mon-Yough," Boxx said. "For six years we had to refer to it simply as the Pittsburgh to Cumberland Trail. The topic was too contentious. Finally, in the fall of 2000 we hired a marketing firm to help us. The meeting was huge—we had eighty people. Many names were floated. Bob McKinley, director of the Regional Trail Council, came up with the word 'Passage.' It could mean the passage through the mountains, or George Washington's passage before the Revolution, or each of our own passages through life. Then we thought 'Allegheny Passage.' Then Bill Metzger called out, 'Hey—the initials are A-P! It could be G-A-P. What starts with a "g"? How about Great!' That did it. We had a name that unified us."

Many skillful and committed people were key to the success of the trail, but everyone credits Boxx for her leadership. She puts it differently. "This was well started by the time I got involved. I just picked up all the disparate pieces and hauled them to the finish line," she said.

The other trail that helped stimulate the idea of crossing the whole country was in Washington State. Its genesis was very different, it took even longer to complete, and like the GAP, it got hung up on nomenclature.

The abandonment, in 1980, was the most shocking of all time. It was the Milwaukee Road's Coast Extension—900 miles from Miles City, Montana, to Tacoma, Washington, all at one fell swoop. Although not every state purchased the resulting land, Washington was farsighted enough to do so. Today that decision has been vindicated, with 224 miles of the corridor slated to be incorporated into the coast-to-coast Great American Rail-Trail. But for nearly forty years the corridor suffered through a political and bureaucratic purgatory straight from the earlier tribulations discussed with the rails-to-trails triangle concept. This trail is a classic case of a triangle that began with only one of its three legs: there was strong state support but no effective advocacy and no plan of action.

The trail's very birth was problematic. In the verdant, more populated west, the corridor was purchased by AT&T, which installed an underground fiber-optic cable and then donated the land to the Washington Parks and Recreation Commission. In the drier, sparser eastern part of Washington, the trail bill was so controversial that it passed by only a single vote in the Senate—and then a technical paperwork error got it placed within the department of natural resources instead of parks and recreation, even though DNR had no expertise in recreation and no staff to manage public use. In the west, parks and rec began a slow, orderly process of turning its segment into a bicyclist- and hiker-oriented trail that they named the Iron Horse State Park. In the east, however, DNR found itself engulfed by antagonistic ranchers on one side and enthusiastic equestrians on the other. The latter were a hardy bunch who could spend all day in the saddle under the blistering sun, traversing fiercely wild backcountry with skin-tearing thistles, expecting to be provided neither food and water nor any other services, and loving it. They knew nothing about more traditional rail-trail users nor about building broadscale coalitions. They were led by a charismatic former navy sailor named Chic Hollenbeck whose devotion to horses was matched only by his worship of the actor John

Wayne (who had no connection whatsoever with Washington, the old railroad, or the Palouse countryside). Through the force of his personality, Hollenbeck succeeded in naming the trail for Wayne, and he also started the John Wayne Pioneer Wagons and Riders organization to stage a colorful annual two-week ride on the bumpy corridor. Simultaneously the ranchers along the route closed ranks against any sort of public trail, erecting barriers, locking gates, lobbying the noxious weed control board, and making sure that the fist-size ballast rocks were not resurfaced with anything that would be more comfortable to walk or ride on. Capping it all off, near the midpoint of the trail flowed the uncrossable Columbia River with the sealed-off Beverly Bridge, discussed previously.

As western Washingtonians gradually discovered the great corridor, with its magnificent trestles and rock tunnels, they came to realize that it actually continued onward all the way to the Idaho border. This would have been more obvious if there hadn't been the nomenclature confusion, but none of the trail advocates wanted to give in, and the two governmental agencies felt powerless to take charge. The facility eventually earned the clumsy compromise name, The John Wayne Pioneer Trail within the Iron Horse State Park. (The width of the former was 10 feet, and the latter 100.)

The rails-to-trails movement was rising to fever pitch in Washington, but as excitement built over a possible cross-state trail, the eastern ranchers' concerns and opposition rose as well. Finally in 2015 the opponents attempted a sneak attack. They prevailed upon two state legislators to quietly slip in a budget amendment transferring 135 miles of the corridor to the adjacent owners. The unnoticed provision passed, but amid the hugger-mugger, the wording of the amendment was garbled. It would have killed the trail forever but it contained a geographical error (". . . from the Columbia River to the Columbia River . . .") and couldn't be implemented. The headline in the *Seattle Bike Blog* blared, "Typo in Law Halts Secret Plan to Give Away Half of John Wayne Trail."

The close call was like an electric shock to trail advocates all over the state who deluged the lawmakers with calls for protection. The long-delayed trail was not only saved, but the state was even impelled to finally develop it. Serious construction money was finally appro-

Map 2. The Palouse-to-Cascades Trail utilizes a single lengthy railroad abandonment to take users from the Idaho border almost to Seattle. After decades of controversy, the trail was put under single management and was finally given a unified name in 2018. Map by Bill Metzger.

priated, ownership was transferred to parks and rec, and in 2018 the agency finally took charge by retiring both the "John Wayne" and the "Iron Horse" titles in favor of something in keeping with its standard naming practice—the Palouse-to-Cascades Trail, honoring two of Washington's most prominent environmental formations.

In 2019, because of the excitement engendered by the GAP, the Palouse-to-Cascades Trail, and other long-distance routings, Rails-to-Trails Conservancy formally returned to its earliest idea. Following several years of political analysis and on-the-ground scouting, RTC announced a preferred route for the Great American Rail-Trail. At the time of unveiling, more than 1,900 trail miles were in existence and about 600 more were on known corridors and in the planning stages. The stretch between Washington DC and central Indiana was already mostly connected, as was the stretch from western Montana to Seattle. The portion from Chicago to western Nebraska was also quite well defined. Only the long stretches of Wyoming and parts of Montana still presented major routing challenges for a complete trail-based journey. When completed it will measure out at 3,773 miles.

"This huge effort," said Ryan Chao, RTC's new president, who was installed just before the announcement, "is not a turning point—it's a growing point. Rail-trails have been transformative for communities everywhere, and now we're bringing them fully up to scale. We think the Great American Rail-Trail will be a national treasure."

Filling the Gaps

17

Of Rail-Trails and Real Estate

WHEN IT COMES TO PROPERTY VALUE, HAVING A RAIL-TRAIL nearby is a proven benefit. Not in every single case, but certainly in the aggregate. Most people like being close to a trail. In an exhaustive overview of thirty-six economic studies and opinion surveys over a forty-year period, John Crompton and Sarah Nicholls found that nearby trails added an average of 3 to 5 percent to the value of a home (with a greater impact in urban areas and lesser in rural). They also found that respondents believed that a nearby trail made it easier to sell a property more quickly.[1]

Despite this, the real estate industry and the rail-trail advocacy movement have been surprisingly slow to come into alignment with each other. Rail-trails, after all, *are* real estate, and real estate professionals can add greatly to the knowledge base about land transactions, development plans, funding mechanisms, and other tricks of the trade. Trail advocates, in turn, can generate wide publicity about the benefits of trails to home values, community vitality, and transportation linkages. Yet even though some brokers consciously place "House for Sale" signs alongside trails, precious few take the step of involving themselves directly with the advocacy movement.

An exception to this lacuna—the man who opened my eyes to some of the possibilities of the profession—is a whirling dervish of real estate and rail-trail activity named Craig Della Penna. Della Penna didn't start in real estate. Growing up in Holyoke, Massachusetts, he fell in love with trains at an early age, first making models (and biking to his local model railroad shop) then getting a job with a short line that once ran the venerable Hoosac Tunnel & Wilmington Railroad (the "Hoot, Toot & Whistle"). Ever curious, he also spent his after-hours hiking and biking rail-trails and abandoned corridors in the Northeast, even writing three guide-books from his findings. Later, in 2001, he and his wife found a rundown old house directly alongside a rail-trail in Northampton, Massachusetts, restored it, and turned it into New England's first rail-trail-oriented bed-and-breakfast establishment. When David Burwell learned of Della Penna, he offered him a job at Rails-to-Trails Conservancy with the missions of organizing advocacy groups and fending off trail opponents.

From doing that work, Della Penna got the insight that the prime reason some people oppose trail proposals is because they assume a nearby pathway will lower the value of their property. But he knew that the data showed otherwise. Della Penna decided to take the bull by the horns and become a real estate broker, choosing the special niche of selling residential properties near rail-trails and other linear parks.

Today, through a combination of computer technology and the force of his personality, Della Penna brings a considerable arsenal to bear in this new role as what might be called a "railtor"—a rail-trail lover who is also a real estate professional. Like all home sellers, Della Penna has access to a database of every property in the state with all its positive attributes, including such amenities as "public transportation," "medical facility," "Laundromat," "golf course," and more. But when he got started in his new business, he was surprised to discover that there was no notation for what he knew was a positive attraction for many people: "bike trail nearby." It took him four years of cajoling and lobbying to get his local board to include that amenity, and today he is instantly notified every time a home comes on the market with a trail in the vicinity. In some cases, through the list of names he has built up over the years, he knows of someone who is specifically interested in purchasing such a property. In other cases he spreads the word among folks who would be particularly likely to care.

Alternatively, if the property itself physically includes an old corridor, Della Penna has been known to go much further. In a few cases he himself has bought the land, excised the rail line from the property, turned the linear strip over to a local land conservation organization for permanent protection, and then resold

Of Rail-Trails and Real Estate

the house and its (slightly truncated) property—carefully seeking someone who is not anti-trail. The ever-sanguine Della Penna hopes that by continuing to work on adjoining properties in this way, he might gradually be able to re-create old corridors that now seem to be hopelessly fragmented—"put Humpty-Dumpty back together again," as he says.

The zealous Della Penna is well positioned to take things further. "If I'm at a public hearing at which someone accuses trails of harming property values," he says, "I have all the latest statistical data from the real estate computer showing that to be wrong. And I'll be talking to the group as a real estate professional, which gets their attention." As an additional flourish, he has a standing offer to any trail opponent: a free night's stay at his trailside bed-and-breakfast. "But they have to come on a weekday," he says, "so that they can personally watch the children walking and biking to school, the mothers pushing their strollers and exercising their dogs, and the older residents taking their after-dinner constitutionals on the trail. I want them to see how safe it is and how good for the community."

There's even more. By closely watching development plans and by being keenly knowledgeable about Massachusetts's rather strong laws protecting corridors, Della Penna has been able to flag and even stop illegal developments that would have blocked or destroyed old railroad lines that were sitting undeveloped in forests or wetlands.

Della Penna has been widely written about, and he has won various conservation and trail awards, but there is still a large unfilled gap between his unique and transformative vision and what others in the real estate industry could do in the furtherance of the rails-to-trails movement. His approach gives a glimpse of a new type of trail advocacy that could arise in the future.

It is interesting to consider Della Penna's activity in the context of a young but already established real estate tool: Walk Score. Walk Score, developed after the invention of computerized mapping, started out as an innovative way for people to compare with each other the feasibility of getting from their home or neighborhood to important destinations without having to drive. Gradually the message moved beyond fun to economic import. As people saw the data and started shifting their thinking about walkability, their home-buying decisions were also affected. Eventually the real estate industry recognized the monetary benefit of the information and found it worthwhile to pay the Walk Score company to include the data on their website. It became a virtuous cycle of public interest and profit.

Perhaps something similar could occur with trails and rail-trails, with the economic force of the marketplace stimulating the preservation of abandoned corridors as well as the creation and expansion of trails. Instead of the full weight of trail creation being carried by idealistic, overworked volunteers, others who can envision a financial benefit from the work would also be involved.

Of Rail-Trails and Real Estate

18

If You Want to Count, You Have to Count

FIFTY YEARS AFTER THE BEGINNING OF THE RAILS-TO-TRAILS movement the nation had about 18,000 miles of rail-trail.[1] For context, that's more than the Appalachian Trail, the Pacific Crest Trail, and all the other national scenic trails combined. It's about the same size as the trail network within all the national parks, even though the Park Service had a fifty-year head start. On the other hand, when the railroad industry itself was fifty years old, around 1880, it had already laid about 90,000 miles of track—five times as much as rail-trail builders had been able to save over that same period of time. Of course, the railroads were doing it for profit, wealth, and power, while trail enthusiasts were doing it for—what?—a jumbled mixture of health, conservation, clean air, alternative transportation, rural economic salvation, and the desire to maintain a historical connection with the past. Or maybe something simpler like the pursuit of happiness. Is happiness only one-fifth as motivational as profit? Of course that discussion is for a different book.

In the early days of the Rails-to-Trails Conservancy, we basically counted only two measures—the number of rail-trails and their total mileage. Our goal was to make known each existing trail and to demonstrate to America that this could be a full-fledged program. Once that was accomplished, it was time to move on to mission number two, showing that there was a sufficiently large resource to work with. We knew the largest extent of the rail system back in 1916, and we knew that it was declining, so where were all the old corridors?

We had a general idea. The maximum size of the railroad network was about 254,000 miles. In 2020 about 137,000 miles were still being used by railroads. About 60,000 miles had been abandoned

Table 19. U.S. trail mileage by type

Type	Miles
U.S. Forest Service Trails	158,000
Trails in State Parks	42,400
Rail-Trails (portion on corridor)	18,000
Rail-Trails (portion off corridor)	6,000
Trails in National Parks	18,000
National Scenic Trails	13,100

Source: American Hiking Society and Rails-to-Trails Conservancy

before 1970 and have largely been plowed under, converted to roads, or otherwise lost forever. About 23,000 miles are now either trails, being worked on for trails, or being held in a "bank" for the future by the states. That means that about 34,000 rail miles—almost the size of the interstate highway system—are unaccounted for. An unknown percentage of those corridors still might be available for conversion to trails. This is the unmined natural resource that the next generation of rails-to-trails aficionados should be concentrating on.

Frustratingly, the data needed to carry this analysis further does not presently exist. The federal government doesn't collect the numbers, nor do any of the states, nor do the railroads. The Rails-to-Trails Conservancy makes a valiant effort (which is where I got most of the figures I worked with here), but there are still significant gaps. RTC is a nonprofit whose primary mission is advocacy. The organization does plenty of research, of course, but that goes toward providing the rationale to create more trails. There is no one to pore through old three-by-five cards at the National Archives, or to call trail managers with a series of questions, or to sort and re-crunch old data in new ways. The bottom line question is: How much of the old rail network is still available for saving and converting into new trails?

Back in the early days, before RTC, no one cared about—or counted—rail-trails. As a result the rails-to-trails movement itself truly did not count. Today it's different. The movement counts for a lot—a lot of usership, a lot of tourism revenue, a lot of carbon emission reduction, a lot of physical activity, a lot of coverage in

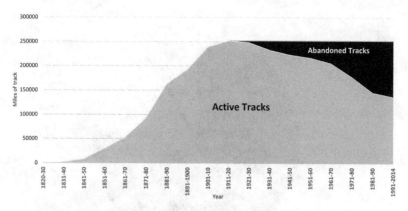

Fig. 6. Miles of railroad track, active and abandoned. Created by author.

the media, a lot of societal satisfaction. Part of the success has been due to the stepped-up calculating done by RTC. But to get to the next level—to really analyze the full possible rail-trail universe—it is now time for some leadership from the federal government.

The fact of a government data void is not due to some agency slacking in its assigned role. No agency was assigned the responsibility in the first place. The Surface Transportation Board counts only what is related to current railroading and to railroad economics. The Department of the Interior, the U.S. Forest Service, and the Bureau of Land Management keep track only of facts related to the lands they specifically own. The Department of Transportation only devotes attention to money that is appropriated in the much broader category of "bicycle/pedestrian," not specifically rails-to-trails. The one federal entity that briefly and enthusiastically tried to rise to the challenge of documenting rail-trails—the Interior Department's Heritage Conservation and Recreation Service—was abolished by President Ronald Reagan's interior secretary, James Watt, in 1981.

To peer into the future and project a likely trajectory for the rails-to-trails movement, it is necessary to answer the following questions:

- How many existing rail-trails contain additional corridor land on either end (or in the middle) that hasn't been developed yet, and what is the mileage?

- Beyond the existing rail-trails, how many miles of abandoned

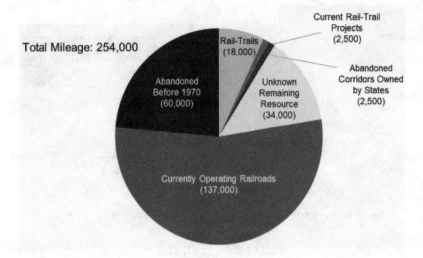

Total Mileage: 254,000

Rail-Trails (18,000)

Current Rail-Trail Projects (2,500)

Abandoned Before 1970 (60,000)

Unknown Remaining Resource (34,000)

Abandoned Corridors Owned by States (2,500)

Currently Operating Railroads (137,000)

Fig. 7. The fate of U.S. railroad corridors, in miles. Created by author.

corridor are already owned and banked by counties, cities, and towns?

- How many miles of abandoned corridor are still owned by railroads and by other entities such as utility companies?

- How many more miles of active railroad lines are likely to be abandoned?

- How much federal, state, local, and private money is currently being spent on rail-trails every year?

These are humdrum questions, but large edifices are built from small building blocks. With hard information like this, we would have a much better idea of the size of the remaining resource, where it is located, what its conversion cost might be, and in what direction the whole movement could go.[2]

Even if these facts are brought to light, numerous unknowns will affect the future of the rails-to-trails movement: the price of gasoline; the evolution of electric bikes, scooters, shared bikes, wheelchairs, and other trail-using technologies; car-sharing, ride-sharing, autonomous vehicles, mass transit, telecommuting and other innovations that could reduce the number of vehicles and free up road space; Americans' attitudes toward fitness and health; governmental

If You Want to Count, You Have to Count

responses to climate change, epidemics, and related environmental and health problems; and, perhaps most important, what role Congress will take in the promotion or restraint of active transportation.

But money and smart car-free policy directives aren't enough. Rail-trails are specialized and highly challenging constructs. They are more difficult to "haul to the finish line," as Linda Boxx put it, than most other bicycle/pedestrian facilities. If money is the only lubricant provided, the result could well be variations of nonmotorized options—bike lanes and other politically easier but lower-quality solutions—that could crowd out rail-trails. We will need a package of laws, regulations, and procedures that will propel a robust rails-to-trails movement into the future. We will need to better protect corridors. We will need to more strongly encourage railroads to negotiate. And we will need to keep trail funds from being siphoned off to use for highway construction.

We will also need better coordination between advocates, governments at all levels, and the railroad industry. Railroad companies are in an anomalous position between public and private: they operate on highly public corridors yet they are capitalist entities with those attendant rights and goals. Improving the relationship between the public and the railroads is critical. This could include holding regular annual meetings between transportation planners, recreation planners, and railroads regarding future line abandonments or reconstruction projects, and doing more to facilitate the rails-*with*-trails concept, including redefining the railroads' liability burden for any such project that benefits a state or locality.

There could also be better coordination with adjacent landowners. Not all the controversies can be unraveled, but some are due only to misunderstandings, a lack of communication, and minor resolvable disagreements. Possible steps could include setting up dispute resolution departments within state transportation and agriculture departments, and creating state legal mediation offices to analyze railroad land deeds to head off lawsuits before they occur.

• • •

RAIL-TRAILS HAVE HISTORICALLY BEEN THOUGHT OF IN TERMS of active motion—places of recreation and transportation, build-

ing upon the speed, purposefulness, and romance of the locomotive. And that is still the dominant motivation and sensibility.
But some urban and suburban rail-trail advocates are also seeing
them as oases—places to move much more slowly, with lush, high-
quality plantings, benches, outdoor art, even performance spaces.
New York's High Line, of course, set the standard on this, but it is
even happening in modest locales. The small Pittsburgh suburb of
Oakmont (population 6,500), for instance, contains a single railroad track sandwiched between the Allegheny River and Allegheny Avenue. There is no fence, and the Allegheny Valley Railroad
runs only one train per night. With the track bisecting the community, there had been no town center or square, and along the
whole mile-and-a-quarter length of track there was only one official crossing—along with 120 informal footpaths. When the Oakmont Garden Club met in 1989 to decide on a centennial gift for
the town, they came up with the concept of the Arboretum Trail,
a rail-with-trail corridor. The goals were beautification, economic
development, safety, environmental education, recreation, and commercial development. Club members planted trees and hung flower
baskets, and the surrounding shops have responded with new
awnings, fresh new paint jobs, and an overlay zoning that includes
a pavilion where the old train station once was. "Our motto," said
Patti Friday, one of the project's instigators, "was 'revive what was
faded, eliminate the negative, camouflage what you can't change,
and enhance the innate character.' The trail did that, and it now
provides Oakmont with a sense of place."

A similar phenomenon happened with the Bloomingdale Trail
in Chicago. As merely a rail-trail route, the concept wasn't quite
strong enough to achieve political support, and by the late 2000s
the proposal had gotten bureaucratically stuck. There were many
reasons for the quagmire, but one was that the corridor formed
the somewhat fraught border between two distinct neighborhoods.
"We were frustrated," said Friends of the Bloomingdale Trail director Ben Helphand, "so we met with the mayor, and he agreed to
appoint a trail point person for the city. That helped a lot. We started
a photo-documentation project called 'Reframing Ruin,' and got
hundreds of photos. We held an idea competition, which brought

in great concepts and raised expectations. That led a foundation to fund a design charette in 2011. That became the beginning of the official planning process, and it was so much more robust than anything we had done previously. A wonderful plan came out of it. It became so much more than just a bike trail."

The fact that rail-trails are perched on the cusp between transportation and parkland gives them great power today and continuing relevance into the future. The population is aging, so there is a growing need for quiet places of contemplation and escape. And there is also a critical need for off-road, car-free travel. Personally, I am gradually transitioning into new ways of using rail-trails. My legs, damaged many years ago by childhood polio, are now slowly weakening. Fortunately I've been able to stay active with the help of an electric pedal-assist bicycle. Perhaps at some point I will need an electric scooter or wheelchair to continue enjoying these great places. Whatever the technology—even if it eventually comes to sitting on a bench and watching younger generations of users hurtling or stumbling past—I know that these preserved, renovated, and embellished corridors will be providing me and countless others priceless enjoyment.

Faster or slower, coast to coast, or just around the neighborhood, the quirky, surprising rails-to-trails movement still has myriad possible directions—or maybe even all of them simultaneously. Built upon the foundations of the greatest economic and industrial enterprise of the nineteenth and early twentieth centuries, rail-trails have the opportunity to continue that legacy and play a major role as the parks and byways of the America of tomorrow.

NOTES

Introduction

1. Peter Harnik, "Vive la Velorution!," *Environmental Action*, July–August 1981, https://digital.library.pitt.edu/islandora/object/pitt%3A666957476/viewer#page /30/mode/2up.

2. Peter Harnik, "Free the Vegetable Car!," *Environmental Action*, December 1981–January 1982, 15–18, https://digital.library.pitt.edu/islandora/object/pitt %3A666957587/viewer#page/16/mode/2up.

2. Why Were There So Many Rail Corridors?

1. Richard D. Stone and Michael Landry, "Sunsetting the ICC: Is It Really Dead?" *Essays in Economic and Business History* 22, no. 1 (2004): 213–28.

2. Richard D. Stone, *The Interstate Commerce Commission and the Railroad Industry* (New York: Praeger, 1991), 2.

3. Paul W. Gates, *History of Public Land Law Development* (Washington DC: U.S. Government Printing Office, 1968), 357.

3. Meanwhile, the Bicycle

1. Judith Crown and Glenn Coleman, *No Hands: The Rise and Fall of the Schwinn Bicycle Company, an American Institution* (New York: Henry Holt, 1996).

2. Charlie Sorrel, "The Bicycle Is Still a Scientific Mystery: Here's Why," Fast Company, August 1, 2016, https://www.fastcompany.com/3062239/the-bicycle-is -still-a-scientific-mystery-heres-why.

3. It later picked up the name "ordinary," an appellation that has bedeviled later generations of bike history readers. The ordinary is a high wheeler, not the kind of bike that everyone uses today, which is why that confusing name is not used in this book.

4. Bruce Epperson, *Bicycles in American Highway Planning: The Critical Years of Policy Making, 1969–1991* (Jefferson NC: McFarlane, 2015), 25.

5. Bruce Epperson, "How Many Bikes? An Investigation into the Quantification of Bicycling, 1878–1914," in *Cycle History 11: Proceedings of the 11th International Cycle History Conference, Osaka*, ed. Andrew Ritchie and Rob Van der Plas (San Francisco: Cycle, 2001), 42–50. The author expands the time period and continuously updates the information in this paper (unpublished). Version used here from July 2018.

6. The early political history leading to road paving is thoroughly recounted by historian Bruce Epperson in *Bicycles in American Highway Planning* (25–35). Bicyclists began the campaign but didn't have the political unity to consummate the victory. Ironically, according to Epperson, the eventual breakthrough success of the Good Roads movement was due mostly to a decree by the U.S. Post Office that it would provide rural free delivery of mail only if a road could be traversed year-round by carriers. (The postmaster general at the time happened to be John Wanamaker, scion of the Wanamaker Company, a major purveyor of catalogue sales.)

7. Actually the decline in bicycling may not have been as absolute as it seems to modern historians. In a brilliant 2016 essay, "Cycling, Modernity and National Culture," Harry Oosterhuis posits that the new lower-class cyclists may have been just as enthusiastic as their well-connected predecessors but were simply incapable of leaving as robust and widely disseminated a written record of their activities. Regardless, cycling fell off the front pages of newspapers and magazines. Harry Oosterhuis, "Cycling, Modernity and National Culture," *Social History* 41, no. 3 (2016): 233–48, https://doi.org/10.1080/03071022.2016.1180897.

8. Epperson, *Bicycles in American Highway Planning*, 35, citing Sterling Elliott, "The League of American Wheelmen: Its Origin, Growth and Prospects," *Harpers Weekly* 39 (March 1895): 284–86.

4. Dark Days and a Seismic Shift

1. Technically the Interstate Commerce Commission was eliminated by Congress in 1995, but that was only a paper fiction done for political reasons. The agency was renamed the Surface Transportation Board, and it continues many of the old ICC functions. (It even kept the same address, telephone system, and many employees.) In this book, both names—Interstate Commerce Commission and Surface Transportation Board—refer to the same agency at different times in its history.

5. Is This Idea for Real?

1. "May Theilgaard Watts," Rails-to-Trails Conservancy, https://www.railstotrails.org/our-work/trail-promotion/rail-trail-champions/#watts, accessed October 4, 2020.

2. Waldo Nielsen, *Right-of-Way* (Bend OR: Maverick, 1992), 23.

3. Nielsen, *Right-of-Way*, 23.

4. "Outdoor Recreation for America," University of Michigan Libraries, https://babel.hathitrust.org/cgi/pt?id=mdp.39015014160447&view=1up&seq=1, accessed October 4, 2020, or also https://babel.hathitrust.org/cgi/ssd?id=mdp.39015014160447;seq=1, accessed October 4, 2020.

5. "Special Message to the Congress on Conservation and Restoration of Natural Beauty," LBJ Presidential Library Research Collections, February 8, 1965, http://www.lbjlibrary.net/collections/selected-speeches/1965/02-08-1965.html.

6. "Trails for America," Bureau of Outdoor Recreation, U.S. Department of the Interior, December 1966, https://www.americantrails.org/images/documents/trails-for-america-1966.pdf.

6. Congress Steps In

1. John Jacobs, *A Rage for Justice: The Passion and Politics of Phillip Burton* (Oakland: University of California Press, 1995), 353.

2. The full text of Section 208 can be found at Public Law 98-11—Mar. 28, 1983 (page 6), https://www.govinfo.gov/content/pkg/STATUTE-97/pdf/STATUTE-97-Pg42.pdf.

7. It's Perfect! Who Could Be Against It?

1. For the full story of this program, see Bonnie Nevel and Peter Harnik, *Railroads Recycled: How Local Initiative and Federal Support Launched the Rails-to-Trails Movement* (Washington DC: Rails-to-Trails Conservancy, 1990).

8. The Movement Gels

1. "Policy Path to the Great Outdoors," Report of the Outdoor Recreation Resources Review Commission, October 2008, https://media.rff.org/documents/RFF-DP-08-44.pdf.

2. Many years later, the effort was revived piece by piece by some of the towns along the route; a classic "never say die" effort, it is now scheduled to become the westernmost portion of the coast-to-coast Great American Rail-Trail.

9. Fighting for Rights in Court

1. Danaya C. Wright, "Rails-to-Trails: Conversion of Railroad Corridors to Recreational Trails," ed. Michael Allan Wolf, 78A *Powell on Real Property*, 78A1–23 (2007).

10. Building the Political Base

1. "Trailblazer," *Rails-to-Trails Conservancy* 3, no. 3 (July–September 1988): 5.

11. Breaking into the Money Vault

1. Samuel H. Morgan, *Environmental Recollections* (St. Paul: Sexton, 2000), 45.

13. Bridges and Tunnels

1. Bill Metzger, *The Great Allegheny Passage Companion* (Confluence PA: Freewheel, 2020), chapter 10.

2. Rick Sharp, *The Burlington Bike Path and Waterfront Park* (Burlington VT: Onion River, 2019), 88.

3. Alex Beam, "Dean's Conversion Experience," *Boston Globe*, December 11, 2003.

4. Sharp, *Burlington Bike Path*, 89.

17. Of Rail-Trails and Real Estate

1. John L. Crompton and Sarah Nicholls, "The Impact of Greenways and Trails on Proximate Property Values: An Updated Review," *Journal of Park and Recreation Administration* 37, no. 3 (Fall 2019): 89–109.

18. If You Want to Count, You Have to Count

1. The total mileage of so-called rail-trails is more than 24,000, but that includes the portions that were constructed "off corridor" to extend trails or to fill in gaps where certain railroad properties were lost.

2. The Surface Transportation Board seems the most logical and best-positioned agency to undertake the research and build the data library. The STB already has voluminous files of old relevant information, but the data is not available to the public, and the agency has no staff to do the research itself. A mandate to do the work (along with the necessary funding) would need to come from Congress.

SELECTED BIBLIOGRAPHY

This book was written largely from personal experience, from interviews with many people who created rail-trails, and through perusing the archives and resources of the Rails-to-Trails Conservancy in Washington DC. There is no other book that tells this history; therefore, it is not possible to present a traditional bibliography here. The selections below fall into two major categories: items of current interest from the Rails-to-Trails Conservancy and items of historical interest covering the four components of the movement's creation—railroads, the bicycle, trails, and property law. But be forewarned: other than materials from the Rails-to-Trails Conservancy, none of the listed resources make more than slight references to rail-trails, and many make none at all. They are provided here only for additional context.

Rails-to-Trails Conservancy

Eaken, Amanda, and Joshua Hart. *Tunnels on Trails*. Washington DC: Rails-to-Trails Conservancy, 2001.

Ferster, Andrea. *Rails-to-Trails Conversions: A Legal Review*. Washington DC: Rails-to-Trails Conservancy, 2017.

Knoch, Carl, and Tom Sexton. *Maintenance Practices and Costs of Rail-Trails*. Washington DC: Rails-to-Trails Conservancy, 2015.

Pack, Kelly, and Pat Tomes. *America's Rails with Trails*. Washington DC: Rails-to-Trails Conservancy, 2013.

Rails-to-Trails (quarterly, 1999–). Rails-to-Trails Conservancy, Washington DC.

Trailblazer (quarterly, 1986–98). Rails-to-Trails Conservancy, Washington DC.

"Traillink." Rails-to-Trails Conservancy. https://www.traillink.com.

Railroading

Clarke, Thomas Curtis, ed. *The American Railway: Its Construction, Development, Management and Appliances*. New York: Skyhorse, 2012 (reprint).

Douglas, George H. *All Aboard!; The Railroad in American Life*. New York: Smithmark, 1996.

Goodrich, Carter. *Government Promotion of American Canals and Railroads, 1800–1890*. New York: Columbia University Press, 1960.

Harwood, Herbert, Jr. *Rails to the Blue Ridge: The Washington & Old Dominion Railroad, 1847–1968*. Fairfax Station: Northern Virginia Regional Park Authority, 2009.

Hilton, George F., and John F. Due. *The Electric Interurban Railways in America*. Stanford CA: Stanford University Press, 1960.

Holbrook, Stewart H. *The Story of American Railroads*. New York: Crown, 1947.

Jackson, David, ed. *A Guide to Trains*. San Francisco: Fog City, 2002.

Lyon, Peter. *To Hell in a Day Coach: An Exasperated Look at American Railroads*. Philadelphia: Lippincott, 1968.

Middleton, William D., George M. Smerk, and Roberta L. Diehl. *Encyclopedia of North American Railroads*. Bloomington: University of Indiana Press, 2007.

Nielsen, Waldo. *Right-of-Way*. Bend OR: Maverick, 1992.

Reutter, Mark. "An American Tragedy." *Wilson Quarterly* (Winter 1994).

Saunders, Richard. *Merging Lines: American Railroads, 1900–1970*. DeKalb: Northern Illinois University Press, 2001.

———. *Main Lines: Rebirth of the North American Railroads, 1970–2002*. DeKalb: Northern Illinois University Press, 2003.

Solomon, Brian. *North American Railroad Family Trees*. Minneapolis: Voyageur, 2013.

Stilgoe, John R. *Metropolitan Corridor*. New Haven: Yale University Press, 1985.

Stone, Richard D., and Michael Landry. "Sunsetting the ICC: Is It Really Dead?" *Essays in Economic and Business History* 22, no. 1 (2004): 213–28.

Stone, Richard D. *The Interstate Commerce Commission and the Railroad Industry*. New York: Praeger, 1991.

Stover, John F. *History of the Baltimore and Ohio Railroad*. Lafayette IN: Purdue University Press, 1987.

White, Richard. *Railroaded: The Transcontinentals and the Making of Modern America*. New York: W. W. Norton, 2011.

Bicycling

Crown, Judith, and Glenn Coleman. *No Hands: The Rise and Fall of the Schwinn Bicycle Company, an American Institution*. New York: Henry Holt, 1996.

Epperson, Bruce. *Bicycles in American Highway Planning: The Critical Years of Policy Making, 1969–1991*. Jefferson NC: McFarlane, 2015.

Friss, Evan. *On Bicycles: A 200-Year History of Cycling in New York City*. New York: Columbia University Press, 2019.

Guroff, Meg. *The Mechanical Horse*. Austin: University of Texas Press, 2016.

Harnik, Peter. "Vive la Velorution!" *Environmental Action*, July–August 1981, https://digital.library.pitt.edu/islandora/object/pitt%3A666957476/viewer#page/30/mode/2up.

————. "Free the Vegetable Car!" *Environmental Action*, December 1981–January 1982, 15–18, https://digital.library.pitt.edu/islandora/object/pitt%3A666957587/viewer#page/16/mode/2up.

Herlihy, David V. *Bicycle: The History*. New Haven: Yale University Press, 2004.

Longhurst, James. *Bike Battles: A History of Sharing the American Road*. Seattle: University of Washington Press, 2015.

Reid, Carlton. *Roads Were Not Built for Cars*. Washington DC: Island Press, 2015.

Smethurst, Paul. *The Bicycle: Toward a Global History*. New York: Palgrave Macmillan, 2015.

Vivanco, Luis. *Reconsidering the Bicycle: An Anthropological Perspective on a New (Old) Thing*. New York: Routledge, 2013.

Trails General

Chamberlin, Silas. *On the Trail: A History of American Hiking*. New Haven: Yale University Press, 2016.

Crompton, John L., and Sarah Nicholls. "The Impact of Greenways and Trails on Proximate Property Values: An Updated Review." *Journal of Park and Recreation Administration* 37, no. 3 (Fall 2019): 89–109.

Elkinton, Steve. *A Grand Experiment: The National Trails System at 50*. Charleston SC: Palmetto, 2018.

Property Law

Gates, Paul W. *History of Public Land Law Development*. Washington DC: U.S. Government Printing Office, 1968.

INDEX

The letters *t*, *f*, and *m* following a page number denote tables, figures, and maps, respectively.

Clean Air Act (1990), 140, 141
Cleveland, Cincinnati, Chicago & St. Louis Railway, 8
Climax Tunnel (PA), 172–74
Clinton, Bill, 143
Coalition for the Capital Crescent Trail (CCCT), 149–50
Coast Guard, 162, 164, 167
Coleman, Glenn, 26–27
Colt, Ralph, 51
Columbia Trail (NJ), 95
Commission on Americans Outdoors, 139
Commoner, Barry, xxii
compensation payments, 106, 109, 110, 111–12
Connecticut: Farmington Canal Trail, 6t, 128; state-run rail-trails operation, 96
Connecticut Trust for Historic Preservation, 105
Conrail, 85, 91, 99, 128, 162, 185, 196
Conversion of Abandoned Rights-of-Way Act, 64. *See also* Railroad Revitalization and Regulatory Reform Act
Coolidge, Calvin, 53
Costantino, Ray, 176
Costello, Brian, 171–72
Costle, Doug, 89
court rulings: on federal land grant ownership, 110–11; on public travel, 103; on railbanking, 103–7
Cowboy Trail (NE), 129, 203
Crandall, Derrick, 134, 139–40
Crawford, Joan, 37
Crompton, John, 211
cross-country skiers, 83
Cross-Ohio Trail (OH), 201
Crown, Judith, 26–27
Crozet Tunnel (VA), 7
CSX Corporation, 43, 105, 117, 126–27, 128, 166
Cumberland Valley Rail-Trail (PA), 170
curves and grades, 3–6, 7, 154

dandy horses, 28–29, 30f
Dave v. Rails-to-Trails Conservancy, 110
David, Joshua, 196–97
Dean, Howard, 172
Delaporte, Chris, 120
Delaware & Northern Railroad, 185
Della Penna, Craig, 211–13

Denver & Rio Grande Western Railroad, 44
Department of the Interior, 62, 64, 71, 217. *See also* Bureau of Outdoor Recreation; Heritage Conservation and Recreation Service; National Park Service
Department of Transportation, 64–65, 71, 217
Depression, Great, 40, 48
DeQuindre Cut (MI), 128
Des Moines & Central Iowa Railroad, 42
Dickinson, Bill, 178
Dionne, Dave, 168
Discover Michigan Trail (MI), 201
Dominion Energy, 177, 178–79
Douglas, Stephen, 21
Douglas, William O., 64, 150
Douglas State Trail (MN), 59
Down East Sunrise Trail (ME), 155
Drais, Baron Karl von, 28
Draisine, 28–29, 30f
Dukakis, Michael, 99
Duluth, Missabe & Northern Railway, 86
Dunlop, John Boyd, 33
Dyson, Rob, 166

East Coast Greenway, 201
Eastern Promenade (ME), 128
Edward T. Jones Investments firm, 126
Elkinton, Steve, 54
Elroy-Sparta Trail (WI), 52–54, 56, 92, 101, 126, 200
eminent domain, 97, 102
Emmanuel, Rahm, 141
Environmental Action, 87
Epperson, Bruce, 32, 35, 223n5, 224n6 (chap. 3)
equestrians, 75, 82, 208
Erie Canal, 11
Erie-Lackawanna Railroad, 44
Eristoff, Simon, 128–30
Evans, Craig, 67, 68

Fairbanks, Douglas, Jr., 37
farmers, 59, 60, 92, 101, 119, 125, 189
Farmington Canal Trail (CT), 6t, 128
Federal Emergency Management Agency, 193
ferries, 172
Ferster, Andrea, 107

Fillmore, Millard, 21
Fisk, Jim, 18
Fitzwilliams, Jeanette, 70, 88
Fixing America's Surface Transportation
  Act (2016), 139
Florida: General James A. Van Fleet Trail,
  147; Pinellas Trail, 116–18, 128; RTC
  assistance, 129–30; Withlacoochee Trail,
  106–7
Ford, Gerald, 65
Forester, John, xxii
Forest Service, U.S., 155–57, 175, 217
Fort Dodge, Des Moines & Southern Rail-
  road, 42
Foster, Ernie, 117
4R Act (1976). *See* Railroad Revitalization
  and Regulatory Reform Act
Fowler, Marianne, 124, 138, 144–45
Friday, Patti, 220
Frisco (St. Louis–San Francisco Railway), 86
Frisco Greenway Trail (MO), 147
funding: fund-raising, 117, 164, 167, 172,
  188, 192; philanthropists, 125–27, 129,
  166; recreation vs. transportation designation, 132–33; salvage value, 92, 129,
  131. *See also* ISTEA; Railroad Revitalization and Regulatory Reform Act

Garvin, Alex, 125
Gary L. Haller Trail (KS), 185
gasoline taxes, 134, 135, 139, 140
Gateway Trail (MN), 106
General James A. Van Fleet Trail (FL), 147
Georgia: Atlanta Beltline, 125, 128; citizen
  advocacy, 122–23; rail-trail losses, 92;
  state-run rail-trails operation, 124–25
Gillum, William, 57
Gilman, Daniel, 77
Giuliani, Rudolph, 197
Glacier Park Real Estate, 132
Glen Echo Trail proposal (DC), 148, 150
Glenn, John, 120
Glennon-Beirne, Cuma, 117–18
Glosemeyer, Maurice and Jayne, 105
Good Roads movement, 33–34, 36–37,
  224n6 (chap. 3)
Gould, Jay, 18, 127
Gould, Kingdon, Jr., 127, 148
government and agencies: Bureau of Land

Management (BLM), 155–58, 217; Bureau
of Outdoor Recreation (BOR), 62–63, 71,
120; Department of the Interior, 62, 64,
71, 217; Department of Transportation,
64–65, 71, 217; Federal Emergency Management Agency, 193; Heritage Conservation and Recreation Service (HCRS),
71–72, 217; National Park Service (NPS),
xix, 62, 63, 72, 74, 126–27, 150, 155–
57, 162; Outdoor Recreation Resources
Review Commission (ORRRC), 54, 90;
railroad land grants, 20–22, 40, 110–11;
state and federal landownership, 74, 75,
97–99, 98–99t, 106, 107, 119, 155–58,
205, 208; subsidies for modes of transportation, 41; U.S. Forest Service, 155–57,
175, 217. *See also* ICC; legislation
grades and curves, 3–6, 7, 154
Grand Illinois Trail (IL), 201
Grand Trunk Western Railroad, 128
granger roads, 60
Gravel, Ryan, 125
Great Allegheny Passage (MD and PA), 1–2,
170, 184–85, 203–7, 206m
Great American Outdoors Act (2020), 146
Great American Rail-Trail, 203, 208, 210,
225n2 (chap. 8)
Great Depression, 40, 48
Great Falls & Old Dominion Railway Com-
pany, 76
Great Northern Railway, 43, 161
Great Western Trail (IA), 81
Green Bay Trail (IL), 181
Guernsey Trail (OH), 81
Gumb, Dana, Jr., 177
Guroff, Margaret, 33

Hammond, Robert, 196–97
Hank Aaron State Trail (WI), 189
Harahan Bridge (AR to TN), 170
Harlem Valley Rail-Trail (NY), 147, 188
health consciousness, 145
Heart of Iowa Nature Trail (IA), 155
Heineman, Ben, 42
Helphand, Ben, 199, 220–21
Herbst, Robert, 59, 66, 134
Heritage Conservation and Recreation Ser-
vice (HCRS), 71–72, 217. *See also* National
Park Service

Heritage Trail (IA), 169
High Line (NY), 196–98, 199
High Steel, 168–69
highway funding reform. *See* ISTEA
Highway Trust Fund, 87
high wheelers (velocipedes), 29–32, 31f, 223n3 (chap. 3)
Hill, James J., 18, 161
Historic Preservation sites, 161–62, 171
Historic Union Pacific Rail-Trail (UT), 147
hobby horses, 28–29, 30f
Hollenbeck, Chic, 208–9
Hoosac Tunnel (MA), 7, 172
Hudson River memorial, 166
Hudson Valley Rail-Trail (NY), 176
hunters, 86–87

ICC (Interstate Commerce Commission): Burke-Gilman Trail involvement, 78; decision-making speed, 62; establishment, 47; and railbanking law, 105, 106, 150; railroad abandonment regulations and notifications, 86, 90, 91, 105; and railroad preservationists, 80; rulings in favor of shippers and small towns, 41. *See also* Surface Transportation Board
Illinois: Bloomingdale Trail, 128, 141, 198–99, 220–21; Grand Illinois Trail, 201; Green Bay Trail, 181; Illinois Prairie Path, 49, 50–51, 101, 160–61; Jane Addams Trail, 118–19; Millennium Park, 199; railbanking, 107; rail-trail losses, 81–82, 92; Rock Island Trail, 145
Illinois Central Railroad, 21, 25
Illinois Commerce Commission, 105
Illinois Prairie Path, 49, 50–51, 101, 160–61
inclines, 3–5, 154
Indiana: Big Four Bridge, 8; Pumpkinvine Trail, 188; railbanking, 107
Inslee, Jay, 171
Interior Department. *See* Department of the Interior
Intermodal Surface Transportation Efficiency Act. *See* ISTEA
Interstate Commerce Commission. *See* ICC
interurbans, 22–24
Iowa: Cedar Valley Nature Trail, 95–96; Great Western Trail, 81; Heart of Iowa Nature Trail, 155; Heritage Trail, 169;

rail-trail losses, 59–60; Wabash Trace Nature Trail, 169
Iowa Trails Council, 95–96
Iron Goat Trail (WA), 128
Iron Horse State Park (WA), 208. *See also* Palouse-to-Cascades State Park Trail
ISTEA (Intermodal Surface Transportation Efficiency Act, 1991): bipartisan support, 141–43; Congestion Mitigation and Air Quality Improvement Program (CMAQ), 140–41, 142t; grant recipients, 140, 141, 147, 162, 166; Mica amendment, 146; proposals and ratification, 137–39; Recreational Trails Program, 139–40; renewal deliberations, 143–45; and Surface Transportation Efficiency Act, 136–37
Istook, Ernest, 144

Jacobs, Jane, xix; *The Death and Life of Great American Cities*, 135–36
Jane Addams Trail (IL), 118–19
Jefferson National Forest (VA), 152
Johnson, Harold "Bizz," 157
Johnson, John, 33
Johnson, Lady Bird, 54–55
Johnson, Lyndon, 54, 55
John Wayne Pioneer Trail within the Iron Horse State Park (WA), 209. *See also* Palouse-to-Cascades State Park Trail
Jones, Ted and Pat, 125–26

Kansas: Gary L. Haller Trail, 185
Kanwisher, Joan, 96, 97
Karotko, Bob, 72
Katy Trail (MO), 72, 105, 125–26, 193, 203. *See also* Boonville Bridge
Katy Trail (TX), 193
Keene, Jack, 168
Kelly, Linda Armstrong, 144
Kempthorne, Dirk, 140
Kendall, Richard, 97, 99
Kennedy, John F., 51, 54
Kentucky: Big Four Bridge, 8
Kienitz, Roy, 141
Kinzua Bridge (PA), 173–74
Kucera, Ron, 126

Lagerwey, Peter, 121–22, 182
LaHood, Ray, 145
Lallement, Pierre, 29–30

Meijer, Fred, 129

Metzenbaum, Howard, 120

Metzger, Bill, 170, 207

Mica, John, 146

Michaud, Ernest, 29

Michigan: DeQuindre Cut, 128; Discover Michigan Trail, 201; rail-trail losses, 92; shared rail-trails, 175; state-run rail-trails operation, 92; White Pine Trail, 188

Michigan Bell Telephone, 175

Midtown Greenway (MN), 192–93

military transportation, 22, 40–41

Millennium Park (IL), 199

Milliken, John, 179, 189

Mill Valley–Sausalito Path (CA), 72, 76

Milwaukee Road, 13, 43, 44, 85, 171, 208

Mineta, Norm, 137

Minneapolis & St. Louis Railway, 13–14, 42

Minnesota: Cannon Valley Trail, 6t, 131–32; Douglas State Trail, 59; Gateway Trail, 106; Luce Line Rail-Trail, 189; Midtown Greenway, 192–93; state-run rail-trails operation, 102–3; Stone Arch Bridge, 8, 161–62

Minnesota Historical Society, 161, 162

Minuteman Bikeway (MA), 106, 115, 133, 147, 189

Missouri: Boonville Bridge, 166–68; Frisco Greenway Trail, 147; Katy Trail, 72, 105, 125–26, 193, 203

Missouri-Kansas-Texas Railroad, 105, 125, 193

Mobile & Ohio Railroad, 21

Mohawk-Hudson Bikeway (NY), 72–73, 76

Montange, Charles, 87–88, 107, 150, 151, 167

Moore, French, Jr., 152–53

Moore, Maryanne, 153

Morgan, Samuel H., 102–3, 132

Morse, Mark, 157, 158

Moses, Robert, xxvii

motorized drivers, 82–84, 133–35, 139, 140

Movement Against Destruction (MD), 135

Moving Ahead for Progress in the 21st Century Act (2012), 139

Moynihan, Daniel Patrick, 136, 138, 140–41

Murphy, Tom, 205

narrow-gauge railroads, 24–25

National Association of Reversionary Property Owners (NARPO), 109–10, 112

National Limited (train), 44

National Parks and Recreation Act (1978), 66

National Park Service (NPS), xix, 62, 63, 72, 74, 126–27, 150, 155–57, 162

National Trails System Act (1968) and Amendments (1983), 54, 55, 65–70, 88, 90

National Wild and Scenic Rivers Act (1968), 54, 55, 90

National Wilderness Act (1964), 54, 90

National Wildlife Federation, 86–87, 90

Native American lands, 81

Nebraska: Cowboy Trail, 129, 203; rail-banking, 107; rail-trail losses, 92

Neenan, Tom, 95–96

New Hampshire: railbanking, 107

New Haven Railroad, 86, 176

New Jersey: Columbia Trail, 95; Paulinskill Valley Trail, 155, 188; state-run rail-trails operation, 96

New Jersey Conservation Foundation (NJCF), 95

Newman, Charles, 170

New Mexico, Santa Fe Rail-Trail, 128

New River Rail-Trail (VA), 153

New York: Adirondack Mountain Preserve, 80; Central Park, xviii–xix; Harlem Valley Rail-Trail, 147, 188; High Line, 196–98, 199; Hudson Valley Rail-Trail, 176; Mohawk-Hudson Bikeway, 72–73, 76; Riverside Park, xxvi–xxvii; state-run rail-trails operation, 96; Walkway Over the Hudson, 8, 116, 161, 162–66; Wallkill Valley Rail-Trail, 123–24, 128

New York, New Haven & Hartford Railroad, 13, 43, 96

New York, Ontario & Western Railway, 42, 51

New York Central Railroad, 43, 72

Nicholls, Sarah, 211

Nielsen, Waldo, 51–52, 196; *Right-of-Way*, 52

Nixon, Richard, 53, 167

Norfolk Southern Railroad, 86, 153, 176

Norfolk & Western Railway (N&W), 86, 152

North Bend Rail-Trail (WV), 174

North Carolina, American Tobacco Trail, 188–89

Northern Central Railway, 5, 73–74, 176

Northern Pacific Railway, 15, 43, 76, 77

rail-trails: conversion rates, 190–91t; dynamics of rural, 152–59, 154t, 156t; dynamics of urban, 148–51, 151t, 156t; genealogies, 6t; number and mileage, 194–95t, 215, 216t, 217f, 218f, 226n1. *See also* bridges; funding; landownership; legislation; tunnels; *and specific trails*

rail-trails advocacy: agency support, 116, 117–22, 123–24, 127–30; bipartisanship, 141–43; collaborations and compromises, 75, 115–16, 140; conflict between types, xx–xxiii, 82–84; early movement, 49–55. *See also* RTC

rail-trails opposition: farmers, 59, 60, 92, 101, 119, 125, 189; preference for corridor disappearance, 80–82, 152; preference for highways, parking, and building complexes, 59–60, 76, 77; railroad preservationists, 56–57, 80; safety concerns, 69, 82, 160, 162, 167, 180, 181–82; utilities, 82. *See also* landownership

Raynor, Pete, 67–69, 88, 148

Reagan, Ronald, 67, 70, 72

real estate: property value near trails, 211–14; railroad divisions, 131–32

Redbank Trail (PA), 173

Redmond, Jim, xxv

Register, Richard, xxiv

Rhodes, James, 119

Ridge, Tom, 204

right-of-first-refusal, 92, 97–99, 97t, 98–99t, 114, 122

Rinaldi, Chuck, 68

Riverside Park (NY), xxvi–xxvii

Robinson, Ellis, 89

Rock Creek Park (DC), xix–xx, xxv–xxvi

Rockefeller, John D., 86

Rockefeller, Larry, 90

Rockefeller, Laurence S., 90

Rock Island Railroad, 86

Rock Island Trail (IL), 145

Roe, Robert, 141

Roosevelt, Theodore, 47

Royal Gorge Bridge, 44

Royer, Charles, 121

RTC (Rails-to-Trails Conservancy): "active transportation" slogan, 145; buying and selling corridors, 128–30; cross-country trail efforts, 201–3, 210; early ambitions, 93–94; establishment, 89–90; and 500th rail-trail celebration, 143, 147; legal counsel, 89; and railbanking law, 88, 103–5; rails-with-trails study, 180, 181–82; state alliances, 95; technical assistance, 123–24, 187–88; website, 195–96; win–loss record, 109, 146

Ryan, Karen-Lee, 123

Ryun, Jim, 143

Safe, Accountable, Flexible, Efficient Transportation Equity Act: A Legacy for Users (2005), 139

safety bicycles, 32–33

safety concerns, 69, 82, 160, 162, 167, 180, 181–82

Salisbury Viaduct (PA), 8

Sansom, Andy, 174

Santa Fe Rail-Trail (NM), 128

Santa Fe Railway, 40

Sayler, John, 184–85

Scenic Western Maryland Railroad, 184–85

Schaedtler, Frederick, 195

Schaeffer, Fred, 165–66

Schaeffer, William Donald, 74

Schenectady & Troy interurban, 72–73

Schroder, Jim, 125

Schumacher, E. F., xxii

Scribbins, Jim, 13

Seaboard Coast Line Railroad, 43

Seaboard System, 86

Seattle, Lakeshore & Eastern Railroad, 77

Sepe, William, 163–64, 165

Sexton, Tom, 186

shared trails: with railroads, 75, 125, 180–86, 181t, 219, 220; with utilities, 175–79

Sharpe, Rick, 171

Shining Sea Bikeway (MA), 86, 96–97

Sidepath League, 36

silk trains, 14

Silverman, Bob, xxiii–xxiv

The 606 (IL), 128, 198

Sizemore, Aaron, 154

skiers, cross-country, 83

Ski Industries America, 90

Smart, Richard, 58

Snohomish County Trail (WA), 107

Snoqualmie Pass, 44